By CONSTANCE HELMERICKS

We Live in Alaska

By CONSTANCE *and* HARMON HELMERICKS

We Live in the Arctic

Our Summer with the Eskimos

Our Alaskan Winter

The Flight of the *Arctic Tern*

The Flight of the *Arctic Tern*

Bud and Connie chat with the Mounties

CONSTANCE *and* HARMON
HELMERICKS

The Flight of the
Arctic Tern

WITH ILLUSTRATIONS

Little, Brown and Company · *Boston*

LIBRARY OF CONGRESS CATALOG CARD NO. 52–5523

Published June 1952
Reprinted August 1952

Published simultaneously
in Canada by McClelland and Stewart Limited

PRINTED IN THE UNITED STATES OF AMERICA

To flyers, to airplanes,
to the dream of the ages: flight

CONTENTS

CONTENTS

ILLUSTRATIONS

The Flight of the *Arctic Tern*

1 AWAY TO THE NORTH

THE MANAGER OF SEA WINGS at Westport, Connecticut, stood on the ramp and pointed out the best channel to take, for the tide was out. It was my first ride in a float plane. Bud himself had made only three water take-offs to get his license. We were dressed in a strange way for amphibious adventuring, for we were due at a press luncheon being held in our honor by our publishers, at the Parker House in downtown Boston, at exactly 12:30 that afternoon.

Our Cessna 140, the *Arctic Tern* rocked back on the heels of her new silver floats, sending a stream of fiery ocean spray flying toward the morning sun. There was just enough breeze to make her step out. Slowly she climbed upon the step, pat-patting against the tops of the waves, gathering speed under Bud's amateur hand. In the restricted bay a large dredge sat nearby to create a mental hazard, and the high cables of the power line and the railway bridge cut off escape up the end of the bay. With a sigh the *Tern* left the water in plenty of time, Bud swung sideways around the rusted iron dredge, and we climbed out and up over a little creek.

"It's probably impolite to fly low over people's country houses and lawns so early in the morning," I thought. But we couldn't help it. Bud remarked that the airplane seemed sluggish. We didn't have our full load yet, either.

Bud and I had been flying only three months at this time when we took off to explore the arctic of Alaska and Canada. As a matter of fact we live in Alaska and are Alaskans. Our profession is exploration. In an ever-expanding world of consciousness and an ever-contracting world of physical horizons, the freedom of flight is no luxury. To get an airplane of your own, what you have to do is economize on the little things. Rather than small petty vices choose instead great freedoms. The saving accounted for by the lack of their accustomed petty expenditures would buy an airplane for many people.

Bud, my husband (and coauthor), learned to fly on the government's time as a veteran of World War Two. There were 400,000 men who took this training, although it is interesting to note that only one eighth of them finished their courses through Commercial Pilot's License and Instrument Rating. Aviation is an education you have to work at. To be a pilot is still something rather special. Pilots don't mean to be clannish, but if you yourself are not of that elevated group, you will notice that to you a pilot will be polite enough, but it is always as though he were looking right through you and seeing something behind you.

You'll notice something else, too, that's peculiar about pilots: they never grow old. Many a pilot is no spring chicken, but due to total unconcern with those small annoyances of life which are regarded seriously by others, the pilot of fifty is often taken to be a boy. Perhaps his youthfulness derives from the fact that his is a profession in which there is freedom and adventure. The flyer is the counterpart in modern life of the old cowboy, the trapper, the Indian scout. Upon his shoulders rest lightly civilization's woes, and he has its joys.

You have to talk to your airplane, sing to it, when you are alone in the cockpit up there. For the willing airplane opens up vast and strange reaches of the earth for you as it beats over the miles. It opens up a new world that kings before would not have dreamed of.

Our Cessna 140 was an all-metal ship and it carried just the two of us. It cost $3666. Its cruising speed was 108 miles an hour; its engine was an 85 horse Continental. There was a gas tank in each wing holding 12½ gallons or 25 gallons total, and it burned less gas to get you some place than most people's cars do — making in still air about 22 miles to the gallon. Its instruments were: a sensitive altimeter, tachometer, gyro turn and bank indicator, oil temperature gauge, oil pressure gauge, air speed indicator, rate of climb indicator and compass; it had instrument panel lights, landing lights, an eight-day clock and a two-way air radio. It had an electric automatic starter, carburetor heater, cabin heater and ventilators.

A large single-piece windshield of safe Plexiglas gave excellent vision on all sides; all the controls operated easily. Radio programs and music could be heard through the earphones or loud speaker during flight, while the pilot could talk back and forth with the men in the radio towers within a twenty to fifty mile radius. I must add, however, that our flights were to take us beyond the range of communications.

"Is there such a thing as an airplane that will be safe in all storms?" I had inquired of a flight instructor.

"No," was the reply. "We haven't learned how to make an airplane yet of any size that the right kind of storm can't tear in half. But — " cheerfully — "you learn to fly around storms and avoid them. That's what we try to teach you guys in ground school."

The insurance we paid on our airplane was to amount to around $450 yearly. We figured there was one chance out of four of losing our plane in the arctic because at any time we might be forced to abandon it in some inaccessible place, perhaps simply through the breakdown of some minor part. If we lost it, we would have to walk out. But after all, we were used to walking in the arctic in the first place.

There were two specific jobs which were taking us to the arctic.

Cornell University, whose Dr. Bill Hamilton is a leader in zoological research, wanted small mammal specimens from north Alaska. It seemed possible that entirely new subspecies might be discovered. We collected specimens for three years; this was able to be done only by flight.

Columbia Concerts Lecture Bureau in New York City wanted to manage us for lecture tours. Would we go to the arctic with modern means and make colored moving pictures? If we would, they would book us for a tour the following midwinter, guaranteeing to the sponsors that the pictures would be made.

We knew nothing of motion picture photography, and as little about aviation. So we bought a very fine moving picture camera with a book of instructions — the 16 mm. Kodak Cine Special — and, along with the "still" cameras we already had, decided to set out for the arctic with the new airplane we had just learned to fly. We believe it was — and still is — good work. Apart from the beauty of nature in the arctic, which we wanted to show people, there is the study of arctic survival problems, a specialty which should be of concern to all the people in North America since it is a part of their land.

We named our new silver Cessna 140 the *Arctic Tern* for the small bird which in its yearly migrations flies nearly from pole to pole. An arctic tern was painted on each side of our ship. If the smallest of birds can manage to withstand those wild untrammeled scenes of nature, so can the smallest of airplanes. For a bird's survival lies not in brute strength to withstand the elements, but in its wily skill.

Flying over the wooded New England countryside was pleasant in the pastel shades of early morning before the smoke smudge boiled up for another day. Rains had washed down the sludge and the wind was blowing out to sea. The winding scenic highways below were a maze as we cut easily across their networks, heading northward. From the air we could see a four-lane highway narrow to three lanes, then to one lane, and at last in some interval shrink into a sort of primitive ox trail which would finally squeeze through a toll bridge.

"That's how they pension off their old politicians in these parts," Bud said cheerily. "They just give 'em a concession on a toll bridge and they're fixed for life."

"Did you find out anything about the seaplane anchorage marked for Boston?" I asked.

"Nope. Couldn't find any pilot who had even heard of it."

When we got over Boston and studied the situation there, there was no hint of where a float ship might come down in the murky waterfront, full of tugs and obstacles.

"I was just afraid some fool thing like this would come up the last moment," I said. "They'll be waiting for us below at the Parker House."

We searched the map for an alternative for the Boston area. Water anchorages for seaplanes — marked on the aviation maps by the symbol of a tiny red anchor — were far less numerous than landing fields. We headed for a little lake inland from Boston which was indicated as a water landing, and within a few minutes had come to rest upon it.

A surprised summer cottage attendant met us on the shore. He said an airplane had landed here once before, years ago. Soon a crowd gathered to see the airplane.

"Has anyone got a telephone?" These were my first words as I stood out on the slippery wet pontoons in my lizard-skin pumps and caught a rope. It was windy, and Bud had to approach the dock with idling propeller very carefully from the downwind side so as not to crash into it.

Some kindly people took us into their cottage where Bud made use of their telephone. The zero hour for the luncheon was all but here. Bud tried to describe the location of the little lake to our publisher and his wife so that they could get us. But they couldn't understand his description of it because he had the airman's point of view and as such his descriptions of the country were to them quite undecipherable. It seemed that the little lake we were on was to Bostonians quite far from Boston, and moreover, it bore a peculiar Indian name. As if this weren't enough, it developed that there were *two* lakes of this same peculiar Indian name in the Boston area. You wouldn't think such a name could occur twice.

The cottagers to whom, of course, there was no other lake in the world, described to us a maze of local roads, the directions to which we endeavored to give over the telephone. Our chief editor's wife and loyal friend, heroically poured the coal into the family car, drove forty miles altogether through Boston traffic, and delivered the explorers for lunch just in time.

A fellow who had a small concession stand on the shore of the lake — the man of odd jobs — was one of the several unsung heroes of the operation. It was he who had the presence of mind to get the ropes with which to tie up our airplane. It was he who watched over it day and night during the time we were in Boston. Once he saved the air-

plane from actual disaster when she dragged her anchor in a wind —
and it is no unheroic task to tow an airplane with a rowboat!

At Boston the city clothes and suitcase we carried were left behind,
while cameras, rifle, and duffle bag took their stead. How would we
pack all the necessities for life in the arctic into this small plane
mounted upon floats? We found we could pack them in but we could
not take off. It was at Boston, with a 100 pound overload which we had
had no opportunity to make a trial with, that we learned that it is not
possible to raise a float plane off the water by faith alone.

"What day are you going to take off?" the reporters asked. "And
what time?"

To the average person not acquainted with the probabilities pertain-
ing to airplanes on floats, it is irksome not to have a definite answer. I
said tomorrow.

Bud said seven in the morning. Audible groans all around.

From 7 o'clock in the morning until 10:15 a little group of determined people of good faith stood on the banks of the small lake with
the long Indian name near Boston, or sat staring from their cars. Our
anxious audience saw the *Arctic Tern* make rush after rush across the
water as a spray-throwing speedboat which had no inclination to fly.
The airplane was too heavily loaded. Bud, with just five hours' training
on floats at this time, was doing his best to give as good a show as he
could at that awful hour of reckoning.

If a float ship is too heavily loaded the drag of the water holds it
back and regardless of how long the run, the airplane will not fly!
As the load increases so does the speed necessary for the airplane to
fly; yet the deeper it sinks into the water, the more the water resistance increases. Even a little increase in weight greatly affects the
seaplane's performance in getting off the water. Nobody had told us
this.

Conditions of wind, waves, air pressure, temperature and altitude
all vary, making it almost unpredictable as to what load any float plane
can take off with on a given day. A seasoned float-ship pilot knows by
the feel of the ship right away whether a take-off is possible.

Time after time, after waving good-by, we attempted to take off, and time after time taxied back to shore to discard precious items into the arms of waiting friends. I saw our editor and his face looked gaunt and worn with worry. What more could we throw out? The irreducible load was merely ourselves, full gas and oil, and that equipment without which the arctic trip would be meaningless: namely, the battery of cameras and their cases, lenses and film. Unfortunately, the Cessna 140 is designed to carry only 80 pounds in its baggage compartment.

We discarded our aluminum cooking kit. We discarded all our supply of emergency ammunition for the rifle, keeping just one box of 20 shots. Then we discarded our Eskimo-made furs. When I had to give up my parka for the arctic, I really felt depressed. At last, as a final sacrifice, we discarded all our maps of North America except the immediate one we were using.

"When a pilot can't even take his maps and papers with him, I say that's the last straw!"

"If I can only get her up on the step just once," said Bud, "I know I can take her off."

Weary faces watched as we plowed across the rolling waves. The wind rolled down over the trees of the opposite shore. It would be hard to climb above those trees, Bud knew. The air poured over the trees like an invisible but powerful waterfall, and the airplane would have to climb up the falls on the opposite shore to clear the impediments.

When the airplane left the water at last, I was limp. Nearer and nearer came the trees rushing at us. But Bud with steady nerves made no effort to climb the plane. We had to have more air speed first.

There is no turning back when you once take off with an airplane. The landsman who is afraid of handling all this power with wings must learn, if he becomes a pilot, that power is his friend. Power is the only thing that can save him in some predicaments.

"Pull her up, pull her up!" I cried involuntarily. But, holding the airplane in level flight and rushing straight at the trees, Bud watched the air speed indicator record 85, 90, 100. At the last moment he pulled the airplane up in a steep climb, and we cleared the top of the invisible waterfall as though there was nothing to it.

At 100 miles an hour the small lake and waiting cars slid beneath us. Bud tipped once good-by, straightened out, and we were on our way.

"What will we do about our other equipment?" I asked faintly.

"It will have to be shipped on to Alaska," replied Bud. "We'll just have to get it when we can.

"I wouldn't do that again for anybody," he said. "But we were scheduled to leave today, and I didn't see any other way out."

"Yes, I know, dear," said I.

It didn't take long to leave Massachusetts; and northern New York, into which we passed from Connecticut within sight of Vermont, was pleasantly reminiscent of the beginnings of the arctic in places. Wild forests and bogs of a tundralike composition gave to the air traveler a peculiar insight into climate and geography not enjoyed by the ground dweller. In this general region the last Ice Age has left visible traces and Dorset-type Eskimo skulls tell that Eskimos lived here not long ago, while caribou roamed here within the memory of living man.

"Look, over there's Maine," said Bud.

"Oh, Maine!" I said. "It's the only state I haven't seen yet."

"You've seen it now," said Bud as we flew on.

Our cruising speed with an engine r.p.m. of 2300 had been 105 miles an hour on wheels, but on floats we noted our mileage fell back to 90 miles per hour with the same engine setting. One drawback to float flying was that it shortens your cruising range about fifteen per cent.

Lovely great Lake Champlain loomed in the offing. Soon we were getting lunch at a village and the airplane was getting gas. It was a cold northern spring; rain fell. Take-off two days later even on that vast expanse was difficult for our overloaded ship, but once in the air we sailed along across the line to Ottawa, Canada.

The seaplane landing there was on the Ottawa River right beside the Rockcliffe Airfield.

"Looks like lots of match sticks floating in the river down there," I observed. "That must be driftwood."

A boom of pulpwood logs had broken loose just about the time we arrived, filling the river with floating logs. We circled, waiting for most of the logs to drift by and hoping the wind would drop. The wind seemed to increase as we made a trial run over the river. A good pilot always does this: He looks over a strange place and makes a low pass at it a couple of times before he drops in. I didn't have to ask Bud what those little men were running about for beneath at the margin of Rockcliffe; it was plainly a contingent of the Canadian Air Force per, sonnel manning the crash boat to stand by.

When we came in for our landing we were at too steep a glide and too fast a speed. Overshooting the quiet water in the crook of the river, Bud settled down just beyond this haven in the midst of fast riffles — the worst place in the ordinarily safe river a pilot could have chosen. These rapids today were exposed to an upstream wind. A mountainous wave erupted in this spot. Clipping the top of this wave, the *Arctic Tern* sprang into the air, Bud caught her with a little throttle, pulled up into a sharp stall, and we plunked into a trough with almost all forward momentum gone. This is the only way to land in very turbulent water: stall and drop in. The six-foot-high wave rolled over the wing tips and the tail disappeared for a moment, observers noted. Drifting on the current downriver to where quieter water enabled us to turn, we taxied back through the side of the river to the dock. The helping hands of an air force mechanic grabbed the ship, and I leaped out and must have scraped my knee on the dock, for the next thing I knew I felt something warm and wet and I saw that blood was running down and filling my shoe. I never did learn how the injury occurred as I felt absolutely nothing. "We thought you were in for trouble," remarked one of the calm Canadians.

"So did we!" I piped up.

"A Norseman just landed before you did, and it all but stood on its head."

The Norseman, one of Canada's own planes which she manufactures herself, is capable of carrying a gross ton and is a favorite with the air force and with the mounted police.

"You Americans is daring chaps, isn't you? We here, now we thought you was going to lose your plane in the river. But I see you must be used to doing that. What kind of a little ship do ye say that it is?"

The men gathered around agreed it was the littlest ship they had ever seen. When it was pulled up on the ramp, safe from the river, they eagerly looked it all over from stem to stern. "All metal, hey?" they noticed. "A Cessna, you don't say? Will ye look at that little instrument panel now? And Edo floats, just like a little Norseman."

Bud and I fairly swelled with pride.

"Lucky fellows, you Americans, that you can buy an airplane like that," we were told. "As for us now, it would cost a man a thousand dollars just for the tax if he could get it, and he kin not get it."

We waited on the ramp for the arrival of the customs official. He came and glanced over our ship casually. He checked our Scientist's and Explorer's Permit and said we were free to travel anywhere we wished in Canada and her territories. His manner gave one the calm assurance that all was right with the world, that he had faith in humanity, and that he did not expect every man to have a black motive. That Canada was extremely thorough, however, there was no doubt, because later we learned they had checked on our character by writing letters to numerous people before we arrived in the country, and they had a fund of information on us that probably would have surprised us could we have seen it. Quietly the customs man came and was gone.

"Is is possible to get a hotel room?"

No, not a chance. The town was packed.

"Why don't you sleep right here inside a Norseman?" somebody suggested. "There are all kinds of sleeping bags and even electric lights."

We thanked the air force and said maybe a Norseman would indeed make a good hotel. Therefore, while it rained two days more, we set up housekeeping inside the spacious fuselage of one of these aircraft, camping out in the middle of Canada's capitol.

Author Richard Finnie and his wife Alyce to whom we had a letter of introduction from Stefansson, came in from their country home 22 miles with their car, and showed us the town. We saw the Parliament Buildings where debates take place in two languages — English and French. One could only imagine the confusions which could easily occur between these two diverse national groups.

"It's the truth," said the Canadian authors, "and Canada pays for it every day."

We ate at restaurants where food was surprisingly cheap, and where, when you asked for a cup of tea, the waitress answered, "Aye, mum." One evening we spent at the home of Taverner, the great ornithologist, author of *Birds of Canada*, a book which we had carried previously by dog sled and canoe on our trips. But "unfortunately," as Bud put it in his diary, Taverner had died just a week before. Here at Mrs. Taverner's home we enjoyed the great privilege of meeting kindly, white-bearded Dr. Martin Porsild, who with his son had just arrived from Greenland the day before. The son was Canada's ambassador to Greenland, where the family had maintained a scientific station of observation for over forty years.

Suddenly, even though I was having a good time in Ottawa, I was impatient to leave. I wanted to get north. Talking with the Greenlanders did it. I had always felt that try as I might, I could never really capture and grasp the arctic — our corner, that is. The days of the dog sled and the canoe were still recent in memory, and never let it be said that they were not great days. But something new lay ahead. I was wondering if the acquisition of an airplane would help us to comprehend our arctic better: to comprehend it in modern terms. I was wondering if this first airplane would lead in time to bigger airplanes for further exploration. To the flyer only belongs the over-all view.

At Ottawa Bud decided reluctantly that to lighten our load we must ship our Kodak Cine Special movie camera in its big velvet-lined case and its film to Fairbanks, Alaska, as we plainly could not carry it further with us.

But why worry? In the meantime there was before us an experimental flight westward all across Canada and up the Alaska Highway to reach our destination. Not only this, but we must figure it out flying floats, landing on *water* all the way.

2 FLYING CANADA WESTWARD

FROM OTTAWA to the little settlement of Trout Mills, Ontario, was only 190 miles, and it was over beautiful country. Cutting across a corner of Quebec near Montreal, we winged over small farms where the French-Indian people below could be seen plowing with cows and oxen hitched up for draft animals in the style of Normandy 300 years ago. "Quaint old Quebec," the posters call it.

"Just how far can a farmer get on cow power today?" Bud wondered.

"Well, it's all the way you look at it," I said, just for the sake of argument. "Is a highly mechanized world necessarily a better world?" That's a big question that has no simple answer.

I thought of those gaily-colored posters which adorn all the modern airlines offices. Posters depicting "romantic" and "picturesque" people — the people whose women carry water gourds on their backs and whose children have never gone to school.

We were heading over Canada going westward.

What does the airman see over Ontario? He sees endless miles of green forest with blue sky above. It is not farming country but pulp-wood country. Every stream is choked with logs; big booms of logs rest in quiet lakes. Logging trails and fire trails below look like spider webs, merging upon great piles of sawdust by the mills. There are large burned-over areas where forest fires in the past were stopped short in sharp contours. The streams and lakes gave us a new confidence in float flying, for wasn't each one of them an emergency landing field if needed?

"Say, sometime we ought to canoe some of these chains of lakes. Just look at those beautiful waterfalls down there. I bet trout are easily caught right below those falls."

Yet while there are still some good hunting and fishing areas in Ontario, man's unnecessary exploitation and pollution in connection with the lumber industry has often ruined what must at one time have been a paradise. The sawdust spewed out by the mills into the streams gets into the gills of the fish and kills them; wherever logs are floated fish are hard put to survive. Ten million dollars have been put into the study of stream pollution by the lumber industry itself in the last ten years, however, with the result that it is now known how to counteract many of the evils quite successfully.

Trout Lake lay in gently rolling country with the timber pressing right down to the water's edge. At the far end of the lake were two float planes anchored on the water. The lake lay like a piece of crystal.

"How will we know the wind direction when there's no wind sock?"

"You can tell by the waves and the streaks of foam," answered Bud. "But today it won't make any difference. We can come in any way."

It takes a particular skill to make a water landing when the water is perfectly still. You can't tell from the air if you are fifty feet above it or five feet above it. The altimeter is not to be depended upon when dealing with these small fractions, and it would be easy to smack right into the water in a serious crash. Water is not soft; crashing into water is to be compared to crashing into a stone wall.

In landing upon glassy water the pilot dares not trust his vision or his common sense to tell him where the water lies. He puts his airplane into a landing attitude plenty high and settles *under power* until contact is made.

Landing can be made upon smooth water so gently that it is hard to tell when you meet the water until the ship sinks down into it from the step as it slows up. Bud had never made a landing upon glassy water until now, but he had been coached on it.

"First we circle the landing area to make sure there are no underwater obstructions or floating driftwood. Then we'll come down on the water parallel to the shore so we can gauge our altitude by it."

From above, a person couldn't tell if what he saw was the surface of the lake or the lake bottom. Bud put the *Arctic Tern* in a landing attitude about fifty feet high and had no trouble settling slowly upon the mirrorlike surface.

As we taxied up to a small dock three men were seen approaching. "How do you want to tie up?" they asked Bud.

On the inland lake where there was little danger of waves or tides, Bud thought it would be all right to pull the airplane up on the edge of the shore for the night. This is the way we often did it: We simply lifted the tails of the floats up on land as far as possible. I was to have my turn at this many a time. You must be sure to lift on the tail where it is marked, "Lift here only," or you may damage the tail. The airplane is secured ashore by tie-downs on each side of the wings. The floats may rest on planks, as they did here, to prevent them from moving against a rocky shore during the night. Ordinarily, of course, we did not have the advantage of planks and would always have to choose sandy or muddy harbors. In this way you have the airplane in a tail-high attitude that has reduced the lifting power of the wings to zero and the wings are held secure. If you tie the tail with a third rope to the trees ashore and lock the controls back with the seat belts no winds can harm the ship. Bud figured this position out for every situation North America had to offer.

We stayed that night at an inn near the water's edge. The only other guests were a group of four men who were flying an old klunker of a two-engined flying boat. The old airplane dated back to about 1930 and had been built for the British Navy. The party was on their way to southeastern Alaska where they were to haul freight with it for a mine. They had been stuck at Trout Mills several days working on their ancient craft, installing a new engine, as an oil line had become stopped up and one engine was ruined.

"Your little ship travels faster than we do," they said, "but it wouldn't do for you to try to follow us."

"What do you mean by that?" we asked.

"Because parts may start flying off at any time." We all laughed.

The next hop was to Remi Lake, 260 miles. A red airplane on floats rode beside a small dock there. We made a trial drag and came gliding in beside it. Here we had tea and pastry with the Air Service Division of the Department of Lands and Forests. The Canadian Government has a fondness for long and boring titles, as do all governments, so that the stranger is hard put to realize that what he is dealing with is simply a policeman, or in this case, a forest ranger. The forester is on a small monthly salary and he is a pilot who patrols for forest fires.

In former years these pilots with the forestry service used to be paid by the hour for their flying time and bachelors as they were, theirs was one of the world's romantic professions. Today, forestry men have little bungalows furnished for them by the government with permanent quarters for their families. All over the north generally — in Alaska as well as Canada — we find the same tendency, after years of struggle against tradition, to at last let a man have his wife and children with him in the northern wilderness, and make of his job a stable lifetime profession.

During the last ten years women with their children have invaded the wilderness to the very top of the continent. There is talk of permanent weather observation stations being established on the most remote islands in the Arctic Ocean belonging to Canada, and if so, there seems no reason, under the conditions of modern housing and communication, why women and children should not soon be stationed even there within a short distance of the North Pole itself.

It was explained that everybody in northern Ontario worked for some government service. This had its evils, but it was an orderly life.

Right now "Canada" was composed of a strip of land about 500 miles wide bordering the northern United States; it had two railroad tracks and a single automobile highway running from East to West. There was nothing to speak of north of that. Almost every town along the railroad called itself the "gateway to the North."

After our pleasant teatime we headed on to Mackenzie Lake, near Armstrong, Ontario, 300 miles. Two women were the only people about when we landed on the lake. It was a summer resort and the town of Armstrong, a railroad town, was a few miles away. These kind people took us into town in their car so that we could buy some groceries and returned us to their summer cottage, where they said we could use the facilities and spend the night, as they were not now occupying it.

Bud and I are meat eaters and we had been living upon vegetables long enough, so we thought. At the railroad town we expected to get a good steak. You can imagine our surprise when we found at the little grocery that we couldn't even obtain wieners.

"You are now in the north," the peaceful old grocer informed us.

We looked at him, remembering the fine butcher shops of Fairbanks, that is still in the temperate zone although a thousand miles north of here and many thousand miles west. We thought of the meat we were used to eating 350 miles north and west of there yet. That's really the best eating of all. That night we ate canned fish and bread — the closest we could come to meat.

The lack of fresh meat, fresh fruit and fresh vegetables gave the little railroad store a primitive appearance that was entirely inconsistent with the actual conditions. The people admitted that their fresh milk came in daily in refrigeration cars from Winnipeg. Yet they seemed to live largely on canned and preserved foods because these were their food habits.

Another informer had told us we were too far north for farming. Yet a look at the map would convince even the most naïve that Canada's richest wheatland lay north of here.

There was one unusual business we found here, though, and this was the delivering of fresh fish daily by airplane. The fish were caught by native Indians and Eskimos, north at James Bay, where bush pilots got them for the cities. Sturgeon paid $1.00 a pound while their prized roe for caviar paid $3.00 a pound. The pilot we were talking with glanced at a sad looking dead fish as he remarked, "They go to New York, you know. But darned if I can see why people pay for a thing like that."

"How come these people around here speak of this as being the north?" Bud asked the bush pilot.

"Oh, I guess the American tourists have told them that so often that they believe it now," he said.

Leaving a $2.00 Canadian bill on the table inside the summer cottage of the railroad wives, we flew a compass course toward Sioux Lookout, Manitoba, in the wheat country.

Shallow prairie lakes began to replace the deep forest lakes. We flew at 5000 feet, for to fly lower than this leaves a pilot with little choice as to possible emergency landing places. To have some gliding range is desirable when flying cross country, even though engine failure is unlikely.

Rain came flying at us like water shot from a hose. It cascaded up over the windshield and ran in little streams over our silvery wings. The landing lake at Sioux Lookout was a gray leaden mass with logs floating here and there upon an indistinguishable surface. Several float ships were moored below near a dock to give a friendly welcome as we came gliding in.

In Alaska even the most down-at-the-heels Indian trading post can furnish the proper gasoline and oil for practically any make of airplane — not so in Canada, even in its larger cities. Almost without exception the only airplanes are those large craft which belong to the airlines, and use a high octane gas. For a small plane to try to burn the gas they use is almost ruinous to its engine. So when we tried to get 80 octane gasoline we could get only 91, and 91 we used.

Blue sky showed ahead as we flew on across prairie landscape. It was a drier land, and we must veer northward yet off the regular airways in order to follow water. The sun broke through; we turned the ventilator cups on each side of the windshield to direct a stream of cool air into the cabin. The little farming town of Lac du Bonnet on the Winnipeg River ahead was to remind us of a small town in rural Iowa. Farmers' trucks and cars stirred the dust of the unpaved streets while blackbirds and crows called from nearby fields. Bud tried to get gas and oil. Although there was a gasoline sales service here, the station had neither gas nor oil of the proper kind for our ship. Several airplanes were stationed here on the water but they used 91 octane. By the time Bud had rounded up fuel, the water was dead calm.

Now came another lesson in the long series of dealing with the take-off on water. The water was perfectly glassy. When there is no breeze, there is no float ship in the world, no matter what its power, that will be able to take off with a heavy load. The smooth water allows no air to get under the floats which would jar it loose from this sticky grip. We made run after run but only succeeded in getting the engine hot. Sometimes a pilot will run his airplane in circles on the water and attempt a take-off over his own waves. But even this expedient did not work for us.

Another troublesome factor, too, was becoming apparent as we went westward. The land gets higher in the prairie provinces, from 2000 to 3000 feet above sea level. An airplane does not have as much lift for take-off in the higher altitudes. In plotting our course on the map we must try to select for our landing lakes only those of a reasonably low altitude.

Frustrated in taking off from Lac du Bonnet on this most beautiful of all flying days, Bud found a fisherman and with his boat secured the *Arctic Tern* out in the river on a buoy. Saturday night was upon us, as we walked up to the one small, new hotel. We asked for a room with bath, and to our surprise the woman who ran it announced that "only regular customers can take a bath here." She was prompted presently to further explanation:

"You see, sir, the town has a poor sewage disposal system, and only people who live here may take a bath."

The room we were given was neat and clean, but right below our window a door opened into the men's ale shop. Saturday night and a room over the saloon is probably the same in any land.

We wished we had slept on the dock in our sleeping bag. About sunrise a big fight started which rolled out into the street below, where victor and vanquished ended the joust in a verbal battle that would have put pirates to shame. Long before daylight came we were ready to leave, and just as the first sleepy rays began to steal over the town we were down on the wharf. There the *Arctic Tern* rode calmly at anchor, but there was not a single boat in sight that we might use to retrieve her with.

After hours passed Bud located a leaky craft and managed to get to the *Arctic Tern* and tow it ashore. Just as the church bells for late services began to ring, calling the faithful from wherever they were hidden, we opened up two furrows in the river and climbed into the blue sky of a gorgeous June morning, our heads still spinning round and round with barroom roars and the crash of glasses.

Farmland and prairie stretched away. So this was North America! I don't believe that I had ever really seen it before. Flying over North America gives one the feeling of seeing a giant slowly awakening.

Next stop: The Pas, Manitoba. In a downpour of rain we came sliding in upon the anchorage lake amid myriad waterfowl. This part of our continent produces millions of wild ducks. They merely moved over to make room for us. Two other float planes rode, tied to a makeshift dock, and we tied the *Arctic Tern* beside them. The rain beat down for a few moments while we sat waiting inside our metal ship, and then the summer squall passed on. Instantly a swarm of mosquitoes arose to look for someone to bite.

Everything around here seemed completely deserted of a Sunday afternoon, although there was a road leaving the lake in two directions. We hadn't eaten food this day. "Say," said Bud, "did you notice when we were landing, just which direction the town lies from this lake?"

"No," I replied, "I always get mixed up when we bank and circle. I thought it was over *that* way."

"Well, I think it is over *that* way," said Bud, pointing differently.

"I was so busy circling that storm when we came in, and so busy watching to make sure we didn't hit any ducks," he explained, "that I had my hands full. The town seemed right nearby when we were in the sky. But everything looks a lot bigger when you get down on the ground, doesn't it?"

"These mosquitoes are fierce," I said slapping. "It's a cinch we can't just stay out here all day." We decided to pick a direction and start walking for the supposed town.

"Wait," said Bud, "it's muddy. We'll sink to our eyes. I guess right now is a good time to get out our mosquito head nets and our Eskimo wading boots, too."

The Eskimo-made summer boots, of scraped sealskin, had lain rolled up in a bundle in a trunk in Arizona for months, and when we packed them to take north, they were as stiff and hard as parchment. It would have been impossible to put them on in that condition. But we had carried them inside one of the floats as we traveled, and the moisture condensing in the float had been absorbed by the boots and so they became pliable once again. The boots were in perfect condition. We dipped them into the edge of the lake before putting them on, to insure that the sinew thread had swelled in the seams to make them completely waterproof. Then, having adjusted a couple of pairs of long wool socks on our feet, we got out some dry felt insoles, and pulled the boots on. They came to just below the knee; they tied with sealskin thongs that now were soft and ready to use. We carried no footwear other than the Eskimo type with us, not only because it is light to carry, to pack and to wear, but because in our experience we had found it is the only possible thing for arctic summer walking through the bogs.

For some time as we trudged down the boggy road in our sealskin waders with clouds of mosquitoes trailing us, we had doubts whether we might not be walking in the wrong direction. After three miles of perseverance, however, we arrived in town with wonderful appetites and there enjoyed a four course steak dinner for the nominal sum of 80¢.

The Pas was a frontier town that was going ahead fast. It was reminiscent of certain up and coming Alaskan towns. This might have been due in part to the fact that there lived here one of those enterprising and original businessmen who have a hand in everything.

"Where can we get gas and oil?" we asked, and were directed through the village in search of Tom Lamb, owner of Lamb's Sawmill, Lamb's Airlines, and builder of the road we had just walked over. We found him at Lamb's Apartments.

Mr. Lamb welcomed us and said we should have just filled up our plane, taking what gas we wanted from the barrels beside the lake, leaving the money on top of the barrel there.

"But we don't have a measure."

"You can guess at the amount and price. It doesn't make much difference," he replied. As he drove us back to the lake in his car he told us about his two fur ranches, one being 135,000 acres in extent, over which we had just flown to arrive here.

When it came to paying for our gas he had no change for $10.00. "Oh, well," he said, "you can just send the money to me when you find somebody who has the right change." This we did, from several hundred miles away.

"Be sure you stop when you next come through," he called in parting. "Just circle the house when you come over and I'll come right out to the lake for you with the car."

"You can tell we are getting back north again when people are like that," Bud said, as we flew on.

As we winged over Manitoba into Saskatchewan we began to notice little patches of smoke on the horizon. They were forest fires.

"Better report these the next place we can," mentioned Bud. "Here's the pencil and map. You mark down where each blaze is."

The smoke thickened and soon blazing areas, totaling thousands upon thousands of acres were all around us and under us. During the 220-mile flight we counted over a hundred separate fires burning!

"They must have started from the electric storms," we thought at first.

But so many? This was new farming country, just being settled. Often in some isolated block of timber, flames would be leaping in three or four places.

We were pretty startled when we reported the fires to learn from a forest ranger that these fires were *not* accidental!

He explained to us: "The farmers are setting a lot of those fires. We know they are doing it, but it is pretty hard to catch them. They start the fires every spring to clear land. Often a fire gets out of control, and although it was set to clear ten acres it ends by burning fifty thousand additional acres. But it matters little to these pioneers so long as it costs the individual nothing."

"What an unbelievable crime! What a waste!" we thought, as we stared through our windshield over the smoke-filled sky of Western Canada. The heedless pioneers were now this very day carrying on exactly the same kind of exploitation that our own pioneers once practiced to subdue our West. Yet in subsequent seasons we will all

hear again and again over the radio of the deliberate fires of Saskatchewan, which continue their destruction regardless.

We made Prince Albert at 9 o'clock at night. This is quite a sizable
city in Saskatchewan. Looking it over from the air, Bud said, "Let's go
on north just thirty miles more and sleep at Emma Lake."

He said he was apprehensive that the deep banks of the Saskatchewan River by Prince Albert would be a deterrent to the future take-
off. The river looked sheltered from any breeze and naturally we
did not want to risk getting stuck there several days. Unless a river
is very wide, only two winds are possible for a take-off: an upstream
or a downstream wind, whereas if there is any current to speak of you
may be able to take off only by running downstream. We thought that
a float pilot would do best to avoid rivers in preference to lakes
wherever possible.

Emma Lake was found to be a kind of summer resort with many
cottages clustered around its wooded shores. The sun had just set as
we "dragged" the lake; a rosy glow lingered in the sky until near midnight now. Emma Lake was a jewel in a beautiful setting, but her
water seemed to be draining away from some unknown cause, and
unless changes occurred, only the setting might be left.

We stayed at Emma Lake two nights. We slept in our sleeping bag
inside a house which was in the process of construction, lent to us by
the game guardian; his wife was Ukrainian, "of which," Bud noted in
his diary, "there are quite a few in Canada."

We were unable to leave Emma Lake because we had to send for
gas by truck clear to Prince Albert, fifty miles away. We were unable
to leave then because the man who promised to truck the gas did not
return.

It was one of those spring days of rare freshness, when the dandelions were in full golden bloom and strawberry blossoms scented the
air while birds sang. I slept most of the day away on the dock in the
partial shadow of the airplane's wing. We lived on steaks fried for us
by the manager of the resort dance hall and on ice cream cones at
five cents each — our favorite foods, so this was well. As I insisted on
treating the Ukrainian girl to ice cream Bud found himself pushing her

baby in the buggy around the lake road, the buggy wheels cutting deep into the sand.

Bud awoke me the second morning at 5:45 A.M. to say that a breeze was blowing. There is no use to argue with Bud at such times; he just views my argument as prejudice because I am sleepy and don't want to get up. "Come on. Let's fly to Prince Albert and get our own gas," he said. "I'm tired of it here, waiting around."

But when we reached Prince Albert we dared not come down. The Saskatchewan River was packed almost solid with drift.

"I wonder if we have enough gas to get back to Emma Lake again?" Bud started calculating. "Let's see, we're on our last quarter of the last tank. When the gauge gets down that low it may not be dependable."

When we got back over Emma Lake, Bud said: "Say, I notice there's an airplane anchorage marked over here at Waskesiew Lake pretty near. Maybe we should try to get there."

"Oh, no," I remonstrated sincerely. "We're sure to run out of gas this time."

"There's a tailwind," argued Bud. "It's just forty miles north of here. There's the automobile road running all the way, and lakes all around quite close, and farmers' fields. You can always land on a level field with floats if you have to."

Bud said that the presence of the highway made the risk justifiable inasmuch as if we had a forced landing we could truck out our airplane from a field or small lake to the larger lake if it came to that. This is how it happened that at an early hour when my bleary mind seemed unable to cope with reality I found us flying over the countryside in an airplane which was due to run out of gas at any moment.

It didn't. Bud found Waskesiew Lake and we came down, scattering a flock of snow geese. Tracks on the beach I saw right off were of deer but not a human foot. Freshly felled trees bore the marks, not of the ax of man but of beavers' teeth. There was an old cabin. Bears had broken out its windows long ago. SEAPLANE BASE were the words printed on a sign above its door.

"You stay here and guard the airplane," said Bud.

"Where are you going?"

"To try and find some gas."

Had Bud only let me sleep we would just now be awakening at Emma Lake resort to have our breakfast of steak and ice cream.

Bud had to walk eight miles to reach the village of Waskesiew. Near the end of his walk he caught a ride. Around noon he returned in a jeep. With him was a kindly older man named Tiny Moffat, a farmer. I have seen several men nicknamed Tiny in the North and they were always very large men. Our new friend was no exception to the Northern tradition, being nearly seven feet tall. Bud and Tiny had 80 octane clear gasoline. This octane gas is used principally in lamps, outboard motors, and automobiles. The men brought me a breakfast of canned spiced meat, cookies and a sack of bananas.

"Drop it!" suddenly Tiny boomed at me, as I picked up a slice of meat on Bud's knife. "It's meatless Tuesday!" He shouted this in such an alarming way that I almost did drop the meat. Then I realized he was teasing.

There were two voluntary meatless days a week in Canada at this time as so much was being sent overseas.

The gas tanks filled, we were ready to try a take-off while Tiny stood by. The engine sounded funny. Alas, it would only turn up 1900 r.p.m. on that lamp gas; we needed 2250.

Tiny helped Bud drain the gasoline back into the cans. He would take it back to town and order some from Prince Albert which was now farther away than ever. But Tiny guaranteed that the gas would be here tomorrow. He would also bring us back some grub with his jeep. The countless considerations of friends we have known in our travels mount up to unpayable debts.

The food Tiny brought was steak — even on meatless Tuesday — a sack of potatoes, fresh eggs, bread and butter. We pitched our little tent. While we slept that night a small black bear walked over the tails of the airplane floats pulled up beside us. The bear's lazy tracks were left in the sand.

The garage man ultimately arrived with the proper gas and we took off. Cost of trucking the gas some 70 miles to refuel at this lake was $10.00. The cost of the gas itself runs from 50¢ to $1.00 a gallon throughout Canada, and $2.50 a gallon in some remote parts of its territories. There are five quarts in the Canadian gallon.

It was a rough, windy day as we headed toward Ladder Lake. In order to fly toward our destination we had to "crab" or fly at an angle of nearly 45 degrees to our true course. Fueling up at Ladder Lake we decided to go on to Cooking Lake right by Edmonton, Alberta, as the wind dropped.

The country now lay like a checkered mat with farms everywhere. The prairie was as vast as a sea. Rain clouds trailing their resplendent robes of water against the sun moved on all sides while streamers of light shot from between the black columns of thunderheads. We wove our way in and out among them. The little prairie towns along the railroad, marked by their big grain elevators, ticked by.

In one last rain spurt we broke through over Cooking Lake. Edmonton, a city of over a quarter of a million and one of the largest cities in Canada, could be seen. Cooking Lake was a prairie lake. Few trees fringed its shores and its water was murky and shallow. Spots showed all over the lake that might be ducks. Closer examination revealed that some of the spots were ducks but some of them refused to fly off — they were stones rearing up from the mud. There was plenty of water for an airplane to land in if its pilot chose the right channel, and this he did.

Our stay there amounted to two days. Young Mr. Spooner was in the seaplane fitting and repair business somewhat like the people at Sea Wings in Connecticut, but his clients did not fly for sport. For some reason that I never figured out, Canada has few landing fields in her far north, so that all commerce must be carried on by means of aircraft on floats which land upon what bodies of water they can find. It is true that water up north is practically everywhere. It is true that more than half the year calls for skis on aircraft, landing fields after the freeze-up being almost anywhere north of the trees. Yet it seemed strange that all of the air traffic going to the North from Canada's greatest western city, had to outfit by way of Cooking Lake, with all of the complications which flying on floats means. The Spooners ran an inn where lodgings could be procured at the same time, and many were the bush pilots of the North who had sat at this board or hugged the massive fireplace at Cooking Lake to spin their tales.

From here on, those of us who fly the bush were on our own. Some of us were leaving for the Yukon Territory, others of us for the District of Franklin. And there were many of us with small airplanes, like Bud and me, who belonged up Alaska way.

3 FLIGHT UP THE ALASKA HIGHWAY

To TAKE THE PROPER CARE of a car, all you need to do is take it to the nearest garage and forget about it except for paying the bill. You can do almost the same thing with your airplane provided there is a "garage." In the United States there are 100,000 privately owned airplanes and five times that many pilots, and nearly every airport has competent mechanics. But in Canada there are few private pilots and as for facilities out beyond the principal cities — they scarcely exist. Canadians, used to the vast distances of their land, never remotely consider that anything smaller than a $30,000 Norseman should be in the air.

Our *Arctic Tern* needed her oil changed and a general checkup every 25 hours. After we reached the northern regions there were absolutely no facilities for caring for our airplane, so Bud had to undertake this job himself.

Here at Cooking Lake were the first and last facilities. But this was a busy time. Several airplanes were on the waiting list to get their summer's floats put on. "Help yourself to tools and do your own work if you like," Mr. Spooner told Bud. "I will be glad to help whenever I can, if you need me." With these words he left Bud to his own devices.

There were airplanes sitting all about in various stages of molting and transition. About the only place left for Bud to work on the *Arctic Tern* was at the end of the ramp. A few men helped him pull it as far up on the ramp as they could, and Bud manfully set to work taking off the engine cover. The trick was not to drop the tiny screws and various parts overboard into the water.

A wind came sliding across the ramp, sending things flying, and every time Bud took a piece of the airplane off, he had to weigh it down or it would be blown into the lake. He got the oil drained and was starting to take out the spark plugs for cleaning when a fellow inquired if he would mind moving the airplane for a few minutes while he put his own into the water. Bud carefully picked up parts, and hoping nothing would fall off the plane while it was on the water, they tugged and pushed it back into the lake. Down the ramp came an airplane with a set of wheels under each float. The airplane went into the lake and the wheels were pulled back up the ramp.

Bud got the *Arctic Tern* back in position and resumed work. The engine had been throwing oil badly, and between Mr. Spooner and Bud the leak was traced to a gasket around the oil screen. A man came down the ramp towards Bud as Bud hastened to get the work underway. "I wonder if you would mind moving your ship so we can get an airplane out of the water?"

"Not at all," Bud replied, and again started gathering up the tools and lifting the weights off pieces so they could be moved aside.

The second airplane came out of the water and Bud finally got the *Arctic Tern* back in place so as to resume his labors. He took out the spark plugs and was just starting to clean them when two men came walking down the ramp. "We wondered if you . . . ."

"Why no, not at all," and Bud moved parts and tools and airplane once more.

The usual time it takes for a pilot to give his airplane its 25 hour check is around four hours, but Bud worked from before 8 o'clock in the morning until 10:00 at night. As he was finishing putting the last screws back into the engine cover late that night a man came walking down the dock. "Would you mind . . . ?" the innocent newcomer began.

"Just a moment," Bud interrupted hastily. "I want to finish this job first."

The man looked puzzled and stood around on first one foot and then the other. In less than ten minutes Bud was done. "You can get your airplane now," he told him with a sigh. "I am done here."

The man looked mildly surprised. "I have no airplane," he said. "I only wanted to look at yours."

Cooking Lake lies at an altitude of 2300 feet. The load we were carrying was designed for sea level performance, and in order to get off at this altitude we must have quite a wind. Bud and I drifted around on the lake for several hours and, after two attempts at take-off, climbed into the air. It was a head wind, but we couldn't be choosy. As we proceeded it increased in velocity.

Near Grand Prairie, western Alberta, there was a last seaplane anchorage marked on the map for a lake called Saskatoon Lake. While there is an excellent landing field for wheel ships at Grand Prairie nearby, we would have to land on the water. I shall never forget Saskatoon Lake.

The shallow muddy prairie pond was whipped to a foaming froth by the time we came over it. It looked treacherous, indeed, with ducks and rocks speckled about. Around we came on a trial run to look it over.

There is a peculiar sensation experienced when you make a turn near the ground in such a wind. Your speed forward is confused by the factor of side drift. First, as you turn out of the wind you are traveling over the ground very fast. Then, as you come crosswind you seem to be blown sideways faster than you go forward, while as you make your final turn into the wind for your landing, you hardly move over the ground at all.

About twenty feet above the lashing waves we were straining our eyes for a sight of snags when a down current of air pushed us right into Saskatoon Lake! Wham! We hit with terrific force. The airplane almost doubled up at the impact. The wind blew us back into the water and we walloped another big wave with a crash. The succeeding impacts brought us to a stop.

Bud and I were all right but the windshield had a jagged crack across it diagonally. We had no sooner made a mental note of this than we realized that we were in imminent danger of capsizing.

Bud hoped to get to the shelter of a cove nearby but the wind was too strong for him to dare use power to buck it. The seaplane pilot knows that it is not safe to try to turn a ship in high winds. He must "sail" the airplane like a boat, letting it head into the wind as it wants to do. The keel of the floats and the rudder keep the ship on course, while the pilot uses the engine only enough to hold his own. In this way, he can "crab" across the water in a nearly sideways direction until he reaches his destination.

Bud was trying to do this while at the same time keeping the aileron of one wing up and the other wing down to hold the airplane fast to the water, when we saw that we were already being washed aground near shore.

"Jump out and grab the airplane!" Bud yelled at me. While I had had some training before now in jumping out and grabbing canoes and dog sleds, I was more reluctant to plunge into that cold dirty Saskatoon Lake to grab the *Arctic Tern*. I hesitated, not understanding the danger which the airplane was in.

"Hurry up, jump!" Bud urged, and at last, obedient, I jumped. I had taken off my shoes and socks and rolled up my pants' legs. The slimy ooze on the bottom of Saskatoon Lake squirmed between my bare toes and it was two feet deep before I struck more solid footing which I presumed was the frost line. While the airplane rode in muddy, heaving water scarcely ten inches deep I sank and sank into goo and seaweeds. Up and up the water crept to my hips, while combers rolled onto my braced back. While I hung all my weight to the bow of a float, Bud clambered ashore with the ax and chopped a stout staff which he drove solidly into the lake bottom.

Holding an airplane in a wind is like trying to hold a bucking horse, and I was fast giving out. But Bud soon had the *Arctic Tern* tied by the cleats on the front of her pontoons where she rode soon at ease. Luckily we were in the only even partially sheltered spot on the whole lake. We were behind a very slight undulation of the shore. Outside the point the white waves rolled wild. Screeching at each other in the wind, my hair blown like a mop, we erected our tent and made camp.

It was the first but not the last time we were to deplore the tent we had. In all our previous experience we had always camped in a solid eight by ten foot canvas wall tent, equipped with a tiny wood-burning camp stove and smoke stack. With such a tent and a knowledge of how to use it a person can be comfortable anyplace on earth, and I mean that literally. But on this airplane trip we were unable to carry our canvas tent. It weighed 25 pounds; we couldn't afford the weight. Bud had, therefore, designed and made us a nylon tent which rolled up into a package about the size of a wiener and which weighed only five pounds, inclusive of its aluminum tent stakes. The slender tent pole and two uprights were always carried lashed onto the pontoons.

Now nylon is an unbeatable material for many things but not for a tent. In a wind like this it proved to be quite unmanageable. The fabric was so light that nothing we devised could hold it down. Although we industriously piled hundreds of pounds of rocks on it, burying the tent walls in rocks and sand, the tent walls would work loose, while holes soon gaped in them from the sparks thrown out of the little stove pipe, thus making a very makeshift shelter when reckoned against nature's blasts.

I set to work boiling some drinking water from the muddy lake while the nylon tent popped and barked as the wind tried to tear it to shreds. We had saved two small buckets from the discarded cooking gear, but we had no food.

While I stayed in the tent and fired the stove, Bud set off to look for gas and grub. From the air the homes of the far-western pioneer wheat ranchers seemed nearby. But they really weren't. After some six miles, Bud reached an inhabited farm house. He had a regular farm supper with the family there, apparently being made by them to feel right at home. By the time he returned to Saskatoon Lake he and the farmer had driven nearly a hundred miles to round up gas.

Bud had got some small stove bolts and a drill; he was able to drill and mend the Plexiglas windshield with bolts and iron glue. We thanked the farmer, Mac Prentiss, as best we could, and he drove away through the cold twilight of midnight while Bud crawled shivering and grateful into the loudly flapping tent. "Farmers the world over are like that man," Bud said. "Helpful and resourceful. I know what he's up against here in this country and it's rough to make a go of it."

The wind blew. On the second day we were getting pretty hungry again. Together we walked to the farm house near the lake which had been empty the first time Bud called there. Now the farmer was at home, although he was just preparing to leave for town.

Did you ever visit the farmer when his wife is away for a few weeks visiting her mother? The once-polished wood range in the kitchen is spattered with grease from hard-fried meat and everything is strewn with dust and ashes. The prairie farm without a woman's presence is as forlorn and empty as the ends of the earth. The farmer, hapless soul, has not changed his shirt for a month, and he ambles around in suspenders, only putting on his shoes when somebody comes to the door. He has been working in his fields night and day, for this is planting time. But no one should feel sorry for this man. He is living the way he wishes so far as anybody can; he has no boss. The poverty of the prairie farmer is evident in his thatched roof and sod-walled outbuildings and in his lack of power machinery about the place, yet pity him not.

When it was uncovered that this man had been born at a little town in the mountains of Colorado right near where Bud's people were now living, he offered us whiskey and beer, and when we declined this, after some palaver, he offered us the long-dreamed-of food. He had more heavy cream, he said, than he knew what to do with, but he had no milk since he had already "separated" for the day. Would we accept a pint or a quart of cream to drink, then? From his wife's cupboards he emerged with a whole chicken in a jar that his oldest daughter had canned. Some withered lettuce and tomatoes, bought in town, came with this. That was all the food he could think up. He apologized that he had no bread. But we couldn't *buy* these things. They were only to give away, he said. We made our way back to our tent and our airplane on the lake, where we devoured the pure cream and the other things that evening, with a little saved over for tomorrow's breakfast.

When the waves quieted we thankfully left Saskatoon Lake and flew to large Charlie Lake near Fort St. John, just over the line from Alberta into British Columbia. Near here, at Dawson Creek, the Alaska Highway officially begins; it is 1671 miles long, 1200 miles of it being in Canada.

We had dinner at a roadhouse. While there we saw a couple of cars full of travelers going by, bound for Alaska on the highway. We asked the owner, who was also our waitress, if she saw many travelers and she told us that around 35 cars were said to be leaving Edmonton daily for Alaska, mostly families intending to settle. Built in 1943 in a period of eight months, the road was still regarded officially as a military highway. Although there were road maintenance camps and some tourist courts every hundred miles or so along the wide gravel road, many people brought tents with them and camped. Many also brought rifles and guns of various sorts, feeling that they were pioneering in the wilderness, but their guns were sealed by the Canadian government to protect the wildlife along the road from being fired upon by the eager travelers.

The owner told us of the pioneers: "An awful lot come back this way again discouraged. It seems like most people feel they didn't find Alaska to be as rich or as easy as they had expected, and they probably thought it too much of a burden to stay there and work. When they got there they couldn't see just working at the same old jobs they had left back in the States. I would sure like to go to Alaska, though," she added.

"Why don't you go?" we asked.

"Well, I'm Canadian and we can't settle permanently in Alaska. My folks were Americans from the States, though," she explained.

Now that girl would like Alaska, we thought, as we walked off, and Alaska would like her; she had the initiative to start up her own restaurant business. The United States, Canada, Alaska, and the Northwest Territories are inhabited by the same kind of people with the same hopes and fears. They are related so closely, often by blood ties, that it is impossible to tell a Canadian from an American on sight. Why must there be these petty border problems? Why can't the people of North America travel and live where they like? Every year several hundred people give up their American citizenship to buy properties and live in the open lands of Canada, and every year at the same time hundreds of Canada's young college graduates and technicians are attracted by business opportunities in the United States. There is a constant interchange of citizens going on between the two countries.

At Fort St. John we left the railroad behind. Charlie Lake where our airplane was gassed up had calmed and there wasn't a breeze. The altitude was 2200 feet. I talked long hours with a Canadian wife who was born and educated in New Jersey and she told me in detail about her husband's stomach ulcers. Over tea at their home I eyed this man with not a little awe.

He had lived around logging camps and worked on the Alaska Highway. Surprisingly, it is more usual for loggers, ranchers, miners and mounted policemen to be killed by the food they exist on in the great open spaces, than by the accidents of their trade.

Lovely green forests again passed beneath our airplane's wings and away on the far horizon stood the snowcapped peaks of the Rocky Mountains. We welcomed the sight of those shining peaks which stretch up the North Pacific coast: they portended the panhandle of Alaska. Flying the continental route was much to be preferred to flying that foggy, glacier-studded ocean front not far away.

The Alaska Highway was built to connect a string of airfields inland. Military flyers at first called this staging route the world's toughest airway. It is five times the length of the Himalayan Hump into China. The maps of ten years ago were highly inaccurate, while only twelve weather stations were scattered along it, whereas now there are 125 or more. Twenty American pilots and many military passengers were lost before the end of 1944. Now this inland flight from the United States through Canada to Alaska is standard for us commuters.

At length the steady hum of our little engine cut away the miles with its flashing metal blade, and we were over Fort Nelson. This village existed before Chicago was imagined. But there was no place for us on floats to refuel except to land on the Nelson River, winding in its canyon far below. We had been flying at our highest altitude yet on floats — 9000 feet — and now must go down and down and still down to find the river set deep within its embankments. Bud made a perfect landing before the Indian village of shacks and log cabins.

We were met by Provincial Officer Keith Alexander on the river bank. His little son, age five and incredibly blooming with health, stood beside him. This man's work as game commissioner with one deputy, Batiste, to help him, embraced the patrol of an area of 150,000 square miles. He loved the life. The five-year-old loved being a wild child. Life in the wilderness is wonderful, exhilarating and vital for all men and children. You have never seen men and children at their best until you have seen them in their natural environment where they have not been artificially repressed and molded. Keith Alexander and his little son made a sight which is rare nowadays.

A gusty breeze blew up the canyon next morning. After grateful good-bys Bud and I climbed aboard the *Arctic Tern* and prepared our souls for the most hazardous and tricky take-off of our entire career thus far. If one passes such an examination as this in aviation he can soon be termed an expert. All northern pilots are experts. That's the only kind that survive.

"Watch the second hand on the clock," directed Bud. "If she won't rise in 45 seconds, we might as well give up and try later."

Running down the river through tricky crosscurrents of wind, the plane skimmed swiftly, eating up the distance to the river's bend. Would she rise in time?

Our eyes were glued ahead to spot out treacherous driftwood. Then I saw a gust coming up river to meet us. If we could hit that gust just right, that would provide our lift. The gust was visible by a ruffling of the water ahead. We met it, the plane rose from the water. The gust passed and dropped us in its wake! Down came the airplane, its pontoons lightly touching the water again.

Our take-off space was almost used up and we were traveling at highest speed. Riding the down draft close to the water, Bud urged the airplane to full power, gambling his faith that we could rise from the canyon as the river turned. In less time than it takes to tell, the take-off was an accomplished fact. We were not content until we had climbed thousands of feet above wicked canyon and forest. High over British Columbia we thanked our lucky stars and life was good.

Range after range of bald peaks stretched away, separated by lake-studded valleys. Patches of last year's snow stood out. The steady on-course signal of the radio range came through Bud's earphones to assure him that we were on the beam.

For gas and noon lunch we came down at Watson Lake, Yukon Territory. A detachment of the Royal Canadian Air Force was stationed here, and there were facilities for passengers traveling the Canadian Pacific Airlines which had a lunch stop in the wilderness. The dark-stained simulated log cabin barracks and the neat graveled roads were unusually decorative; here was no ugly gash on the landscape which man's presence but too often portends. We ate a very good meal in the men's mess for a charge of 50¢ each while the *Arctic Tern* rode tied to the dock.

We had to pay a dollar "landing fee." These charges are made at Canadian airports which are in almost all instances government controlled.

In the United States if an airport wants to go out of business quick, it charges a landing fee. In the case of some big city airports, a landing fee may be charged with the hope of scaring all small aircraft away to make room for the commercial traffic.

We were asked by the officer in charge what routes we were traveling.

"Why, on clear days we fly the radio beam, and on days of poor visibility we follow prominent landmarks or we don't fly," Bud answered, wondering what the officer was getting at.

"You will fly over the Alaska Highway and not leave it from now on," the immaculate moustached officer directed.

It was only then that we learned that in Canada private aircraft are rigidly controlled. The pilot is not the captain of his own ship in the sense that he is in the United States; he is not allowed in Canada to embark upon flight from any airport until permission is given, and then he must follow a carefully given flight plan. This regulation is meant to save private aircraft from getting lost over Canada's vast terrain.

Yet this regulation was much questioned by the pilots, for while flights are regulated strictly from all the fields along the Alaska Highway, pilots do get caught in fog, storms or darkness, and then they are caught away from their radio range, and really lost! The end of several good pilots, including one woman accompanied by her eleven-year-old boy, came while they were trying to follow a winding mountainous automobile road through canyons at over 120 miles an hour.

The only thing in favor of the regulation was said to be that lost pilots or their bodies are more easily found if they fly along the highway. Canada feels she can't take the responsibility of letting these pilots fly freely all over the Territories on their way to Alaska. If pilots are to be handled like children this may be a good rule. In Alaska we have wilderness, too, but in Alaska the rules of the game are reversed. You fly when, where and as you like as long as you obey the civil air laws. If you want to fly in storms, why go ahead. If you get lost, that's your tough luck.

We followed the Alaska Highway, winding through mountains over the divide and into the Yukon watershed. The clouds descended; soon we found ourselves in fog and rain with a low ceiling under which we barely sneaked along, trailing the yellow ribbon of the muddy automobile road. A moose ran down the road ahead and occasionally we passed over cars or highway camps. Over the divide the great lakes which head the Yukon River were turquoise blue, surrounded by majestic snow-capped peaks.

We reached the town of Whitehorse in the Yukon Territory. It is the terminus of the old Whitehorse Railroad which connects to Skagway, Alaska, with ocean communications on the North Pacific with Seattle. We flew over the town where we must get gas, but since a water landing had to be made, the spacious airfield at Whitehorse might as well not have existed for us. Bud called in by radio to the tower as we traveled onward ten minutes' flight to Upper Lake Laberge.

"Wish I dared land on the Yukon right in front of the town," Bud said. "But the man in the tower says there's a seven-mile current there and I'd hate to try to get off it with a loaded ship."

"Are there any facilities or any people at Lake Laberge?" I asked.

"Man didn't say. Look, what are those tents or houses down there?"

From long memories of the past I knew the look of those tents. They were Indians at their fishing. We came in during a lull. Just previously the big lake had been wild and it quieted long enough for Bud and me, wading again in the ice water of a rocky beach, to haul our plane up safely on two drift planks and tie it by weighting a packing box filled with rocks on either wing.

A congenial Indian woman helped us do this, Mrs. Agnes Slim. There "on the marge of Lake Lebarge" where the mythical Sam McGee was cremated by poet Robert Service, we pitched our tent right beside the airplane.

Mrs. Slim marveled as a complete camp unrolled quickly from so small a bundle. She saw that we had with us no food.

"Here is dried fish," she said softly. "You can boil him." Soon smoke was issuing from the tiny stovepipe and the kettle simmered. I found a piece of bread left over from Waskesiew Lake, Saskatchewan, and a little cream from Saskatoon Lake, Alberta. The kindly Indian people said there was plenty of fuel in their woodpile. It was not the first time nor the last that the Indian and Eskimo people of the North have helped out a pilot!

Next day Bud flew the *Arctic Tern* back to Whitehorse to get gas, leaving me there in the camp. Although it was a flight of only ten minutes, the same trip to town by power boat was said to take 4½ hours upstream. Landing on the swift, infant Yukon before the town with an empty ship, Bud returned as quickly as he could.

Whitehorse is a more or less modern city with hotels, flop houses, garbage dumps, electricity and the rest of it. In 1898 it was founded by the Gold Rush, when thousands of men, women, and even children poured over the trail where the Whitehorse Railroad now lies to stake their claims, and by canoes and rafts floated down the rapids to Lake Laberge and down the Yukon to Dawson in hopes of getting rich. Fabulous were the fortunes made by a few. Thousands met disillusionment, poverty, suffering and death. Some froze in the winter, some were shot by robbers and outlaws, some were drowned under ice. They did not have the proper clothing and they did not know how to take care of themselves in the wilderness.

This fact holds true of the pioneers of today as well! They too are ill-clothed, ill-housed and disillusioned. It would seem as though humanity in these years has learned little or nothing about living in the North, outside the protection of its cities.

The people of old were from the cities; from them has come down to us a vast accumulation of story and legend, much of which is completely without basis or fact, upon which most of the American public still bases its "information" on arctic life today.

The city of Whitehorse, while it is in Canada's Yukon Territory geographically, comes under some psychological American influence because its railroad runs through Alaska to reach it from the Pacific. Canadian and American products vie with each other on the grocery shelves. The land of five quarts to the gallon ends here.

Bud and I awoke in our tent on the shore of Lake Laberge the third day. It had rained in the night. The spruce forest was wet and somber, and fog hung halfway down the mountain. Outside our fumigated tent the mosquitoes wailed in their thin tiny voices, and we heard all kinds of bird songs, long absent to the ear: Gambel's white-crowned sparrow, the junco, the myrtle warbler.

The old familiar sights and sounds came suddenly as though we had never left them. Everything fell into focus. I had never really felt as though we were getting North when we were flying over it with our airplane, viewing it with detachment. It was necessary to come down into that Indian camp and hear the chained dogs wail and have the Indians give us fish. Unexpectedly my happiness went clear to the bone. This might be Alaska now. We were almost home in Alaska!

4 HOME TO ALASKA

AT WHITEHORSE Bud had talked with the customs inspector, as it was a port of embarkation from Canada. He had radioed the airport in flight that he was landing on floats, and a customs official met him on the bank of the Yukon River before the town. Together in a taxi they rode some blocks to the customs office. When they got out the official beat a retreat into his office and the taxi driver looked straight at Bud.

"The customer pays," he said.

"Doesn't he always?"

"Yes," the cab driver admitted with a grin, "but in this case, you happen to be the customer."

"Oh! How much?"

"One buck."

In the office the inspector inquired of Bud if he had had a pleasant trip through Canada. As commander of a vessel Bud must answer a few questions. How many passengers aboard? What was the tonnage? (Both smiled at that.) If you are merely crossing Canada and not taking anything into or out of the country there are but few formalities. Briefly they are: You must clear a customs office before leaving the United States and you must land at a recognized port of entry in Canada. At both ends of the line you must state your business, what you intend to do, and give your aircraft identification and particulars.

Low clouds hung over the mountains but the weatherman on the radio reported clear sky ahead Alaska way.

Weather is sent every fifteen minutes over the regular radio range. You can tune in on the beam and listen. The weather is given for all the surrounding country so that pilots may know what the exact weather is at any point in a radius of several hundred miles. The pilot can also call in and ask for detailed weather in any particular place.

The radio is likewise useful for filing "flight plans." A flight plan is a detailed account by the pilot to the airfield of the trip he is going to make. He gives his time of departure, his compass course, his hours of fuel on board, the mileage involved, his cruising speed, and his estimated time of arrival at his destination. This information is wired ahead or radioed ahead to alert other airports for the pilot's safety. The only flaw in filing a flight plan is that it *must* be closed. You must report in without fail at the end of your journey at the time stipulated.

In the United States and in Alaska there is so much flying that experience has proved it very expensive, confusing and almost impossible to keep track of all these pilots, just as it is impractical to try to keep track of all the automobilists embarking from the various cities. An American pilot is accustomed to being responsible for himself, and he does not have to file a flight plan. Not so in Canada. Filing a flight plan is not optional along the Alaska Highway but mandatory.

Now, there is an Air Search and Rescue unit in Alaska which was established in 1945 and which is very alert. If a pilot is reported flying on a schedule and he becomes as much as half an hour beyond his fuel supply a search plane departs from its base immediately and a rescue operation is underway.

For these reasons we did not want to file a flight plan when crossing into Alaska with a float ship. We had found what happens when you must land on rivers and lakes far from all communications. Our radio had a sending range of only fifteen to twenty miles.

Yet as we left Whitehorse for Tanacross, Alaska, we had to file a flight plan to comply with Canadian regulations.

Taking the plane's telephone mouthpiece from its hook, and tuning in on the air radio, Bud called. Here is what I heard, which may be presumed to be a typical communication of this kind:

"Whitehorse Radio. Whitehorse Radio," said Bud. "Cessna N89149 calling Whitehorse Radio. Do you read? Over."

The metallic reply came back at once: "Aircraft Cessna 89149 calling Whitehorse Radio. Go ahead."

Bud: "Cessna N89149 en route from Lake Laberge to Tanacross, Alaska. Contact flight along Alaska Highway. Estimated time of arrival, 3:05. Fuel on board, four hours. What is the weather at Kluane Lake? Over."

The weather at Kluane Lake was given as "600, thin scattered, visibility 20 miles, temperature 61, dew point 54, wind west seven, altimeter 001. Visibility east, 4 miles, south, 1½. Scattered to variable broken clouds."

Bud came back with "Roger," and said, "Thank you. Over and out."

There is no room for excess chatter on the airways for this system is like a party line; some other aircraft may be waiting his turn to talk.

It is quite simple to communicate by talking back and forth over the radio telephone unless there is a lot of static to contend with. In this case communication may be impossible. There are also some mistakes made at times that may prove embarrassing.

Water had got into the airspeed indicator somehow at Lake Laberge and it didn't register; the rate-of-climb indicator also was struggling about unreliably. Storm clouds pressed low into the great mountains of the Yukon Territory as again we followed the thin ribbon of the Alaska Highway. Our aeronautical map, the only one we could get, was four years out of date. It showed the Alaska Highway as a straight line and forgot to mention the side roads. At last we came to a fork in the road. Which way?

As rain clouds spilled their burdens on all sides we decided, of course, upon the wrong road. We followed it, believing we "identified" one lake after another. Then doubts began to assail us. A half hour later we were getting into rugged mountains. Bud switched on the radio. To his surprise he got an A signal where an N signal should have been.

"This road has led us astray," he muttered, and turned the controls over to me while he started pawing the map. "Either both this compass and the radio are wrong, or we're on the wrong road."

We swung around and headed back over the miles we had just come. We had wasted one hour's gasoline when we got the mistake corrected. There would not be quite enough gas left to fly on to Tanacross, Alaska, and still have a good margin of safety.

"Guess we'll just have to land on Kluane Lake," Bud said. But Kluane Lake was given as 3050 feet. Would the airplane be able to get off from there with a load on floats? We tried to reach some station by radio to report our changed plans, but no luck; the rain storm had the air waves jammed full of static.

Kluane Lake was a deep apple green that changed tones as the lake deepened. We got gas at Burwash Landing but there was no radio station there. Because it was the fourth day since we had eaten a real meal, we took guilty time off to gobble one at the roadhouse. Meanwhile, the wind dropped. We waited and waited, drifting on the big lake. At length a black cloud bore down the lake with lightning streaking across its front at intervals. As we watched, a streak of rumpled water came rushing forward. Bud opened the *Arctic Tern* up to full throttle and went smashing toward it. The wind met us head-on and up into the air the airplane lifted. Bud swung around the frowning cloud and we were on our way. For a while we had discussed the possibility that I might have to take the O'Hara Bus Line, which made three trips a week from Edmonton to Fairbanks.

Sunset found our small airplane following the broad valley of the familiar Tanana River northwestward. There were endless hours of twilight for flight, if we wished to extend our time, for we were bordering the "land of the midnight sun" in the subarctic, where during the summer weeks it never gets dark at all. Northern bush pilots seldom rest during the summer.

I suppose our first flight to Alaska would not be complete, to crown a liberal beginner's education, if we did not have some experience in getting lost and rescued. We were destined to enter Alaska with a real salute, and here is how it happened.

The storm clouds were behind. An arctic sun highlighted the peaks of the Alaska Range as we crossed the border into Alaska. The mountains had slid back to march along at a respectful distance on either side, where broad gleaming glacial streams came crawling out of their gorges to join the infant Tanana River on the plain. We flew over a country of green swamps and forests into which full summer had already stolen. Although we had not seen this part of Alaska before, it was all home now.

As we passed over Northway, a big weather station and airfield, Bud called in on the radio to explain why we were somewhat late. There was already a tracer or alert signal out to all stations to be on the lookout for our plane; now they could cancel it.

It was late in the day and we were tired and sleepy when we flew over the village marked Tanacross, Alaska. There was a new airfield there and I flew around it at 1000 feet while Bud tried in vain to rouse the tower and close our flight plan for the evening. At last Bud gave up on that; we couldn't establish contact.

"Count off the seconds on the clock," he directed me, "and I'll make a pass at the river there by the town."

"Why?" I asked.

"Well, if I know how many seconds it takes to skim over that bend, then I'll know if we have enough room to land there and take off again."

The count I made was only 35 seconds. Bud said the bend of the river was too short. Later we learned bush pilots on floats did land here but Bud's judgment was beyond a doubt right for us, considering our load. If it had only been feasible to land, a lot of the misunderstanding that subsequently occurred could have been avoided. We could have taxied on the Tanana River right over to the edge of the landing field itself, reported in personally, and got our gas. We were low on gas. We had to find some nearby water to land on quickly.

Just six miles off lay a lake marked Mansfield Lake, with a village by it. We looked the village over. Indians.

Back over the Army transport field we buzzed again. This time Bud got the tower on the radio.

"Cessna N89149. I am landing on Mansfield Lake," he repeated. "I am landing on Mansfield Lake. Do you have 80 octane gasoline and

40 SAE oil. I am low on gas. I am low on gas. I need ten gallons of gas and one quart of oil. I'll come in in the morning and pick it up."

Although the static was bad, the confident "Roger" of the man at the field assured us he understood.

We made a landing upon serene Mansfield Lake. To our surprise there was no village upon its forested shore; not even a path could be seen. Actually the village was half a mile back where the Indians were just winding up their spring muskrat hunting in the swamps.

"Think I'll taxi up into this slough here," Bud said. "Maybe we can reach the village by these winding channels." Soon the lake was lost behind as our little airplane was swallowed whole by an enveloping jungle of green.

"The airplane will be safe from waves here anyway," Bud said, "and if we can't reach the Indians we can just make camp and sleep."

I was well acquainted with the winding waterways of the northern forests. They are usually very deep, currentless, aimless, and almost endless. That was why it might be foolish to leave the airplane to walk to the village; it was doubtful if a person could reach it without being cut off by water.

Shortly after our river forked, therefore, we halted and waded in slimy swamp to tether our airplane. The thorny brambles were shoulder high; they were wild primroses.

Not much to our surprise, an Indian arrived with his obedient little son between his knees perched lightly in a kayak so frail it was like a shell.

"You are hungry?" asked the man in good English. "My wife is cook for you. Come, eat."

"Say, those're the best words we've heard yet."

It was a real welcome home to Alaska, even if not the hot bath and comforts I had hoped for in Fairbanks. Bud and I stepped very carefully into the shell-like canoe. Could it carry us all? We sat very still as the water rose to the gunnels. Blood in the bottom of the canoe showed something had recently been killed.

For half an hour up the winding slough the man silently paddled. He pulled up beside a fish trap and we stepped out into the village.

There were tents pitched upon the greensward. The Indian and his round, shy, smiling wife, mother of six, gave us food in their tent. It was surely nice to get into a good canvas tent again. They wordlessly gave us the best they had. The food was chunks of moose (the loin, fried white-man style in a skillet for our especial benefit), hardtack, canned butter, store cookies and canned pineapple rings. We ate moderately because our stomachs were shrunken, then pressed $2.00 into the man's palm.

"I will take it. For my children," he smiled. "I am poor man, not catch much last year."

All across Canada and now in Alaska we heard of the severe drop in fur prices which was impoverishing the northern people whose only income was derived from fur. As if that weren't all, it had been the coldest winter in years. Day after day of 60 below and 70 below and once even 80 below zero weather throughout British Columbia, the Yukon, and interior Alaska, hung on even into March.

The numbers of fur animals caught took a drop because nothing moves when it gets that cold. The Indian told us how a wolf slept near his house of nights, trying to catch one of his dogs.

Conveying us back to our airplane with silent dripping paddle strokes, our friend watched interestedly while we quickly pitched a camp in one of the most unfavorable locales, in high brambles amid swarms of mosquitoes, that we had ever attempted. But soon the wet briars were tramped down, the stove was erected inside the tent, and we crawled in with an armload of wood. Content that the white people were all right and safe, the watchful Indian went home. Inside the tent we fumigated with the DDT fizz gun and fell exhausted into the sack.

At 4:30 in the morning, with the early sun promising a scorching day, with a thrush calling in the forest and the insects humming, a terrific noise came suddenly into our jungle solitude to penetrate our heavy slumber. It was a $75,000 army observation plane. Over our little green nylon tent it came diving down from a yellow sky with a roar that catapulted us out of the tent.

I stood there full in a beam of sunlight in my red shirt to reassure our "rescuers" — something was up which meant that this could be no less than a rescue! Hundreds of mosquitoes which had waited patiently outside the tent as we slept made dives upon me at the same time and enjoyed an early breakfast.

We couldn't know why, but we were plainly being rescued! The airplane came roaring by again only a few feet above the bushes. It had an army star painted under each wing. The early morning sun stained its silvery form a blushing red and streamers of fire seemed to fly from its flashing propeller blades. Just then we saw an orange streamer flutter down behind as it passed. Plummeting into the brush, the streamer fell with its message across the deep slough. Bud jumped into our tied airplane and tried briefly without success to contact the airfield just six miles away. There was nothing to do but settle this matter at once, and within a few minutes more I saw him take off from the lake and fly away. Not content even with this sign of activity from us the persistent war bird flew along with Bud to Tanacross and there headed in to its runways. Bud circled and came to a landing with the empty *Arctic Tern* upon the river.

He had just finished tying up and climbed the river bank to the army field when a group of five fellows came to meet him.

"Hey, what's up?" asked Bud.

"We brought you your gas and oil. But, say, didn't you burn your motor up flying around like that?"

"Flying like what? There is no danger of burning up the motor."

"But without any oil," the fellows said.

"Why, there is plenty of oil and gas too, left in this little ship to fly on to Fairbanks, if I had to, on a margin."

At this a roar of laughter burst all around. "We figured you would be drifting on the lake," they explained, "since you were given to us as a float ship. But you see, the radio man understood you were out of oil and were making a forced landing. He said you needed 14 quarts of oil and 10 gallons of gas."

"Why, if he had stopped to think, this little ship only holds 4½ quarts of oil total."

The rescuers had intended to drop on Mansfield Lake the 10 gallons of gas and the 14 quarts of oil that were ordered. But how on earth did they imagine that 14 quarts of oil could be contained in the kind of small aircraft we had? Used to dealing with large aircraft, the army did not consider this even a bit strange. These airmen were attached to the Search and Rescue Squadron stationed at Fairbanks and they had been dispatched 200 miles from their home base at four in the morning to perform this particular service for humanity. It was all part of a long-range plan by which the United States Air Force had resolved to become familiar with arctic and subarctic flying. Already since 1945 they had effected many rescues, which were only incidental to the vast general fund of information they were accumulating in their training grounds.

"Say, I know you bush pilots can really fly, but just tell us one thing, please," asked one of the young rescuers earnestly: "How do you Alaskan pilots land your ships in little rivers like the one we saw yours in? Now, I'll say that must take *some* flying!"

Bud had to be honest with him. "Oh, I didn't *land* there," he explained. "I landed on the lake and just taxied in there because I wanted to pitch the tent and go to sleep."

"Oh!"

The members of the squadron were rightly impressed by the stories they had heard about the Alaska bush pilots. They didn't know that Bud wasn't one of those — not yet!

The fellows told Bud that nearly all the Alaska bush pilots that got into trouble with their planes would be found sitting on some lonesome river bar or in some hole in the brush, or floating about the middle of a lake if they were on floats. There would be little or no damage done to either the airplane or its passengers which a few imported materials would not remedy.

"It is different though, with military craft," they sighed. "They get lost a lot because they fly over the overcast. And when you find those guys it's generally pretty sad." As the flyers admitted, "Boy, when they turn up missing, well — they're just gone!" They had lost 80 men during one six-week period.

"Thanks a lot fellows, anyway. I'd better be going now and get back to my wife."

"No trouble at all," they said. "We're glad you didn't need rescuing. Just let us know if you ever need us. That's what we're stationed here for. We need the practice."

"I'll say you need the practice," quipped one to the pilot. "The way you bounced on that landing! You sprung our darn landing gear."

I was waiting with the tent rolled when Bud got back. As we loaded up, the army ship came flying by on its way home — just a few minutes to Fairbanks.

When we reached Fairbanks ourselves near 11:00 that morning we went to the customs official to report in. From him we learned we had run up around $1000 worth of fines in violations, although considering the nature of the case they would not be pressed. The first violation was that of making a landing in the Territory of Alaska without first notifying officials of our arrival from a foreign country. Officials were supposed to meet every entry on the landing field. But if you have to land on floats on a wilderness lake, what then? Such a landing can only be dubbed an emergency landing.

The second violation was that we landed at Fairbanks on the Chena Slough of the Tanana River downtown without first radioing officials to meet us there on the river bank. We just came in, tied up the *Arctic Tern* with the other aircraft on floats near the bridge, and never thought a thing about it. Then we walked uptown unnoticed and had on our minds only a steak, and a shave and haircut for Bud. The shave and haircut in Fairbanks cost $2.50. After that, we saw the customs inspector. He said the next time to just omit the steak and see him first.

It was June 27. We had left Boston on June 5. *It had taken us twenty-two days to fly to Alaska.* I have heard of flights made to establish time records but I believe this must be the longest time record of modern days. In subsequent years we always made it in from three to five days on wheels, following the string of good fields all the way. Other pilots who have flown it on floats admit that they also have known some inconvenience.

Within a couple of days we had found the first and only bath of the year in a real bathtub in Fairbanks and had completed all our outfitting.

In Fairbanks a person always tries to catch up on all the news of Alaska in one gulp. Chuck West, bush pilot, had started an "Arctic Travel Service," and he was distributing attractive folders on the arctic around the hotel lobbies.

I had never had any doubt from the beginning that the arctic would, or at least should, become a world playground in time: its vacation possibilities are stupendous.

Yet there was always that strong antisocial intuition, that inner voice which tells every Alaskan to be cautious when he praises Alaska.

"I have given you everything," the voice says. "I have nurtured you in your prodigal days. Now, even you, too, betray me."

The trouble is that you can't share wilderness. When you share it the wilderness is no more. You can't easily make either wilderness or freedom available to other human beings. Freedom given easily is forgotten and even held in contempt by self-willed slaves. Wilderness given to the tender mercies of 250 million people, is doomed.

Friendly Fairbanks, the end of the road: A "Man-on-the-Street" program, promoted by Station KFAR in conjunction with the very active Chamber of Commerce, was going along interviewing newcomers on the sidewalks asking them what they thought of Alaska and what they hoped to do here. The University of Alaska sat on its hill north of town nearby. But Fairbanks was not the rest of Alaska. Not any more than Mexico City is like the rest of Mexico. Alaska as she is — harsh, primitive, beautiful and cruel, is far from the town of urban dwellers, most of whom in our generation have never known real want, fear or hunger — or loneliness.

"Have you ever met any of these women in Alaska who live out alone, like teachers and missionaries at the remote settlements?" I asked some women at one of the town's innumerable cocktail parties.

"No," they laughed. "And we don't want to."

A certain part of Fairbanks was very cordial, very gay. It was their happy duty to entertain the visiting delegations of senators which arrived almost weekly from Washington to dash off an Alaska report. The little florist shop was ready with its air-imported roses and gardenias for corsages. The shop windows displayed the latest gowns

Above the Alatna Valley

Looking toward the ridge that separates the Alatna Valley
from Takahula Lake

Our cabin and plane at Takahula Lake

The beginning of a take-off

at all seasons, while the town bustled with clubs and organizations, including a $100,000 Country Club with a membership of 100. This was the side of Fairbanks which the visiting senators, generals and foreign personages saw. There was also a diaper service in Fairbanks and modern schools and hospitals.

Another side of the picture was the hordes of homeless people with their families in cars who had traveled up the Alaska Highway. Every day they came now, winter and summer, seeking a new life, seeking opportunity. Alaska needed new people. People with skills and professions, people with capital, people who had the know-how to create their own business in a land crying for business development. Who were the people who came? They were Western people mostly, the kind of people who had migration in their blood. But mostly they were the kind of people who have little to lose.

They set up in Fairbanks in shacks, tents, garages and tourist courts, and by the time their first winter was over the piles of empty tin cans surrounding most of those dwellings were higher than the house, matching only the coffee grounds and egg shells which were thrown out the door. There is no sanitation, no sewage system throughout most of Alaska's cities. Building materials were so hard to come by these last few years, what with the inflation and the steamship strikes which continuously isolated Alaska for months at a time, that it was not uncommon to find people living in a shelter built out of packing house crates picked up from the backs of stores and barrooms; we knew one student of anthropology at the University who, with his wife, built a baribari out of logs and sod and lived in it all winter after the fashion of the Eskimo aborigines whom he studied in school.

It was said in a government bulletin urging Federal housing aid: "No one will ever know the number of people who have gone to Alaska in hopes of settling, only to return to the United States again heartsick and disillusioned because of a lack of adequate housing."

Yet the United States pours millions of dollars yearly into Alaska as it is. There are 52 government bureaus operating in Alaska.

"Why don't you write a little bit about the *Realities* of Alaska instead of giving people these stories about the beauties of nature and encouraging all these folks to come up here unprepared?" a news reporter asked us, without pulling any punches.

"Reality is what you make it," Bud said.

"We do write about real things," I said. "All the things we have written about were perfectly true. You are right when you say there's a lot I don't know about masses of people and their mass social problems. Yet I'm afraid I'll have to leave that to the experts. We write for the individual and for what he can be and do, and I fail to see why the United States Government should be morally obligated to subsidize people to live in Alaska."

We had spent some years in Alaska towns ourselves in half-built houses. I can recall when we used to stuff the cracks in the house with old socks, lots of times. I can recall how those of us who stayed dug our own bomb shelters in the back yard against the advance of the Japanese. Bud and I felt that we had earned the privilege of our present Alaska residence. Now we had an airplane and a tent, and a lot of people stand ready to blame a person for that.

We put up a small order of summer necessities to be shipped to Hughes, Alaska; one hundred fifty dollars spent for one day in town, and we only expected to see Fairbanks twice this year: once going into the arctic and once coming out. It was a kind of home town to us.

Taking off the winding Chena Slough in the heart of downtown Fairbanks was not easy. Just the day before, a doctor had overshot his landing and crashed under the bridge into a riverboat rounding the bend. A perfect network of obstacles — buildings, smokestacks and electric wires — girdled the slough to catch the unwary. The wires stretched on high across the slough at intervals were all but invisible and you had to know where to fly over them or under them.

We started drifting down the sluggish muddy current in our airplane. The crooked slough possessed many a submerged sandbar. The pontoons scraped bottom and we were stuck. Out into the garbage and sewage-fed stream we had to wade to ease the *Arctic Tern* over the bar.

"Don't let her get sideways!"

After several bars and one hour of taxiing and five attempted take-offs we got into the air down by the power plant.

I didn't ask: "What are we going to do, Bud, now that we are back in Alaska?"

He didn't know. I didn't know. We didn't know what life held from one hour to another, let alone from one day to another. It had been this way many times. We would do the first thing at hand, starting from the known and working toward the unknown. How do you feel your way along with an airplane?

We flew along the Tanana River to where it joined the Yukon and then straightened out across the rolling forest toward the trading post of Hughes on the upper Koyukuk, north of the Yukon.

By river from Fairbanks it is a thousand miles. We had found Hughes the first time by canoe. This afternoon it was to be merely a 210 mile crosscountry flight. Perhaps if we flew to Hughes we would find something there that we had found before.

When we landed on the lovely Koyukuk River our old friends, the traders, Les James and his wife burst out of the door and came down the river bank to meet us. Their son, Johnny, home from the army, was there too. They were expecting us, for they had heard the news of our arrival in Alaska over "Tundra Topics," the radio program, the night before. After shaking hands with the 17 or 18 Indian people of the village, we trailed into the big log home of the traders, slapping at mosquitoes.

"Welcome back to Alaska. How was life with the Eskimos?"

"Oh, the States are nice to visit," we said, "but we always intended to come back."

"Had a nice trip out ourselves for a month last year," Les said. "Or was it the year before? The damned fur prices have gone down so our people can hardly make a living. Say, I notice you settled on a Cessna. Why don't you get yourselves a good airplane like our Stinson?"

"So you've gone and done it, too!" we exclaimed. "You mean to say that old crate setting there by the door is your own airplane?" Bud kidded back.

"Yes, we figured it was about time our family got up to date. Well, a person just about has to keep up with the times. You'll notice the field's 2400 feet long now. Not bad, huh? I dug her out myself with our new D-4 Caterpillar tractor that we brought in by river barge from Fairbanks.

"We hardly do any river freighting any more. Johnny hauls just about everything you could think of direct from town with the airplane. Why, our Indians here have been eating fresh grapes and cantaloupes for the first time in their lives. We've seen air freight from Seattle go down from 96¢ a pound to 12¢ a pound, the last two years!"

We learned there were sixteen different competing airlines running into Fairbanks at present.

"What are you folks going to do this season?" our friends asked us over the breakfast table next morning.

"I don't know exactly," replied Bud. "We haven't decided yet. One thing, Connie and I want to fly up into the Brooks Range across the Arctic Circle and take a look at our old cabin where we lived alone that year. I would just like to see how it looks."

"We want to study the Brooks Range," I added, "from the air. You know we have always kind of considered that country as our special country. Do you happen to know if it is still uninhabited?"

The Jameses admitted it was just the same.

"Expect us back in a few days," Bud said. "I guess we'll just fly up there and land on some lake and camp awhile.

"Well," I said, as Bud and I took off the bosom of the Koyukuk with a full load of gas, "today is the day we have spoken of for a long time. Today we're going to know the answers to a lot of things. I never thought I'd see this day."

What did the Alatna Valley look like by air? Where did fabled Gull Pass lie? How close did we ever get to the head waters of the timberless Colville River in our ground explorations?

The airplane opens up all mysteries. No sooner is a wish expressed to see the other side of a mountain than it is done.

Easily we winged across the Arctic Circle and toward those strange mountains which stretch like new Rockies barricading interior Alaska from the far polar sea. The arctic Brooks Range is composed of twelve major mountain groups as yet not all clearly delineated by the geographers. In these remote arctic mountains we had labored and hunted game to live, and nearly starved.

"First we'll fly over the mountains very high to get the over-all view," said Bud.

We flew at 13,000 feet. The highest peak in the Endicott group was given as 8800 feet. Countless other peaks soared in spectacular array, glacier-strewn. Not real glaciers, for there are almost no glaciers in the arctic, aside from Greenland, but very high snow-filled bowls. We had not been able to see these higher crags from our valley floor before. Now we could see how all the peaks, valleys and the streams that drained them, were laid out.

The day was perfectly clear, the lower slopes of the range warm in the sun, the forests of spruce and birch barely visible from high above. Pilots flying over the Brooks Range were quick to say that no kind of life exists there. People had said we would starve to death. I could see now why pilots made that mistake, looking at the country from high up in the fierce peaks where they flew. But down below, hidden deep in these mountains there are valleys that are lush and green. We knew that our valley contained all of the materials upon which a family could live indefinitely.

We flew clear up to the arctic divide, north of the last trees. Then we came back down the southern continental side of the range, retracing our way at a lower altitude, peering into the canyons and scrutinizing each landmark as we reached our country.

Our country. It seemed as though the sound of the tiny airplane in that country was hushed in its bigness. The sound trailed in the wind, eddied a moment, and was lost in silence. It seemed to me as though I was going home, I who had never wanted a home in the conventional meaning of that term. More majestic even than I had recalled were those rock fortresses which guarded the Alatna River Valley. I had not exaggerated.

Our old cabin, when we found it at last, hardly seemed real. Alone it sat on its hill overlooking a bend of the wild river, unvisited by man since we last closed its door. Quite impossible to find unless you knew where to look for it; overshadowed by the great mountain peaks, it stood as a landmark to the smallness of man. Arctic nights had come and gone. Wolverines had prowled about its door.

Sitting there in solitude all these years the cabin seemed like a child's toy in that vast setting. The people who had lived there once, where were they? They had taken their little lives and problems so seriously. They must have been toys, too. They had a toy airplane now.

We flew low over the roof and back and over again. We could not linger. We could not stop. The place was totally inaccessible by air. It would be foolhardy to risk a landing on the steep swift mountain river.

Somehow I thrilled to the idea of its total inaccessibility and was glad.

We looked over most of the lakes in a hundred mile radius. There was great Walker Lake, 20 miles long, winding between the peaks, head of the arctic Kobuk River. Any person could have that lake just for settling there. Sky blue it was; there is an old legend that a great fish lives in Walker Lake which swallows men who venture out upon it. Then there was Iniakuk Lake in the general area. Good moose country there. Lots of willows. Yet, I personally wouldn't care to build on a lake as large as a sea. The kind of lake a person wants, that is if he intends to build a home, is a small lake. A small lake is sequestered and it has a mood.

We had to land some place. We had burned up three hours of gasoline cruising over some of our country in which no human beings had habitation. Coming around to Takahula Lake for the second time, not on the aerial map, we decided to land there. A clever twist and turn over the low neck of land that separated it from the Alatna River, and it was done. Takahula Lake lay just forty miles along the Alatna Valley from our old cabin. It was about one and one-half miles long and a mile wide: just large enough for a landing field for the largest airplane.

It was perfectly tranquil when we came gliding in. The rock cliff at its head, conical Takahula Peak, was reflected in its mirror. It was a very deep lake. Utter peace pervaded there, as our pretty bird settled with a soft swish.

Open went the silver airplane doors. Our floats touched the rocky shore, I leaped off, caught a tossed rope, and made us fast.

We knew then what we were going to do. The feeling grew and took form when we stood on that shore. We were going to build a home here. Bud said, "You know a person needs a place, I suppose, where he can store the stuff that accumulates through the years."

Aloud I said, "Yes, we need a kind of headquarters where we can collect all our equipment for arctic exploration."

To myself I thought, "Of course we'll take trips out from here, but we'll always come back."

It was as though we had never left this country which had had such a formative influence on us that it had changed our whole lives. We were wanderers yet even a wanderer must have headquarters. A writer can make his headquarters anyplace he wishes and as for photography, this whole country had never been touched with a camera, and it would take a lifetime to do it.

There definitely was a need for someone to make studies in the American arctic a lifetime's profession. There was a need for public education. The world was changing fast and in this modern world we saw a great laboratory for a naturalist in the arctic. Already we had from our experiences of seven years a wealth of intimate knowledge of a kind which was irreplaceable and unique in our generation, knowledge which could be compared to that which a student might acquire tediously in the course of getting his Ph.D. in college. Takahula Lake offered a landing field and it offered many other advantages which I shall describe, to make for an unusual home that without an airplane otherwise would not have been possible. It was a dream founded and made to come true by the wonderful age of air.

I can think of no higher goal of life than that of the student and reporter, unless it be the ideals of he who devotes his lifetime to the discovery and conquest of beauty. The country had taken hold of our hearts.

It is interesting that many a writer withdraws morosely from public life. He retreats to the Florida Keys, to Cape Cod, or to a drafty farmhouse in Maine, and every time he suspiciously opens his door a crack, the critics in New York throw stones at him.

There is probably no author who does not realize he is quite unworthy of his job, but he must tackle it anyway in his own way. In this he often seeks solace from the elements: the oceans, the winds, and sun and rain. He knows that the winds and fogs and rains and the warm sun are good things. A contact with them is invigorating and may be necessary to keep man morally lean.

Here where human voice had never spoken since the world began, the mood of nature ruled supreme, spreading a divine benediction over mountain and valley, field and stream. The year we lived alone in the Alatna Valley it had seemed to me that there was a Presence which walked abroad about the silent land.

Some people would call this land desolate for the reason that no humans inhabit it. It was never at any time desolate to Bud and me. The Presence lived in the music of the stream and the call of the lonely raven. It lived in the ways of the wandering moose, which scientists call instinct, having no other name for the mystery, but which the Indians might be more correct in calling the Spirit of the Moose.

How can man explain this instinct which guides each living thing? How can he account for the incredible diversity of nature animated by intelligence?

There are two evolutions going on on earth at the present time. One is the evolution of man. It is a moral evolution, and its confusions and struggles and paradoxes hold many a writer spellbound observing and predicting the great and terrible panorama of human strife. Yet this is not all of the story. There is also another evolution taking place. The nature people know it. They compose three quarters of the population of the earth. They are still very close to it. It is the evolution of the animals and rocks and trees and ferns which make up the lower orders of life and which have no moral responsibility but which have also their place and their rights on the earth.

Understanding this is what is meant by being in tune with the language of nature. The birds sing their songs and the waterfalls tinkle only for those who will approach on tiptoe. Here the evolving Idea or Presence lay undisturbed in arctic purity, stretching out in a great kingdom to the pole of the earth.

5 TAKAHULA LAKE

Bud and i found Takahula Lake the year we spent alone in these mountains. I had left a canoe at the head of this lake in 1945. I never expected to see this place again.

"Come on," I said the first thing. "Let's see if we can find my old canoe."

Applying plenty of mosquito lotion and not forgetting the rifle, together we staggered on weakened city legs around the lake shore and over the weed-grown portage to the Alatna River's bend a quarter of a mile. The giant afternoon shadow of Takahula Peak cut across our trail.

Bud had made the fragile nine-foot canoe out of arctic spruce pieces chopped out with an ax and planed smooth with a pocketknife. He had lashed its frame with twisted wet moose rawhide from some moose of ours of long ago. A canvas cover was added which was waterproofed by a layer of linseed oil.

We had left the canoe hanging by thongs inside an ancient prospectors' cabin. Now when we found the spot, the old cabin, where we had eaten a whole moose in a month, following a period of starvation, was just a pile of logs. The old cabin fell on my canoe and buried it beneath.

"I can see one end of the canoe sticking out," I cried hopefully. Bud then crawled into a hole on his hands and knees and dug. He retrieved my canoe, battered and broken. Only its brave skeleton was left.

"Look," observed Bud. "Before the cabin fell down a grizzly bear ruined it anyway." The grizzly had left the marks of his teeth along the shattered frame, with strands of his silvery hair. He had stripped it of its canvas with powerful claws. Only tiny shreds of the canvas could be found at the site, carried yards away by the squirrels and birds.

"Don't worry. I can fix it," Bud promised.

Gratefully I carried the remains home. You have to have a canoe to get around. It comes even before the house. A little string and new canvas and paint would fix it up, Bud said. Bud carried his old home-made sled. We would be needing both these things again. They were well made to survive the years of our careless absence.

After months of indecision in the United States, at last we had a concrete plan. Our home we would build here in the arctic. We would build it of the native materials at hand — of spruce logs and stone — and it would nestle into the landscape. It must not be a blot upon this beautiful setting but must be a part of it.

A home should reflect the kind of geography in which it is set and it should suit the personalities of the people who are to live in it. The nest of every wild thing suits its requirements. There is the warm snug nest of the deer mouse and the grass-lined nest of the marmot for his winter's sleep. There is the high massive framework of sticks constructed by the warrior eagle and the tiny thistledown nest built by the delicate hummingbird. These contrast sharply with the metal trap nest of the domestic chicken whose only purpose is to mechanically tally the number of eggs laid.

Into the metal trap nest class fall the mass housing projects, where in overpopulated areas human beings must subdue all normal yearning for individuality and live in standardized burrows, hutches and warrens. Our travels had convinced us that people would really like to be individuals but that if they are crowded too closely together — no matter what the cause or provocation — they haven't a chance. We saw the struggles of our friends to build homes. The shortage of materials, and the regulations and restrictions were such that it had become all but impossible for a person to simply build a home with his own hands. We were amazed to find among our friends in civilization that there were relatively few who had acquired even one small spot of sanctuary of their own which was inviolate, or had a great prospect of acquiring it.

Here in Alaska we could build a home without asking anybody's permission or signing a single paper. We could build it ourselves and have the fun of working on it. The materials were free.

Ninety-eight per cent of Alaska is still unsurveyed and most of it is entirely uninhabited. Anyone may build here in the free public lands. Legal title to 160 acres may be acquired under the Homestead Act which yet governs the opening of lands in the West. It calls for certain improvements plus residence on the land for five months out of each year for three years. There is just one difficulty: you have to *cultivate* ten acres into crops, to get a homestead. And Alaska is *not* an agricultural country, despite what the politicians claim. The arctic just isn't farm country, I am happy to say.

There is another possible means by which a person might gain title to ground in the arctic. He might apply for five acres as a home site or business site. We could fulfill the regulations for this except the part which says that the ground must be surveyed by a government surveyor. The government surveyor must be flown in here at your own expense, and since Takahula Lake was not even on the maps you would have to get him personally. Alaska's government surveyors were all dated up with business ten years in advance a thousand miles to the south of us. So we just gave up on that for the time being and took up a kind of self-appointed trusteeship of the whole sixty thousand uninhabited square miles of the arctic Brooks Range without any more bother over it.

Takahula Lake lies about 350 miles by winding waterways from Hughes. It is days by canoe from our nearest neighbors, the store, and post office. Yet it is only one hour's flight across country by *Arctic Tern*. Our home is about twenty hours' flight from the United States and just four hours off the main airways of the world at Fairbanks, Alaska, most important city in our coming northland. We are residents of the Arctic Zone, being just about seventy miles due north of the Arctic Circle, and as far north as the trees go.

There is four hours' time difference between Takahula Lake and

Arizona, for Alaska lies as far to the west as it does north. We are directly north of the Hawaiian Islands. The lake was named by Eskimos and has seldom been seen by modern man. But it can be suspected as a Hawaiian name because many such names have been handed down in Alaska from the language of the mixed whaling crews which contacted the native people years ago. Thus it comes about that we have a lake in the arctic with a Hawaiian name.

At the head of the lake towers conical Takahula Peak, four thousand feet of rock, rising above the dark green spruce forest. There is no incoming stream to feed the lake. It is fed altogether by deep springs and melted snow, and it keeps an almost constant level the centuries through. The lake has but one outlet. Takahula Creek drains over a shallow bar at the lower end and flows meanderingly for eight miles down the valley through blueberry swamps fed by freshets from the mountains on each side, whose courses we have never traced to our entire satisfaction. There are a few muskrats, a beaver dam. There are many smaller shallow lakes along the valley, where the fat whitefish spawn, packed side to side and nose to tail. A long narrow ridge running down the shoulder of Takahula Peak separates us from the Alatna River, although we are really a part of the whole Alatna Valley in all. Takahula Lake with its sheer cliffs, and its swamps and flower-strewn meadows, does not easily give up its mystery. It is sequestered, secluded, unexpected. It is less than five miles around but it is the kind of lake which you cannot see all of at once from any one spot.

We pitched our tent. It was not hard to decide where to build the house. There was only one place on the lake where there was enough timber to last, and this coincided nicely with the place where the airplane would be sheltered at anchor. We called it Airplane Cove. The house was going to go up on a little knoll overlooking Airplane Cove some thirty feet from the lake edge. It was all so mountainous that a level spot would have to be made. Bud started right in the first hour, in his characteristic way, leveling off the hill.

Sparks flew from the shovel as Bud hoed away the blanket of moss and chopped the alders and willows from a spot the exact size of our house. I helped carry rocks from the lakeside to form the foundation.

This was made two feet wide and three feet deep. The stones we anchored down into the permanently frozen subsoil so that the house would never settle. A small rock-lined and rock-covered drain ran around the outside of the foundation and drained into the garden just in case moisture from melting snow should seep in around the house.

These drains subsequently proved to be the runs for a succession of pet ermine that came to live with us.

Easy-Weasel, as we always called him, was never tame, but one evening he arrived, and he remained ever after, streaking about among the logs as we worked and greedily eating what meat or fish scraps we put out for him. He never asked for food or thanked us for it. He simply demanded it as his rightful due. Whether the rock pile that made the house foundation had once been his home we had no way of knowing, but we do know that Easy-Weasel and his silken kind made themselves at home under our cabin, our porch, and even inside the house, rubbing between our legs and lapping from a bowl of warm gravy like a house cat.

"I'll fly down to Hughes," said Bud, "and bring back a couple of Indians to help. We've built log cabins before, just the two of us. I'm thinking that some help would make it go a lot quicker. We'll pay them $100 each for the completed job. Three weeks from today you will have a home standing in this spot. I mean a nice modern home with running water.

"Do you mind staying here alone?" he asked. "I hate to leave you but I don't see any other way."

"Oh, that's all right," I said. "You'll be back in a couple of hours."

It was true. Bud was back before I knew it from those flights he had to make with an empty ship to Hughes, leaving me alone as many as twenty-five times our first year with an airplane in the arctic. Nothing ever happened. It was always all right.

The two Indian helpers, Henry and Joe, were transported to Takahula Lake where they went to work felling trees, Bud himself working the hardest of all. He made a sort of game out of it. The Indians didn't like it here. They were afraid to go out of sight of the tents. They would work only if they liked you. They lived in their own tent and did their own cooking with store grub we furnished; they were strong brown men in faded ill-fitting work clothes with suspenders and beaded moosehide moccasins. Their moccasins were their one redeeming feature as far as beauty was concerned and incidentally the one item which they could call their own.

The trees which went into the building of our home were all from two hundred to four hundred years old. Bud directed the selection of each individual tree to be felled, so as to practice conservation of the timber. We lived with the sound of the axes biting into trees and the creak and moan followed by a crash as each selected patriarch came tumbling down. Then there was the brittle sound of branches being lopped off and the ring of the ax striking the slippery log sidewise as the bark of each log was peeled from it.

The bark of the logs was removed for reasons of preservation of the wood and to make for a clean house, in part. Another reason is that the white wood slowly turns to gold and amber as it weathers, and we planned to oil and varnish it. In time all the woodwork inside we would treat similarly to bring out the natural wood tones. No paint would be used either inside or outside the cabin. Wood colors are the colors of thought and solitude.

Like great ivory candles the peeled forest trees lay amid the slash and ruin of torn bark and lopped-off branches.

"It sounds good to hear those other axes ringing in the woods to help me out," said Bud.

"Please don't cut more than you have to."

"Building any kind of house destroys trees," remarked Bud. "Only here you can see what it takes first hand. But we will clean up the mess and you will never know where those trees came from in a year."

It was true. Later I was to wonder where the one hundred or more logs came from that made up our home, so carefully were they selected that the living arctic forest seemed unchanged.

The log cabins of pioneers in Alaska and northern Canada are too often built out of the nearest available trees which can be dragged up to the door. Thus practically every cabin stands always in the exact center of a cleared space, encircled by the mute protests of mutilated stumps.

The three men soon had the house well along. They sledded each peeled naked log along the ground on a rope, maneuvering it between bushes and over fallen timber. Like a sled on snow the log was skidded downhill from above and rolled alongside the house foundation; then with the aid of two slanting poles they rolled each log up and it fell into place. Bud cut a notch in each log while the Indians brought more. It is a precision job to notch logs with an ax and fit the ends of them together correctly. No spikes or nails were used in the construction — only wooden pegs which Bud made with the ax out of scrap material and pounded into holes which he drilled with the auger. A layer of forest moss, which I gathered by the washtubful, was packed in and around each notched log end to make each airtight as it was laid into place. There is no better insulation material for a climate having radical temperature drops than simple arctic moss. There is no warmer structure existent than a properly built log cabin.

Aside from putting in pins about six inches on each side of where the door and window openings would be, no notice was taken of these openings which would be cut later. The structure looked just like a solid corral fence for the time.

We planned to have two rooms. Their inside dimensions were twelve feet by fourteen feet, and fourteen feet by sixteen feet. "Only one room for winter," we said. "But we'll build a second room for company."

Company? Well, it's a changing world. The arctic today is not as remote from the centers of civilization as our grandparents were when they lived just eight miles out of town with a horse and buggy. We were counting on having a house guest once in a while here in the arctic!

Bud flew to the store and got a new canvas for the canoe and he painted it bright yellow for me.

"To match my new window curtains," I explained. "I'm going to have red and yellow curtains of monk's cloth. We'll hang them, of course, after you get the window places cut in the walls and the window panes flown in."

"I won't be able to cut the windows until I make some big plank shutters to close over them," Bud warned me.

Every time you left the house you must have shutters ready to close over the windows. Otherwise grouse fly into the glass, moose and bears stick their heads through, and pretty soon every varmint in the woods is inside your house. Stout shutters were a peculiar necessity for a house in the arctic in winter. For when the sun left and the arctic night descended a view would no longer be an attribute. The big windows we wanted would permit much loss of heat from the house and would at that season be useless as well as dangerous ornaments. Ultimately we put in big picture windows on two sides, overlooking the lake. We could obtain only rather small panes but set four of them together vertically, making each window six feet long by three feet high, and using a double layer of panes between the house interior and the outside. It gave us a snug kind of pleasure then to think that in winter we could seal off the big windows with the shutters, pile snow blocks up to the roof, and dig in.

The nine-foot yellow canoe was tricky to ride, but I was mastering it. In it you sat crosslegged, Indian-style on a removable frame of slats and skimmed along the margin of the lake with the agility of a waterbug, having two inches of freeboard. It was difficult to get into. You had to brace your paddle crosswise against some solid object such as a rock on shore to hold it steady, then ease your bottom down into it with the greatest delicacy. The advantage of such a canoe is that you can take it up under your arm and travel overland until you reach the next puddle, thus crossing otherwise untraversable country with ease and rapidity.

The clear lake depths hypnotized me and made me dizzy at first. To make it safer Bud tied an empty sealed five-gallon gas can into the canoe. This served at once for a back rest and a float in case of capsizal. I never in my years in an arctic hunting canoe have capsized but I should not advise anyone who had to attempt to leave the canoe and swim to shore through a lake like Takahula Lake.

I made a circuit of the entire lake shore, exploring each cove beneath a turquoise sky, taking a washcloth and towel and a bar of soap of the kind that floats. The sun was warm. Not a twig moved in the stillness. There wasn't an insect. I washed on a rock ledge with the white soapsuds running down my ankles into the water. The lake was so clean I hated to get it dirty by bathing in it.

The Indians at work building the cabin told us there wasn't much game or fish here. They told us this, believing it, when a game trail encircled the lake beaten into the earth and another game trail came through the low pass from the Alatna River to merge right by our house. Probably the belief was held by the people along the Koyukuk because this place was far distant from their villages. These awesome mountain cliffs depressed them. The spirit of nature brooded here strongly. They were essentially correct in their intuitions.

As we worked on the cabin two white objects became noticeable on the bare hilltop overhanging us. Everybody thought the objects were rocks. They did not move, and as Joe said, since he had accompanied the last hunting party up the Alatna River several years ago and secured forty sheep, there were no wild sheep left, and no sheep would be so foolish as to come out on that bare little hill so far from protection. Yet there was something strangely attractive to the eye about those objects. The native people know that "spirit" caribou have been verified by many people.

"Do you think there could be perhaps such a thing as a spirit sheep?" Bud asked Joe. Joe began to think about it.

Next day the two white objects were visible but seemed to be in a slightly different attitude. The binoculars held no answer. Finally the objects moved in relation to each other and it became indisputable to all that they were sheep.

Bud had no intention of encouraging the Indians to hunt. The white Dall sheep is becoming extinct in Alaska since the war and increased means of communication, being reduced to but five per cent of its numbers of ten years ago, according to Alaska Game Commission figures. The Indians told Bud that after mature consideration of the subject they concluded that the sheep were spirit sheep.

"Do spirit animals leave tracks?" I asked.

The Indians thought they might. The subject made them uneasy.

But they were hungry for meat. Asked what would happen if a man should go after them Joe replied, "Well, that can be dangerous for a man sometimes. Besides, you would get nothing."

Joe had been educated by Christian missionaries and he professed to be an absolutely orthodox Episcopalian. But the laws of nature were still strong on him as they are strong on all people who prefer a tent to a house.

Bud said then, "It's awfully lonely up here in the mountains. You know the winters are terribly cold."

"Yes, it must be much colder," the Indians eagerly agreed. "It's in the mountains."

Most people would imagine that, but the year we kept a temperature record in the Alatna Valley we found that two thirds of the year was above zero. While much of southerly Alaska is rainy and foggy, due to the warming influence of the Japan Current off the North Pacific, the interior of this arctic mountain range offers day after day of glorious skies. Winds are rare in our valley, for although there are winds all about the peaks, they have not found our valley out.

Bud flew to Hughes thrice weekly, returning with loads both inside the airplane and out. Planking for door and window frames was lashed onto the floats. The airplane flew with a one hundred pound overload and looked like a flying lumber yard.

"Catch us some fish to eat," he counseled me.

There didn't seem to be a living fish in the lake. When selecting Takahula Lake for a home we had the fish in mind. Something told me that fish were here but I never got closer to one than fifty yards because they could see me coming through the clear water.

First I found three grayling streams in the neighborhood. Arctic grayling are similar to brook trout, which exist in the far northern part of our continent. Aristocrats as they are, and because they are such willing fish, they are eagerly caught out and even now are extinct in their southerly range wherever a town lies nearby. The pioneers and soldiers in Alaska caught them by the thousands, and farmers in the earlier days of Matanuska Valley were known to have used dynamite on them.

A large grayling will not go more than eighteen inches in length, but it is the fightingest fish pound for pound that is now known. Able to exist only in the purest water and absolutely unable to stand the least taint of pollution of their habitat, they snap at little black flies cast deftly by a fly rod, and sometimes a swift icy mountain stream will be black with their back fins and leaping forms.

I fished the virgin grayling streams and my whole body and soul became rested by my exertions. I learned that the grayling streams in our neighborhood would supply us with all we needed each summer and that the same number would be exactly replaced in the identical pools the following year, so long as the original waterways system from which they came was in itself not harmed. Bud, bewhiskered and whistling, was happy at building our walls beneath summer sun and summer arctic rain.

I went down the lake early in the day in the little yellow canoe with my new fly rod, recently arrived at Hughes. Along the shallow mouth of Takahula Creek the spotted pike were staggered like an array of sharp spikes at a gateway. They all lay with tail to the weeds and eyes pointed out into the narrow creek neck. Some were just loafing along; others sped like rockets in alarm as the canoe moved softly in among them.

They were waiting here at this marine thoroughfare for smaller fish. A pike hunts by waiting.

Perspiring and desperate at the marvelous sight, I flicked my flies past the long noses, balancing precariously in my tiny craft. But the pike would not take flies; they wanted meat. Finally I got a strike. I can only say now that there is no more thrilling sport than to manage a pike on a fly rod with a leader of three pound test while trying to keep your balance in such a canoe. Back and forth the pike towed me, as though I were hooked to a wayward whale. He wound me up in line, and when I got him into the canoe he jumped right out again. After his third trip into the canoe I managed to club him with the oar and he was there to stay: fish for dinner.

Pike are not considered a valuable fish in Alaska. We set the net out and they fell into the net easily, for the reason that it is their nature to swim through weeds, and so they in fact sought out obstructions, expecting to pass through.

We suspected presently that other fish in Takahula Lake were swimming around the net. We suspected that and staked much on it.

The arctic is the last place left in North America where it is legal to set your fish net and catch all the fish you need for your daily bread. People count on this in choosing a dwelling site. A good fish net is necessary life insurance in these uninhabited regions. There are several food fish, such as the salmon and whitefish, which do not bite on a lure at any time but must be taken by net. It was a tipsy occupation to set the fish net and take up the threshing food with the little canoe, for to be capsized into his own net would not be a fate to be relished by any fisherman. Sometimes we used the airplane in setting the net.

Beneath the overhanging brow of Sheep Spirit Mountain I worked at making a trail from our house to Airplane Cove. Bud had borrowed a mattock or grubbing hoe from Les James. It was heavy and back-breaking. It had two blades on the end of a long handle: one, a broad flat horizontal one for cutting sod loose, and the other a vertical blade similar to an ax for chopping out the brambles.

The making of even an elementary trail in Alaska's wilderness poses several problems you wouldn't suspect if you have never seen a country which has not had the original layer of moss removed. The solid earth lies so far beneath the moss that your trail may be a foot deep. Mosquitoes roar angrily at disturbance of their ancient moist breeding sanctuary, while unsightly piles of debris collect on either side. Trail making is burrowing. The heaps and ridges of trash accumulate; they should be burned, but drying them out would take most of the first season. Whether our property would ultimately be beautified by these efforts appeared doubtful. Merely cutting off the willows and alders does not make a trail. This brush will grow up with exhilarated vigor next year from the trimming. The earth is a mass of fibrous roots, spreading out upon the surface. To "level" a trail you cannot merely pack moss and fibrous forest peat in a low spot taken from a higher spot. It all rolls underfoot. No, I thought, to have anything bearing a resemblance to a real trail, you have to get down to real earth. Not to remove all the moss is to stagger continuously over sponges.

When you strip any considerable amount of the natural covering of moss from the earth, as in clearing the ground for agriculture, you invite many complications which upset the hydrologic cycle and may even affect the weather. Originally on this continent there were few floods out of season such as the great inexplicable floods that man endeavors by a futile series of dams to cope with today.

There is a great sudden increase of hardy noxious weeds. Dandelions were only waiting for centuries in the arctic to have me come along with my grubbing hoe and clear the moss away. Ragweed, burdocks, goldenrod and hundreds of unwanted pests spring up by millions the following season after clearing the land, following the steps of the white man even here. Only here is there left in North America an area which is like it originally was, where a person can observe the past in the present and possibly predict the future.

I thought about mosquitoes. We often hear that they are terrible in the arctic in summer. What the explorers neglect to tell us is that the mosquito time lasts only for about six weeks out of the year. It is at its worst early in June and through July. After July 15 the mosquitoes do not bite much except on muggy overcast days. The mosquitoes succumb to a kind of fungus in the later generations which incapacitates them. Only the female mosquitoes bite at any time, but lotions are virtually without effect against their hordes, and for the protection of life itself a person must withdraw beneath head nets, bed nets and gloves.

Every reporter on Alaska writes against the mosquitoes. It has been said truthfully that they are the greatest deterring factor against Alaska's colonization. Most Alaskan cities are today sprayed by airplanes each summer, a system which was introduced by the army who spray their military reservations in an effort to make life more livable for the human inhabitants. Recommendations have been made that all Alaska could be completely "cured" of the insect plague by aerial DDT spraying and swamp draining.

But let us give the mosquitoes their fair day in court.

Lake Louise, a body of water twenty miles long, was selected by the army for a recreational area. About sixty miles east of Palmer, Matanuska Valley, the big wilderness lake was made accessible by a road and it was believed that boating, fishing, and swimming would be ideal there if only the mosquitoes could be dealt with. Accordingly, two pilots flying army aircraft were dispatched to give the area the spray treatment.

The pilots used their best judgment in handling the spray and they flew inland not close to the lake margin, but the wind drifted the spray out upon the surface. It was in June 1948 that, three days after the lake spraying, the visiting general was flown out to the lake, where a party was planned inaugurating the resort. What the general and his companions found was a lake surface filled with dead fish floating belly up. Yes, Lake Louise was successfully sprayed so a general could enjoy fishing without mosquitoes — but incidentally, without fish.

You would imagine that the Alaskans would take a lesson from the several mistakes the army made in using DDT, but on the contrary, as soon as supplies of this insecticide became available to civilians after the war, there came a cry from every mining camp and outpost to have their area airplane-sprayed also.

Even Government bureaus are quick to endorse the new "modern" mosquito control measures. The Territorial Department of Health says pompously:

"The enormous expanse of muskeg flats, bogs, and swampy areas throughout much of Alaska, provides almost unlimited breeding places for insects such as mosquitoes. Such pests not only menace health but serve as a handicap and detriment to the economic development of the Territory."

The irony of course is that the very "economic development" of which these people prate *depends* upon mosquitoes! The mosquitoes of the north carry no malaria or other disease. The Pacific Coast salmon industry is tied up closely with the mosquitoes which fill the spawning streams of Alaska. All trout fishing is tied up with them, for it is upon mosquitoes that trout depend for their food. North America's migratory birds depend upon soft insect food in great abundance to feed their young each season during the early weeks of their life. Although the mystery of the cause of bird migration is much disputed, the fact remains, no matter what the cause, that our birds must have Alaska's and Canada's mosquito diet if we are going to continue to have birds.

Much better that man would concentrate his mental powers on seeking means to effectively prevent the mosquito from biting man than to try to eradicate the hated but necessary insect from its natural habitat — the last place on this continent where primeval nature still maintains her cycles of the ponds and mosses.

Why try to make Alaska what it was never meant to be? Why destroy our wilderness resources: the only important crop which Alaska is now producing or is likely soon to produce.

Bud and I arose at 4 A.M. and sneaked off fishing together. Breakfast was leftover cooked rice and raisins hastily bolted with powdered milk stirred into water. Using the airplane as a boat, we paddled to the middle of the lake and dropped our lines off the floats to explore the deep lake bottom. With a big sinker and a hunk of grayling for bait, Bud caught a lake trout between 25 and 50 yards deep. Weighing about four pounds, it was as brightly speckled as a leopard, with scales so tiny that it appeared to have no scales, and with bright scarlet belly fins.

"I'll wager," said Bud, "that there are fish lying on the bottom of this lake that are fifty years old and almost as big as your canoe."

Seeking a constant cold temperature in the depths the year round, the more elderly lake trout lay there unknown. The big ones were never seen. Living a life of seclusion, safe and undisturbed, they were immune to all their enemies, including the roving otter. They would not take baits on a set line; they would not swim into the fish net because they saw the net all summer long until the nights got dark. Yet if we could only contrive a system there were enough trout in that lake to last one family a lifetime on a sustained yield basis. The principal food of the trout seemed to be snails which they grubbed from the lake bottom and munched down, shells and all.

Takahula Lake, overshadowed by the conical peak rising from its head, lay silent and did not reveal the secrets of its munching fish.

We ate all of our first trout eagerly. We had it with creamed potatoes, cheese and tea, when we got home at 2 P.M. *Ten Hours Later.*

"You know it's a bigger country than a man thinks," observed Bud, consulting his watch. "The day's almost gone and I'll have to get back to work with the boys."

Because the sun went around the horizon and never passed overhead, it always seemed to be early morning in the valley of the Alatna. A person never knew a day had passed, and he could hardly know that a year had passed. As the sun swung along each day anew it caught the glint of rocks on far mountainsides; a person spent hours accounting for every glitter upon those highlands while the sun rolled sideways through the top-of-the-world sky.

It was interesting that the question people most frequently asked us later on our lecture tours was, "Don't you get lonesome up there in the arctic?" The removal of familiar boundaries and restrictions left them aghast and shocked at the thought.

To jump ahead of our story I will say that it took two and a half years really to finish up our home the way we wanted it, working on it alternately with exploration and a career out in the world. It was necessary to transport by air into the arctic all the materials and equipment which were not obtainable locally, but we tried in all cases to rely upon the country itself for everything. To us, this was the zest of it. We lived at the cabin over five months out of each year for three years and fulfilled the home site requirements on five acres of property in the arctic, but never a government official has seen it to this day.

We hung a large six-sided mirror on the wall and got hand-painted china dishes, a meat grinder and a pressure cooker. We got a small wood-burning cooking range as well as a cabin heater. Storage bins for preserving foods and arctic survival equipment Bud built beneath the bunks, lining them with strong wire mesh as well as lining the entire floor of the cabin with wire mesh to keep the rodents out. We hung our guns on the walls and built a fireplace in the guest room out of native rock, set with cement flown from Fairbanks at $40 the one hundred pound sack. Bud made our table and our chairs of spruce and moose rawhide.

Two polar bear skins from up north ultimately came to be installed for the floor and lounge. Bud installed his running water system for me, the first running water in the arctic. It consisted of two fifty gallon tanks hung on the wall which drained down by pipes into twin aluminum trailer sinks set in a sideboard covered with green linoleum, and the running water part particularly came in when Bud ran down to the lake every few days and hauled the water in cans to fill the tanks up.

A cesspool for draining the little sinks was put underneath the front yard. We had a gravel walk running around one side of the house to the woodpile and trash pit in back. Bud made the gravel by pounding up big rocks into little ones.

Our fuel of course was wood. The first year we spent in the arctic forests we recalled how we had industriously cut and hauled a great pile of logs which was in the fall time as high as our house. Now we knew there was no need to get fuel ahead for winter. With Eskimo fur clothing no temperature of 60 degrees below zero is prohibitive, so there is not the fear of cold that civilized man has. Fuel can be cut as needed on snowshoes all winter long without any particular hardship. There is no need to shovel snow in the arctic to make a path to the woodpile: it is simpler to just walk over it.

For lights we used gasoline pressure lamps, but no illumination at all was needed during half the year.

"We could put in a little electric generator if you want it?" Bud once suggested.

To install an electric plant is about the first thing the enterprising American thinks of whenever he is in the wilderness, and I can say truthfully that I have seen places where a little American mechanics would go quite well. We thought the matter over in our case. The question seemed to rest on whether an electric plant and electrical wiring would increase the simplicity of management of our arctic home and our enjoyment of it. We decided it wouldn't.

Gasoline lamps are simple to manage. They run eight hours on a quart of gas and all you have to worry about is a new mantel once in a while. Giving efficient illumination, they are put out by the mail order houses in attractive models with pleasing designs in lamp shades, I found to my surprise.

How about radio? How about communication? people have always asked. The Jameses at Hughes dug their own place out of the wilderness and they had it all now: two electric generators, thousands of pounds of stored foods amounting to perhaps $75,000 for trade goods, and their own airfield. Traveling salesmen flew in and stayed overnight. Mrs. James found it necessary to enlarge the accommodations to make room for sleeping a dozen people at a time. Presently the place became a boarding house. Mrs. James cooked meals for these people, and having obtained a radio, she became thenceforth almost out of public obligation a U.S. Weather Bureau observer with fifteen schedules a day, and for fifteen years she had never missed a schedule.

Eventually Bud and I got a transoceanic shortwave radio for the cabin. The mountains created a peculiar condition in which we found it usually impossible to contact any station either in the United States or Alaska; sometimes we could hear Radio Moscow, the Philippines, Colombia or Brazil.

On the little airplane radio we could contact nothing. Takahula Lake remained blanketed with silence. Bud could get a certain station on the Koyukuk River southward when he was within ten minutes' flying distance from the lake. He could notify this station — Bettles — when en route to and from Hughes on his runs, but once having landed on the water at the lake we were cut off from the world.

As a precaution we kept in fairly close touch with the Jameses at Hughes. They observed our unconventional venture with as much detachment as they could muster. During the freeze-up and breakup periods twice yearly when Takahula Lake was totally inaccessible for a number of weeks the Jameses were always much concerned. We had an arrangement with them each fall that if we did not appear by a

certain date after the freeze-up Johnny James would fly his Stinson in
on skis and investigate. However, it never came to that. We always
made our appearance in due course, and Johnny being a bush pilot
busily engaged in local commerce among the Indians on the Koyukuk
River, never had occasion to visit the remote lake in the mountains,
but only saw it in our pictures. No one ever saw Takahula Lake upon
which we made our home except that approximately 100,000 people
each year saw it in the colored moving pictures with which we lec-
tured about the United States and many people saw it on television.

6 THE ARCTIC OCEAN
ON FLOATS

THE BEAUTIFUL CRAGS AND FOREST of the Brooks Range were not all that were offered to a person who built his home at Takahula Lake. There was also our big back yard: the vast prairie stretching out north of timberline.

To live where the trees end, enables one to be a dweller in two lands. The great Brooks Range, leaning to the north, breaks off into the treeless arctic plateaus, the plateaus break eventually into the low arctic coastal plain, and the continent itself leaves off at last into the ice-locked polar sea which is no man's land. We had traveled all these different kinds of arctic country before we built our home. Those pure trackless spaces lying just out there to the north of us made for a back yard which was limited only by the isolated handfuls of people living on the fringes of the next continent on the opposite side of the world.

Perhaps my father put it in the best words, when he wrote: "That you plan for a home, a retreat in which you can find refuge from time to time, will help you evaluate the entire world. This is something which cannot be done in Tucson, Washington or New York City. You have built powerful friendships and firm human relations of enduring value throughout North America, but which would themselves engulf you if you could not reflect upon them from the distance afforded by the Brooks Range."

Bud and I liked to think that with our airplane we could be north of timberline any time we wanted to within a few hours. We could sit in our cabin and dream dreams about that country lying just out there beyond, and the knowledge of its existence was gloriously reassuring. We could get out our furs which arrived in their duffle sacks and dress again like the Eskimos. With the arrival of our furs from the States, with the arrival of the necessary movie camera and its para-phernalia, and with the return of our Indian helpers to their homes upon the completion of their job, we were inspired to start moving.

"Nanny and George will be looking for us any day now," Bud said. "So will Mathew's people. They will be watching the sky. The Arctic Ocean will be clear of ice along the shore, ready for float landings."

Bud had promised the Eskimos we would come back to visit them with an airplane.

Yet we were faced with transport problems now that made our first ones minor by comparison. There is a basic minimum of equipment you must have with you in the arctic at all times to survive. The coun-try is uninhabited and the distances are immense between fuel stops.

"Everything is different with an airplane," I realized. Suddenly catapulted into the modern age of air, you must be ready to meet all environments and be prepared at all times for a possible long walk out. Both summer and winter equipment must be carried. We figured there was one chance in four that we would lose our plane. We could carry almost no food, but we would carry the means to get food in emergency. We were used to taking care of ourselves in the old days with no communications and no outside support. Bud knew the land of the Eskimos like he knew the palm of his hand.

We planned to live mostly on fish. Fish, like meat, is a complete diet. You need nothing else for perfect health. How many people know this or will recognize the fact? Every prospector, explorer and traveler in the North American Arctic has always lived on big game, killed out of season in the summertime. But the possession of modern means of transport poses a responsibility toward the welfare of the game herds, and actually there has never been any excuse for killing big game in summer, in a land where fish is plentiful.

The list of things we carried was similar to that which Canada re-quires all pilots to carry when flying in the Northwest Territories:

Rifle and ammunition (in our case, only a .22)
Mosquito head nets, bed nets, hats with brims
Fish net
Sleeping bag (Woods Arctic 3 Star)
Small nylon tent
Gasoline burner, called a primus stove
Bud's homemade tiny sheet iron stove to burn wood in some
   areas
Ax
Tool kit for the airplane
Cooking pots and eating gear
Emergency sewing kit
Woolen clothing for summer
Eskimo furs and snowshoes for winter
Pocket compass and watch
Knife, matches and waterproof match container
First Aid kit
Ropes and snare wire

Ten pounds food is minimum required by Canada but in Alaska there is no requirement. We carried only a few candy bars and a five-pound nylon sack of yellow corn meal, salt and tea.

With these things a person of resourcefulness can live in the arctic north of tree line for a couple of years — or indefinitely. The peculiar thing about an airplane which you must never forget is that you can go flying off gaily into remote areas where an airplane has never been heard before in the sky, expecting to be gone for a few days, but you might be gone for a few years.

Although most modern pilots would probably dispense with the small wood-burning stove and depend entirely on the gasoline burner, we were much attached to our old stove and so took it along. There is nothing like a wood-burning heater for sheer comfortable living inside a tent. We knew that wood floats down the larger rivers of the world into the arctic, such as the Mackenzie of Canada, the Colville of Alaska, and the Lena of Siberia, where it drifts around in the ocean, lodging upon certain beaches.

Our sealskin waders were the only boots we carried; without them in the summer arctic a person is practically helpless. Rubber boots and shoepacks which we had tried before are but poor substitutes, for they cause the feet to sweat due to lack of ventilation and the cold is conducted right through them. Furthermore, they soon blister heels when you are slipping and sliding clumsily over sphagnum moss. The woolen shirts on our backs were freshly laundered, albeit unironed. We would just wear them all summer. Our long-handled wool underwear went along to be donned as needed and we had our old caribou parkas, now shedding much hair.

Incidentally it is a fact known to arctic pilots that the necessary parkas of caribou go to make yet another aviation hazard which is part of the business: the hairs that shed have been known to get in the gas and clog up a carburetor.

We used tight-weave poplin jackets of the African safari model.

"We can't go straight north over the mountains, I'm sorry to say," Bud calculated. "Can't get off the lake here with full gas. It's the darned photographic stuff. Our baggage limit is officially 80 pounds, and half of that is taken up with the cameras. I believe we'll really enjoy taking a circular route, though, if we can ever get off with our overload at one thousand feet."

I was tremendously enthused, for here was our chance to tour some places we had never seen. A person can live all his life in Alaska and never see it all because the places marked as towns on the map are often totally inaccessible for those not having their own airplane. We started out then, to fly the entire coastline of the arctic. We would land at every village and fish camp even where there were no landing fields.

This was our route:

Takahula Lake	to	Kotzebue	270 miles
Kotzebue	to	Point Hope	150 "
Point Hope	to	Wainwright	230 "
Wainwright	to	Point Barrow	90 "
Point Barrow	to	Beechey Point —	
east along top of the continent			190 "
		Total	930 miles

The mountains around our Takahula cabin

A view of the Alatna Valley near our northernmost cabin

Our closest neighbors, the Jameses, at Hughes 100 miles away

The camp on Victoria Island

A flight of 930 miles would get us to our destination, that part of the arctic where our particular Eskimo friends lived, which actually was just 330 miles due north of our cabin.

How many days our field trip would take we couldn't foresee and cared less. It all depended upon weather, availability of gas and upon finding subjects to photograph. The pilot flying the coast of the Arctic Ocean by summer is likely to be grounded by winds, fog, rain and sleet for uncertain days. It is the worst flying weather in the world.

After several successive days of waiting, we swallowed beans and blueberries hastily at 6:00 A.M., boarded up the two windows so far cut, and put the little yellow canoe inside the house to keep it safe from bears.

Takahula Lake had taken on its look of inverted mountains and forest reflected in a perfect mirror. The mirror surface bent away as our floats opened up a furrow of white. The bows of the floats rose to the surge of power as the engine reached full speed. Jeweled spray boiled in the air for a moment; then we were on the step. Only the propeller blast and a skimming trail rumpled the giant reflected picture. Gently Bud turned the wheel in his hand and rocked the *Arctic Tern* over on her side. He picked one float out of the water. Then he pulled the other remaining float up in the air to join its mate. We circled the lake, while below, the waves began their journey toward each distant shore.

Around the lake we sped, higher and higher, climbing up around the walls of rock. I thought momentarily of the great trout lying asleep on the bottom of our lake. Did the take-off disturb their tranquillity of a thousand years? It seemed unlikely. The jagged peaks and the turquoise water lying unexpectedly among them reminded me of those visions seen sometimes in distant clouds.

I was exhilarated by the swift-moving panorama of our lives, even though I regretted that I could not grasp and hold it all. Over the fierce peaks of the Brooks Range we sat securely in the sky and from where we sat could see great blue Walker Lake, Iniakuk Lake, and Takahula Lake all at once, until, winding down the little-known Kobuck River to Kotzebue Sound, we entered a different geography overhung by the haze of the Chuckchee Sea.

A long arm of lowland jutted out into the ocean, and squatting upon it, a hundred miles due north of Nome, was the town of Kotzebue. Bud made a landing upon the shallow lagoon behind the town; later we learned that pilots always use the ocean directly in front of Archie Ferguson's trading post. The only spectators to our arrival were two little Eskimo boys. Off to our right was a big bustling airfield from which wheel ships took off and landed steadily. Archie Ferguson, trader for fifty years, had bought several small airplanes and established a school of aviation here, instructing Eskimos how to fly.

Kotzebue is generally agreed to be one of the most picturesque spots in Alaska. Its population is said to be around 1800 mixed Eskimos drained from the surrounding area of several thousand square miles and two river deltas. The whites number around forty, most of them being employed by the government. There is a herd of 1500 reindeer. Along the main street, a beaten path beside the waterfront, we walked past racks of rosy split salmon hanging to dry in the sun. Ugrug skins, the skin of the great bearded seal, for boats and bootsoles were pegged out to cure. Sled dogs were chained in long rows along the sandy beach. Eskimos smiled and we stopped to chat. We knew relatives and friends of theirs. The ocean had filled some of their nets with seaweed and several people were cleaning their nets and mending them. One old man sat on the ground by his tent door playing solitaire with a deck of cards on a caribou skin.

Down the path we turned to the only man in sight, at the moment, for information. He was darkly tanned, a Texan with the high narrow jaws and lean shanks common to some Western men. In his late thirties, he was extremely fit and he wore pants that had been lived in for several weeks, topped by a heavy, gray knit "Skiwash" sweater. His eyes were keenly intelligent. He looked like an explorer.

An explorer was what he was. "Well, I'll bet you are the Helmericks. I would know you anyplace."

He grasped our hands, and so it happened that we met by accident right there in the path someone we had been thinking about. He was Louis Giddings, one of our great archæologists of the arctic regions. He had married an old school friend of mine who used to be in my sociology class a few years back in Arizona.

"We just visited Ruth and saw the new baby a few days ago in Fairbanks," was the first thing we told him. "I sure like that log cabin of yours there on the campus."

With a couple of students Giddings had just got into Kotzebue that very hour from his current "dig" up the Squirrel River, a tributary of the Kobuck. He was traveling by powerboat. The five of us gathered at the Farthest North Restaurant. Giddings told us that his rations, when he traveled alone — as he had for fourteen summers — were rice, powdered milk, sugar, coffee, tea, tobacco and raisins if it is before the blueberries get ripe. That was all he ever carried. It will be noted that he had no stove because he couldn't carry one on his back, and therefore he had no way to bake. Consequently, he took no flour. It will also be noted that he carried no frying pan, only a boiling pot. The bulk of his diet was composed of straight fish and what game the natives gave him as he went along. He had been so many seasons at this life that this diet was what he preferred, he admitted privately, to sympathetic ears, although the University required that students accompanying him on field trips must have a "balanced" diet now.

Giddings' dig was a prehistoric Eskimo village, one of many whose secrets lie locked in the arctic burial grounds. An expert in tree-ring dating, who trained under Douglas at Arizona, his business was to estimate the period of ancient villages by the timbers used in their construction. While we drank tea he talked about the Eskimo villages of the past. Many of them Giddings had tracked only by tracing down the ancient legends which he listened to in the tents of his Eskimo friends. Mostly the tales he heard had no basis in fact — but occasionally they had. Sometimes Giddings heard a tale which led him to a certain spot, there to find the moldering remains of what had once been a real flourishing people. It was a work that went deep into the lore of fairyland and mythology.

We learned that by all indications so far uncovered the Eskimo is a newcomer to North America who may not have been here more than 600 to 900 years. It is only a guess because when you go back even 100 years in Alaska you are prehistoric. More evidence waits to be uncovered. It was that confirmation that Louis was after in his lifetime search, and after fourteen years, he admitted to us that day at Kotzebue, that the trail was getting clear, with such an excitement as he found a difficulty to suppress.

"You're onto something big?" we asked.

"Well, we won't say no," was all he said.

Arctic archæology can proceed only inch by inch in the summertime as the ground thaws. To attempt to hasten the process by rough methods would be disastrous to the frail artifacts which the archæologist seeks to piece together and preserve for posterity.

Bud managed to gas up the *Arctic Tern* with the help of Billy, a fifteen-year-old boy, who delivered the gas to the lagoon with a boy's size tractor. There was a cot in a Wien Airlines shack where we could sleep. We had supper at the restaurant: reindeer roast topped off with fresh local blueberry pie. Our walk brought us to the movie house where a crowd was gathering. American people are so well trained that they will fall into line wherever they see a line forming. We fell in.

Inside the frame barnlike structure chairs were set up in rows, where a fly-specked screen hung from the wall. As the mixed audience in their mixed arctic apparel shuffled to their seats the only show of the evening began. At such an outpost it isn't a question of what show is playing at the theater but rather the question is if the film arrived so that there can be a show. Even the projectionist doesn't know what the show will be until he opens the cans. *Hoosier Holiday* was the movie tonight, as we all learned. The acoustics were terrible. The show was hardly underway when slowly the screen sagged while the picture crumpled with it, and as the light flickered to a stop the screen fell with a crash and the house lights came on. Archie Ferguson, owner, operator, head usher and general repair man, with the aid of some of the audience, hung the screen to the wall once more.

It was just as light outdoors when we came out as when we had gone in. Only the sun had glided along to the north. It seemed to be hanging right out over the North Pole, unless looks were deceiving.

Weather along the west coast of Alaska is radical. A nice day can turn to pea soup within half an hour. It looked good today but as we climbed into the sky it was with a certain wholesome skepticism. We flew along directly over the shoreline, heading up the west side of Alaska for Point Hope. Every time we passed a little white tent on the beach we would waggle our wings to the friendly waving of fur-clad figures below. As we flew northward the ceiling came down and down. Presently only a dim undulating line showed where the gray breakers smashed against the arctic shore just 100 feet below. That ocean was far too wild to consider making a landing upon, even in an emergency.

Chill mist clothed this world on all sides as we made a swift swing to turn back. Even the white line of the breakers below was lost from sight. The altimeter said fifty feet as Bud sought not to lose contact with our only guide. To lose the shore of the continent here means being lost in the Arctic Ocean with a westward current drift to Siberia. I mopped at the window on my side. "I see it. There it is!"

The breaker line! We could almost reach down and touch the heaving mountains of water; above the roar of our engine we could only guess at the suck and roar of the ocean as it broke and foamed and retreated again. Although it was a fearsome sight, we were glad for that guiding line of white foam, stretching through the mist. There was a town marked on the map right here someplace — Kivalina.

"Maybe we can get down there."

Kivalina was perched at the very tip of a sandspit, surrounded by water and almost washed into the mighty sea. We came over it flying low. In a high wind Bud held the airplane off with a deft touch and then let her settle into the only quiet water behind the town.

The people, all Eskimos, whose town had no landing field and no radio communications, offered smiling faces and warm hands from out their parkas as we stepped ashore. Competently they helped us tie up. Then we followed the Indian Service teachers, a man and his wife, into their dwelling.

Both the teachers were full Eskimos. Orphaned at a tender age, the woman had been sent away to boarding school in the United States by missionary benefactors. Now she spoke only English. A boarding school child, her life had not been happy. She had married a schooled Eskimo college graduate and today they were the parents of four small boys. They spent much time at tending fish net, gathering driftwood for fuel, or snaring birds for table. This summer had been an unusually productive season for blueberries, not common here.

The teachers' quarters had caught fire and burned down two years past, shortly after the couple came to this post. They had to stay in the rambling disorderly warehouse, a structure impossible to heat at any time. Everybody lived in furs most of the year round.

The kindly couple gave us tea and bread. This is the standard order with which arctic wayfarers are met. Later we had stewed reindeer, fresh fried salmon, and fresh blueberries mixed with yellow salmonberries in huge bowls with sugar and canned milk. Our talk was of hunting, fishing, herding and school.

There was a slender kayak drawn up by the door. Bud asked if he might take a try at it.

"Sure."

"Better be careful, Bud. You haven't had so much practice in these canoes and this is the ocean."

The ocean-going kayak of the Eskimo is made for use in the severest weather in the world. It completely envelops the body of the canoeist, with only a hole for his trunk and arms to stick out. The two-bladed paddle is balanced in the middle of its shaft on a groove of the kayak and is handled by a circular wrist motion. While the kayak is very easy to paddle, it has a precarious center of balance. The factor is that the novice does not want to turn upsidedown in icy seas in a craft from which he cannot easily extricate himself. In the old days the people of these coasts and of the Aleutian Islands, to the southward, used to purposely capsize themselves to negotiate rough breakers, and it is said that water never touched them because of the remarkable water-proof "slickers" they wore which were made of stitched sea animal intestine.

Carrying the sleek hunting craft to the lagoon, Bud climbed into it while the teacher held him against the shore on balance. The craft was painted white to simulate ice cakes. Actually Bud was too large for the space accommodation. His legs were too long.

"How would you like me to make one of these for our lake?" he asked.

"Wonderful. Oh, I'd love to have one there," I called. After we had each taken our timid turn upon the ocean in the kayak we were so convinced of its obvious merits that we set about at once to get the plans of construction from the teacher. It was eleven feet two inches long by twenty-three inches wide, tapering to a point at each end. The hole where a man sat was six feet one and one-half inches back from the bow.

Kivalina, aside from Kotzebue and Barrow, is the only reindeer-herding area now existent in Alaska. Ten years ago there were half a million deer in the Territory. Now there are only a few hundred which cannot begin to fill the needs of the people. If anyone still talks about the "reindeer of Alaska" he is behind the times; his information is out of date. The reindeer have gone.

Where did the reindeer go?

The story of the reindeer is at once sad and silly. In the beginning they were imported by the white man from Norway and some from Siberia. They were never native to Alaska, but it was hoped that an industry might be started. This idea is still basically sound. The oldest domesticated animal in the world, the reindeer was herded five thousand years ago in Northern Asia even before the domestication of cattle was practiced by us, and it is still the favorite food animal of the Northern Hemisphere in the Far East. If it is called a "new meat," it is new only to America.

Because it is a naturally adapted arctic animal, being the close brother of our wild caribou, it is one of the few animals known which

can utilize the forage of the high latitudes of the world and so produce meat for people in areas that would otherwise produce nothing.
The reindeer needs no shelter from arctic blasts. Its fur, in fact, is
invaluable for parkas. It can make its own living the year round by
pawing grass, lichens and plants out of the snow. It needs no hay or
imported food rations. All it needs is guidance by herders and protection from wolves. From the few original deer brought to Alaska thousands upon thousands of them grew up within a few years, with minimum herding protection.

We can blame the Depression, along with the selfishness and short-
sightedness of a small clique in Congress, for the abrupt end of the
budding reindeer industry of Alaska. Reindeer carcasses from Alaska
were sent to Seattle for only a few dollars each, and after the first
shiploads of reindeer meat, the Department of Agriculture certified the
excellence of it, and the sheep and cattlemen of the West got busy!
During the Depression the new meat did not quickly sell and times
were hard for all meat producers. Taking advantage of the right psychological moment, the Western senators campaigned against the
menace of the new competing meat. By subtle lobbying they were
able to convince Congress that it would be wise to take action against
the danger of reindeer!

But the war was not as open as this. What they actually did was
to hoodwink Congress. They could not outlaw the new meat in the
United States — there was no means by which that could be done, although many cities managed to pass local ordinances forbidding the
sale and use of it — but they could convince Congress that it would
be desirable to give all the reindeer in Alaska to the government, to
be managed for and by the native people only, under the Indian
Service!

Thus the Reindeer Act went into effect in 1940. Only the native
people may own reindeer today in Alaska.

In a country where we are supposed to be against all kinds of "racist
legislation" the Reindeer Act has become one of the greatest farces per-
petrated upon the American public. Incidentally, Canada followed
suit by a similar prohibitive law and reindeer may not be handled in

any of her vast arctic grazing grounds except by native peoples. The result? In each country the Eskimos have shot off every single reindeer they could get for human and dog food and turned back to hunting as usual. Reindeer herding is a specialty which a few distraught schoolteachers making $1800 a year were not equipped or trained to handle in Alaska. The remnants of the abandoned herds ran away and joined their brothers, the wild caribou, where they became subject to the wolf and caribou cycle and were swallowed up in the immensity of northern wilderness.

Exclusive ownership of reindeer without competition was supposed to help the Eskimos. Just why exclusiveness of ownership was considered necessary for the natives' success is not clear, but the result is that the "starving Eskimos" are no better off than they ever were, the vast grazing grounds of the arctic world lie idle, an industry of inestimable value was ruined before it got started, and the rest of the world is starving for meat.

This question of more meat for the world is one that is here to stay. Dr. Stefansson over a quarter of a century ago prophesied that the world would ultimately have to turn to the arctic to augment its food supply.

He was right. There is little doubt that the Reindeer Act will be revoked or amended eventually as the result of population pressures in the United States.

The earnings of the Eskimo people from Kivalina northward all along this coast are derived almost entirely from trapping white foxes. A seafaring people who made most of their living from the sea in the past, these coastal Eskimos still live on hair seals, ugrugs, polar bears, whales and walrus. There is a little ivory carving for the tourist market and that is all.

The war, which brought over 200,000 military men to Alaska, gave the ivory trade a great boom. Everybody wanted ivory trinkets to send home. But there is only a limited amount of ivory in the world, since it is produced from animals. Would the natives get ivory and make the trinkets? They would and did, selling them for fancy prices.

The ivory comes from walrus. Although there are clearly not enough walrus to provide ivory trinkets for all the people who want them, this fact was totally disregarded. The slaughter of the walrus by Eskimo hunters turned into commercial hunters had no legal restrictions. There is no limit on the number of walrus an Eskimo may kill under the National Walrus Act.

While only the Eskimos are allowed to kill them, on the assumption that they need them for food, we find in actuality that the ancient picture of primitive hunting as imagined in Washington, D.C., has given way to the power boat; these rare ton-weight animals are now being taken by Eskimos for the market value of ivory, the price of which in turn enables the Eskimo to purchase store food and more power boats. Thus again we see how "racist legislation" created for special groups can boomerang with unexpected results.

The wind blew and the surf boomed all night long as we slept through the blue twilight. We awoke late next day, after the custom of arctic summer life.

"We can get the weather on our radio," Bud mentioned to me, "but by the time we get it, it is so old as to be of little value here."

"When you can see to Cape Thomson the weather is usually clear all the way on to Point Hope," our hosts told us from their experience.

The really heavy fog liked to hang around Cape Thomson and Cape Lisburne. Here the land breaks off from a plateau to fall suddenly straight down into the ocean. The warm summer air from the continent, meeting the cold moist air of the sea, turns into Grade-A homogenized fog.

On the rocky ledges ahead the murres — locally called "crowbills" — banded together by summer in immense colonies. Lining the face of the black cliff in thousands, these sea birds laid eggs having pointed ends especially designed to roll in a circle rather than off the cliff. The birds strongly resemble the penguins of Antarctica except that they can fly.* When an airplane passes over their cliffs the murres launch themselves. They dive off into space to gain flying speed, their short little wings beating like flails. When they turn in flight they can

* Bird lore from Taverner's *Birds of Canada.*

manage only in big sweeping arcs. The wings make a peculiar whistling sound as these enthusiastic birds labor to keep in the air. What murres in the air mean to a pilot is murder!

If you fly near their cliff the witless birds launch forth by countless thousands, and with their poor mastery of the air they are as likely to crash into an airplane as to avoid it. We wanted to pass Cape Thomson on a clear day so as to miss this hysterical rookery.

Below us the ocean front stretched ever northward, while lagoons and salt-drenched lakes lining the shore were numerous enough to furnish emergency landing fields if needed. White sea gulls arose from a black mass washed up on the beach.

"Walrus carcass," Bud said. We had seen several of them, their ivory tusks cut out and abandoned by the Eskimo ivory hunters.

Point Hope lay out on the end of a giant hook that enclosed a large lagoon. The terrain was flat and sandy; the weather the year round was hostile to man, unyielding. A goodly settlement of Eskimos was here, and a handful of whites who administered to them. Here also was a unique human cemetery whose collection of bones had been gathered by missionaries from the surrounding country. The fence was composed of whale jaw and rib bones. How many whales went to make up such a fence? It seemed fitting enough that the people whose lives depended upon the whales should have their graves marked by the very whales they had eaten.

Over one grave of a whale hunter stood a mammoth whale jaw, many feet high. This was the largest whale ever known to be killed at Point Hope and the man who had killed it was, as logically follows, the mightiest hunter.

An archæologist's paradise, Point Hope each summer opens new cavities under its thawing banks where bones of human beings and whales lie intermingled from the ages past. The native people make pocket change by doing a little digging in their spare time and are paid to exhume grandfather and his trinkets on a commission basis according to the pieces they collect.

The Eskimos have always lived as solitary wanderers, as independent as the wolves. They had no tribe or class society or chiefs to lead them as many primitive people have had. They never owned money or property or slaves. Accordingly they were innocent of many evils, and at the same time they remained innocent of many sophistications, as a result of their environment.

The only way human beings could exist in the arctic world was by scattering over a vast area. There was no way to accumulate goods for a people who were always wandering, and hence no need of book-keeping or a written language. The existence of such a village as Point Hope was caused by one factor: food. Wherever the most and best food is, any people, animals, birds or fish that depend upon it will be, regardless of climate. Eskimos from time back forsook the sheltered inland climate of the arctic to congregate on these hostile blustery coasts. At Point Hope the currents keep the ice of the ocean pushed away from shore for year-round sealing, and the giant whales, largest animals of the earth, pass in their summer migrations close by, enabling the people to approach them.

Splashing to a landing in the lagoon, we tied the *Arctic Tern* to a whale vertebra and buried this in the sand. We could get fifteen gallons of gas at Point Hope, stored here for the personal use of Wien pilots, due to the charities of pilot Bernie Story, who gave us his permission at Kotzebue. We started walking over the long spit toward town. Bill Gordon met us half way.

Bud and I had attended the Alaska wildflower wedding of this missionary and his bride a few years ago in a town in southern Alaska. We hadn't seen our friends since. Bill was just about our age and had started off on his fortunes in Alaska at almost the same period as we had.

"Well, hello, hello. Welcome to Point Hope. Where have you been keeping yourselves? So you've got an airplane now. Shirley will be disappointed she missed you."

Bill explained that only a half hour before our arrival Shirley had embarked with a pilot for Kotzebue because their little girl had been mauled in a dog fight between the dogs of their team. Nothing serious, but they thought a doctor should properly disinfect the bite.

"Oh, I almost forgot. Here's a jar of blueberries. Compliments of your friends down at Kivalina," I said. No blueberries grew near Point Hope.

We walked toward the Native Service building and met a Mr. and Mrs. Alexander there. With their grown daughter who kept radio schedules in their home for the U.S. Weather Bureau, the Alexanders completed the Caucasian community.

The ceiling, never very high, had dropped until it touched the ground, leaving the short brown grass soaking wet, even as we walked. Shore birds called, while murres commuting between Cape Lisburne and Cape Thomson passed single-mindedly overhead. Making themselves busy about the human dwellings, the plump snowbirds twittered. Bill's mission stood nearly a mile from the rest of the scattered village of sod burrows and shacks, and we traveled a path worn away by countless mukluk-clad feet. At regular intervals along this path a whale rib was thrust up in the sand to keep travelers on course during winter storms.

"Do you remember, Connie, at Seward, at your house you gave me my first lesson in cooking? It sure has come in handy out here. I can't tell you how many times I've thought of that."

"You always said a missionary had to be practical and know everything. Bud, you'll be interested to know that I finally became a good carpenter and an electrician, too."

"People have been telling us about your dog sled trips all up and down this coast here," I said. Then I asked, "How did the lecture tour go last year in the United States?"

"Maybe he can give us some tips," Bud added.

"Wore me out," Bill admitted with a laugh. "What they do is they kill you with kindness. The worst part about it is being constantly entertained. Well, you'll see."

"Do you get fat?" I asked. We all laughed.

We saw an airplane coming in for a landing with wheels on the improvised strip. Its passenger, an Eskimo soldier newly discharged from the army, had made a charter trip from Kotzebue to get home from World War Two. His entire family clustered about him, helping to carry his duffle. He had a guitar under his arm. We could well imagine the "plinking" and "planking" that would take place in a tent or sod igloo as tales were recounted of distant lands — perhaps China, Japan, or the U.S.A. Alaska Indians and Eskimos, when they can pass the physical and literacy tests, are drafted into the army, just as are the American Indians on United States reservations, although neither can vote in the country for which they fight. They, as well as all Alaskans must pay a Federal Income Tax: taxation without representation.

Fuel is the chief factor which limits human progress at Point Hope. How can people live in a decent house if they can't heat one? How can a person buy fuel with the limited income of fox trapping? How could anyone, other than a millionaire or a person supported by an outside agency, afford to buy fuel at Point Hope at $120 a ton for coal delivered by steamship?

Nature furnishes no trees, not even a low bush. There is almost no driftwood. The sole source of fuel has been in the past the oil of sea animals that at the same time were also needed for food. The question arises: "Is it better to be warm than full?" Or, "Should I let my dog team go hungry because I must burn their food to warm my house?" These problems press at times in all arctic lands. It is true that today you can buy kerosene at 85¢ a gallon to $1.10 a gallon, or stove oil at similar prices. You can also buy the limited amount of coal which is brought in by steamship. But you can't buy these things without money. The resident arctic people, call them Eskimos if you wish, are just like people anywhere, in that progress for them is not possible without the physical means.

Bud and I knew what these people were up against. We had lived in igloos. We had moved around from one beach to another to find a few sticks to cook our meat. We had lived with our parkas on in the house. We had shared houses where fifteen people crouch in a twelve by fourteen foot space five feet tall at its highest point. It works out all right with good caribou furs and it may even be comfortable in its way for a primitive people who spend most of their time out of doors hunting. But for a more settled civilized people who are trying to build up a town, the conditions are impossible. For a people who are being invaded by tuberculosis, venereal infections and epidemic flu, the conditions are tragic.

Before the white man came here, these people were healthy, warm and happy. The white man's coming brought a much more interesting way of living but one that the old means could not support. In this we have the underlying source of the great problem the whole world faces. Today the people are trying to adopt new ways but they have only the old sources of wealth to support them. Yet they must go forward because it has become impossible to go back.

Maybe there is, however, a solution to the fuel and housing problem in many places north of tree line. Nature hasn't forgotten these people after all: many parts of the arctic are rich in coal and oil.

Less than a hundred miles from Point Hope by water lies a deposit of high grade coal that can be worked on the surface! The practical Episcopalian Mission bought a vessel to serve the village in hauling coal, but the ship was lost in the first storm and another one had never been obtained. Coal cheap enough to be within reach of all would be the biggest blessing Point Hope could receive.

People ask: "How can I make a living in Alaska?" To anyone who knows anything about chronic Alaska shortages a hundred answers are obvious. The newly established business in every case, while giving employment to the local people, would at the same time give them buying power.

Bill waved a comradely good-by as he shoved us off into the ocean in the *Arctic Tern*. We didn't know then that he had just been appointed the Bishop of all Alaska. Bishop of Alaska at the age of twenty-eight!

The person who flies the arctic coastline in summer had better get used to fog, for it will be his constant consort. We climbed up to 3000 feet and for a while it was fun. Then a gray blanket stretched across the sky ahead. It was like a wedge with its sharp side toward us. We dropped lower and lower to keep free of the heavy, moisture-laden clouds; the temperature outside was exactly 32 degrees — the most favorable temperature for forming ice on your wings.

Where Cape Lisburne reared up a thousand feet from the sea, the murre rookeries made a hazard. The cloud wedge pushed us down under a thousand feet; we would have to hug the cliff so as not to lose sight of land. Growling under his breath, Bud finally was obliged to turn out to sea. Fog had moved in before and behind during the last ten minutes. We were flying between two layers of clouds, although here and there the sun shone through and there were holes in the fog below with whitecaps rolling below that. It was a situation that could become bad at any moment.

For half an hour we flew onward with the two cloud layers slowly coming together. At last we knew we were clear of the headland. From here on we could turn landward because only flat beach extends around the top corner of Alaska from here on to Canada.

"Might as well get underneath this soup and keep low. There are no obstacles. Perhaps we should land on a lagoon and camp until clear weather."

We began looking for a camping spot as we flew along right over the beach line with mist driving in from the ocean. The strong wind blew balls of foam which rolled along the beach like white rabbits scurrying.

We were nearing Point Lay, 175 miles up the coast. If we could reach that, we wouldn't have to camp, but could visit. We sat tight and presently the tiny settlement appeared — a smaller reproduction of Kivalina but without any schoolteachers at present, and north of the blueberries.

Point Lay was out on a reef surrounded by seas of water. Only the white line of the breakers beating against that slender dark spit of land reassured a pilot that he was still on this earth. We landed in the lagoon.

To our surprise we were met by a party of five explorers for the U.S. Geological Survey.

They had reached Point Lay the day before at the termination of a summer's trip boating down a river from the interior. They expected an airplane to pick them up any time. We were also met of course by the entire village of Eskimos, including the Eskimo store manager.

At nearly every Eskimo village there is a small store called the

"Native Store" to distinguish it from other stores which may be run by independent traders. These Native Stores, encouraged by the Native Service, are a very good thing because the Eskimos have their chance to be in business for themselves. Jointly owned by the entire village or by all-Eskimo stockholders, some of these stores are valued at many thousands of dollars. We have known of a single Eskimo holding $10,000 worth of stock. Such stores are managed by a board of directors or by an individual appointed by the board. The store is there to make a reasonable profit, and it does. No advance credit is issued to the store patrons — a harsh rule, but the only rule that has been found workable in this country. Some towns have more of a co-op set-up where the profits are divided among the people who buy the goods, in the form of rebates. The Native Service works toward the latter.

Usually in the arctic the trade goods are just dumped in piles on the beach as they are hastily unloaded from the ship and they are sold right there and gone. To keep anything at all on hand for year-round trade is a problem. Here we found the store to consist of one little sheet iron building about twenty by thirty feet, freshly painted and immaculate inside. Its weighing scales were new and shiny, the small counter and shelves were neat. But there was absolutely nothing to sell inside.

Five or six tabby cats of various shades and sizes — the property of the absent Eskimo teacher — slept near the iron heater, and this room was turned into a kind of village social center or recreation hall. We were served tea and raisin bread.

While we were eating one Eskimo woman noticed Bud had worn a hole in the protective patch on one of his sealskin boot soles.

"I fix?" she asked shyly. She took the boot from Bud and capably went to work on it right there on the floor with a needle and sinew thread taken from some place inside her voluminous skirts. With a motherly smile she handed the boot back in a few minutes with a new ugrug patch neatly stitched in place.

"That was nice of her," Bud whispered to me aside. Then he added as an afterthought: "But her sewing can't compare to Nanny's, can it?"

We knew relatives of nearly everyone here and we carried on a conversation partly in Eskimo and partly in English.

"Why don't you come on over to our tent and join us in a square meal?" the Survey fellows invited.

We entered the large flapping tent of the white men and made out well there on dehydrated vegetables and sauces and things which lent themselves admirably to the principal course, which was caribou meat.

The United States Government, under its various branches, has been sending out these survey parties to map and explore Alaska for a very long time. The parties have increased greatly in number and scope during the last five years, while at the same time the airplane has given such exploration a terrific boost. The procedure is to take a party of around four to ten men up to the head of some river and land them and their equipment wherever a landing spot can be found. The party then makes its way down to the seacoast, drifting on the current in their convertible boats. Caches of supplies are dropped ahead for the explorers at prearranged spots along their route. What always amazed and amused the Eskimos and others native to the country was the outsize amount of equipment the men saddled themselves with. Of course, the Eskimos always considered boxes of scientific instruments and cases of rock samples which the men returned with, as supplies.

What really is incredible, however, is something that none of the local people would think about at all. It is that these government-supported explorers in our present modern day should feel free to live off wild game in a Territory of the United States. Game killed in the summertime, out of season. Game killed without hunting licenses because these people are nonresidents who have no right to hunt.

Formerly the U.S. Army and U.S. Surveyors lived on game in our old West. It has been a historic practice. Today these parties of young men out in the wilderness are leaving dead and crippled big game from one end of Alaska to the other as each summer passes. It is a plain fact, not exaggerated, from the many instances Bud and I know. During the war the 200,000 armed men in Alaska with government rifles and time on their hands did more to plunder Alaska's wildlife resources than can be related in one book.

Both by the sins of omission and the sins of commission our government is guilty of plundering Alaska. By negligence of conservation, by the lack of funds for the inadequate Alaska Game Commission and the Fish and Wildlife Service, and by overt acts of aggression, the United States Government itself has been the greatest personal enemy to wildlife in Alaska.

We ate the caribou meat, and were glad to get it.

In the evening the Eskimos of the village gave us all a party. We whites changed our shirts — put on the other one, that is — and the Eskimos put on their brightest calico print snowshirts and fanciest boots. Inside the Native Store, while the cold rain poured down outside, there was the beating of a single Eskimo drum and chanting, as each dancer took his turn before the assembled crowd. The dances of the Eskimos are interpretive, telling a story. Even the good-hearted Survey fellows rose one by one and celebrated the occasion by doing a dance to the drum.

We were flying under a hundred foot ceiling following the white breaker line from Point Lay to Wainwright. We flew with the cabin heater on full blast. The outside temperature was 34 degrees.

It was the kind of weather, with temperature and dew point close together, that causes carburetor icing: Ice which forms inside the intake of a carburetor when gasoline turns from a liquid to a gas. It is the same action which is involved in a refrigerator. This action causes the temperature in the carburetor to fall several degrees. When the humidity of the air is high, condensation will take place inside the carburetor, forming ice. The ice builds up until it closes off the fuel intake just as an invisible hand might close off the throttle.

To avoid carburetor ice, which may occur at any time, the pilot uses a heat control valve to shoot a stream of hot air from the exhaust stacks through the carburetor. A person could fly with his carburetor heat on all the time along the west coast of Alaska except that it cuts the power slightly. The ear of the pilot is his warning of when carburetor heat is needed; at the first sound of roughness in the engine and a loss of power, the pilot is alert to this danger.

Some airplanes are worse about carburetor ice than others. The test we gave the Cessna in this most difficult of moist atmospheres proved it well.

Steam formed inside the cabin. I was kept busy wiping it away. At last out of the storm came the cluster of houses and tents for which we looked: Wainwright.

Again a big lagoon lay behind the town and we headed for it, swinging out to avoid any high towers or radio antenna that might rear from the mist.

On such nights as this, I thought, only the Eskimos come down to the beach to meet the wayfarer. Those dependable, weathered faces upon whom one relies when all else fails!

This is no criticism of the whites. They are busy at their indoor jobs for which they are stationed here, while the Eskimo urchins stand in the rain to catch a tossed rope for entertainment.

Through a marsh we floundered wetly with this soggy parade. We left them to enter the large white frame Native Service Building.

How could we guess that, from coming out of the wild night, we were to drop into the middle of one of the most remarkable families we have ever known?

They were united in a common cause of sorrow. The flower of their group, the lovely golden-haired child, had become a victim of multiple sclerosis at the age of thirteen. This malady often appears like infantile paralysis, the origin of the symptoms being spinal. A rare kind of degeneration of the nervous system, similar to that which Lou Gehrig the much-loved baseball player had — this disease is not understood at the present time. There is no known cure. The girl's family had had her at the Mayo Clinic for a whole year. Nothing more could seemingly be done. After that, irrelevant as such a course of action might seem at a glance, they embarked for Alaska.

The young girl showed almost no symptoms of her illness to the casual observer. I didn't treat her like a child; nobody did. She was more adult now than most adults ever are. The family talked freely about her illness. She said she had learned to live every minute right now, without hoping for anything else and without regret. Looking at me with serene pure eyes she said, "I think people should learn to enjoy life and accept it for what it is, for life is always difficult in some ways for everyone." Strange words for a girl of fifteen!

Conversation with the transplanted family in their arctic home — mother, father, young son and young daughter — was witty, scintillating, subtle and at times even brilliant.

The father, we learned, left the principalship of a city high school to join the Native Service and live here alone with his family in an all-Eskimo village. Why? These things aren't easily explained. An intellectual of fastidious disposition, the father admitted quite freely and at intervals with brilliant sarcasm that he didn't like the arctic or the solitude of nature. The rest of the family professed to love it. "Oh, come on now, Father, snap out of it. This will make you a true philosopher," said the children.

"It's a good thing we can't look ahead in life and see what's coming next," the golden child told me in her low full voice, so amazingly mature. "For you know, it would spoil so many nice surprises."

It seemed incongruous that here in such a place would be found fine minds of civilization willfully repudiating the ease of civilization. But there you are: This again is one of the unexpected things you may find in the arctic on some stormy night.

Inside the warm government school, Bud and I quickly forgot about our airplane which Bud had tied to some small pieces of driftwood that he buried in the beach. We slept that night as guests of the government in our sleeping bag laid out on the floor of a vacant room and didn't hear the wind slowly rising. Once Bud awoke in the night and uneasily noted the crashing of the ocean on the beach outside the lagoon. The lagoon was sheltered from the ocean's wildness by a strip of land. It was a low strip, and the lagoon opened by a big mouth right into the ocean.

Next day it was with a slight apprehension that we made our way along the shore of the lagoon where we had left the *Arctic Tern*. The fog had lifted. We were ready to fly on. But where was our airplane? The spot where we had left it was empty!

Away to the far horizon the ocean outside the big lagoon was calm and vast. Bud gazed with unbelief at the empty scene. I didn't fully comprehend the meaning because I never paid much attention to how Bud tied the airplane or just exactly where along that monotonous beach we had left it.

The shore jutted out with a high cut-bank hiding a small bay behind. The only place where the airplane could be! It was a slim chance indeed. With heavy heart Bud walked around the curve after me and just then I called, "Well, look Bud, our airplane has broken loose and it is drifting on the water here." Unknown to me was the fact that Bud almost collapsed with relief and regained his composure all in one breath.

The *Arctic Tern* was just drifting conveniently in to touch the shore as I walked up. A broken rope trailed from each wing while another from the tail towed a small pile of sticks behind it. We looked the ship over. How far out to sea had she gone? Lucky for us the off-shore wind had changed shortly after it rose or the *Arctic Tern* could have landed in Siberia.

The experience was reminiscent of the plight of Sig Wien of Wien Alaska Airlines one time. Sig, who is doubtless Alaska's most famous living bush pilot of the old school, had brought a seaplane to Cross Island. This is a tiny sand reef in the Arctic Ocean north of Alaska about halfway between Point Barrow and Aklavik, Canada; Bud and I spent three months there once in our dogsled days. Sig was helping to fix a propeller on a damaged land plane there and he forgot for a moment about his own seaplane. When he next looked, his airplane was quite a ways from shore and drifting rapidly towards the North Pole.

Sig looked around desperately for some means to rescue his ship. There was nothing at hand but a 55-gallon gasoline drum, that was empty. There were a few small pieces of driftwood on the sand reef that would at first glance seem to be of no consequence.

Did you ever try to ride one of those hobby-horse rolling barrels they keep for amusement in public swimming pools?

The intrepid Alaskan pilot mounted the rolling barrel, and with some driftwood outriggers and a shovel for a paddle, he charted his way through the drifting summer ice cakes of the Arctic Ocean until he reached his runaway airplane and brought it back.

The moral of the two experiences is: tie a float ship securely and then tie her again, even if you are working right by the airplane, and sleep right beside her.

We got off from Wainwright at 5 in the afternoon and were at Point Barrow, on the exact top of the continent, by 6:15.

"Watch out for Skull Cliff," we had been warned. There was a brand new 700 foot tower erected there. It sat far enough back from the beach so that an aircraft following the beach line in a fog would not be apt to crash into it. Skull Cliff is the first in a line of three towers of very high frequency which have been erected around the top of North America to establish a means of modern polar circumnavigation for aircraft.

Over the radio at Wainwright we had already heard about the operations going on at Barrow. The navy was unloading their year's supplies for a thousand men in residence. Point Barrow saw such operations in the old whaling days when dozens of vessels passed beside the point each season; only radio with its high-powered news coverage wasn't known then. Yet there was something different, too, between our times and the olden days. As we winged over the point and saw five old gray tankers anchored there, we thought: "There is something different. Our times have come to stay." Uncle Sam's most far northern sandspit is becoming year by year a permanent modern city, with its own telephones, electric light system, air beacons, and big runways upon which airplanes land every hour of the day.

We landed upon the lagoon, back of old Charlie Brower's Store, taking care to miss all the sunken barrels and whalebones in its midst. Charlie Brower, who wrote the book *Fifty Years Below Zero*, died just a couple of years ago. He was a former whaler turned trader who for fifty years lived at Point Barrow as Uncle Sam's most northerly citizen. From his two Eskimo wives were born a total of fourteen children. One of them became a lieutenant-general in the U.S. Army and five of them now make their residence in California. From the Brower family stock a considerable portion of the village of Barrow is today descended.

The temperature was 45 degrees on the button, one of the most balmy evenings that Point Barrow can expect during any year. Here the polar ice pack presses mountainously against the shore, even some years threatening to slice away the very village itself — for the currents and winds here seldom take the pack out far to sea. Ships must watch their rare chance to slip around the Point and not get caught. Today airplanes scout ahead for the ships and hasten their passage through the ice lanes in a program co-ordinated by radio. Just six miles from Point Barrow stands a stone marker erected to the memory of veteran pilot Wiley Post who with Will Rogers crashed to death when they were trying to find the fog-shrouded village of Barrow some years ago.

We staked the *Arctic Tern* to the sand and looked about. Groups of U.S. sailors were walking along taking their first look at the top of the world. Many of them brought their cameras. We set off along the filth-saturated path past houses, cardboard shacks and tents of every description. Past dog teams chained to a cast anchor. Past trash and tin can heaps. To build yourself a sixteen by twenty foot frame shack eight feet high here — labor furnished by yourself — costs $1600. But Barrow mines its own coal. It freights it by tractor from its own mine one hundred miles away. The Eskimos manage this. At Point Barrow some government people and some Eskimos also burn natural gas today, from nearby gas wells.

We hadn't been in town five minutes before we got most of the news and learned where old friends had been transferred in the government services. A free-lance bush pilot "Red" Crosslin, was new to Barrow. From California, he had met and married Barrow's new schoolteacher, who had come up from Arizona. Doreen was as cute and pretty as a Powers Model and no schoolteacher like that could last long there. Red and Doreen planned to make Barrow their future home, getting their livelihood servicing the Eskimos with their Piper Cub Cruiser: floats by summer, skis by winter.

"Rusty" Herlene, an artist who had wandered far afield from Westport, Connecticut, was living at Barrow and working with Eskimo art.

Sig Wien had abandoned managership of his million-dollar airline to his brothers and their offices in the principal Alaska cities southward, in order to make his bachelor home in one of Barrow's shacks where he could get a little peace of mind. Always the hardest-working man in Alaska, detesting the routine of city life, the pioneer flyer found plenty of elbow room here, helping the Eskimos with one hand and with the other playing nursemaid to the navy. With the navy he had a contract to deliver mail and supplies to Umiat, their oil-drilling camp. For the army he flew also to Barter Island in the eastern ocean, and he organized their survey parties for ground exploration; both the army and the navy depended on this one man's intimate knowledge of Alaska's arctic north of tree line, when they started in here, whether or not they were openly admitting it.

There is no hotel at Barrow. Somebody should start up a good hotel. It is the most disorganized place of all the places I have been where diverse people gather. In the dusk of midnight after prolonged talking with various friends we pitched our tent in the sand beside our airplane, kicked out the beach trash, and crawled in to sleep. My old igloo and trail companion, Ruth Ahtongarook, with whom I once lived a year helped us pitch camp. The Eskimo girl had moved with her family 240 miles along the coast from where I saw her last. Accompanying her was a bespectacled, cross-eyed and much lipsticked belle of Barrow, her "city" girl friend.

Abraham Stine and Dora, with an infant, came to see us at the Presbyterian Rectory when they learned we were in town. Of half Eskimo blood, Abraham gave us intimate news of the arctic eastward. The news was dismaying for a photographer for only a few people still lived scattered eastward and remained true to the old-time ways we expected of Eskimos.

Eastward then along the top of the continent we would fly.

7 MY FAVORITE ESKIMOS

WE CALLED at the naval base which lies a few miles out of Barrow Village near the end of Point Barrow. Presenting our credentials to the commanding officer, we got his O.K. to go ahead into the 30,000 square miles of the United States Naval Petroleum Reserve which was where our Eskimo friends happen to live. It was easy to hop a ride on a Weasel along the gravel road back to town. The Eskimo driver was a reckless fellow, very self-important. One side of the tracks flopped with loose cleats, while people scattered along our way.

The Arctic Contractors, a private concern under contract to develop oil for the navy, were employing quite a few Eskimos with results which seemed fairly satisfactory to all concerned. In this way Barrow was prospering and the arctic people had a future not solely dependent upon their trapped-out countryside. Many of the ancestors of the Eskimo people were English sailors and South Sea Islanders, incidentally, so that when we speak of Eskimos today we must bear in mind that we are speaking of people actually of mixed races and a much-mixed arctic culture.

At Barrow we met Johnny Tukok whose sad story we learned from Abraham Stine:

"Johnny Tukok, he lost his whole family, his wife and two kids. They live at 20 miles above Foggy Island. Last fall on December 19 they leave for Barter Island for Christmas. They caught west storm — this side of Brownlow Point. They didn't know when they go out on the sea ice. When Johnny find out where they at they try to go to the land but the dogs half froze.

"They couldn't travel, so they build snow igloo and camp on the ice. But when night come the ice start to moving and bucking. The ice come piling in and few minutes later the two kids gone and afterwards Johnny's wife she caught her leg in ice crack. Ice closing in. They could not get her. Johnny with two hunters drifted one week and finally landed at Old Lynd's place. Everything lost. Dogs and sled lost, too."

Johnny's wife had often had tea and cookies in my igloo. Her name was Virginia. The two children, Donald age two, and Dora age four, were the most adorable little Eskimo packages you ever saw. It didn't seem real that the cruel polar ice had taken our friends in such a way.

Johnny Tukok stood around while Bud changed oil. Already the Eskimos had a name for the airplane. They called it *"Mitgodialuk,"* which in Eskimo means *Arctic Tern.*

We had been able to get hold of one pound of tea to carry eastward. That's all we could manage. A pound of tea means unbounded pleasure to those who have nothing else and who love tea as only an Eskimo can. It meant another pound overload for us.

On the take-off from the short lagoon we stayed on the water so long I feared we really wouldn't make it that time.

The top of our continent eastward from Point Barrow, Alaska, is low and filled with innumerable lakes. It is not possible for a person afoot to walk along the Arctic Ocean coast during the summer; he would be stranded until freeze-up. Sometimes as much as one third of the earth's surface as seen from the air is under water: green water, red water, muddy, murky, sour water. Blue lakes surrounded by fields of pink flowers amid which the curlews call. The lakes are of every imaginable shape, but most typical is the exactly square lake or the six-sided or eight-sided lake with square corners. Nobody knows why the corners are square but it has something to do with winter frost action pushing against the ground.

Because the subsoil is frozen eternally just a few feet below the surface these lakes cannot drain off beneath, and neither can they drain off the surface because they are choked and clogged with moss. The water level, in perfect balance between the mean precipitation and evaporation, remains constant. Precipitation is but fourteen inches a year here, which means that the arctic, north of tree line, is so dry that actually it would be a desert if it were located elsewhere.

Yet a remarkable incubator, with its undrained puddles and ponds and its luxuriant carpet of mosses, is this arctic prairie for breeding its famous mosquito hordes in the summertime. The arctic is kind to insect life. The constant cold temperatures of winter which have no intermittent thaws make for perfect refrigeration of the life processes during the period of sleep.

As we flew over the lakes, the soil polygons and frost rectangles * we noted a strange recent additional feature: The tracks of Weasels and Caterpillars crawled over the green plain below us, in and out among the lakes. Modern arctic tractor trains with their heavy equipment pulled on giant sleds had crossed this country during the wintertime. Throughout the whole area lies oil.

They had commenced drilling their test wells in 1945. It was now hard to get permission to enter this area. Formerly we hadn't needed permission because we were living there before the Arctic Contractors under the navy came to develop it. Ultimately, all of our films had to be censored by both the army and navy via a personal trip to Washington, D.C., before we could show them.

We used to always consider it 240 miles from Point Barrow to Beechey Point by dog sled or ocean boat but by air this was cut to 190 miles direct. We could see the ground as we flew, and flocks of what experience told us were brant and pintail ducks were alarmed from lake shores as we passed; the small white elongated objects were swans.

Dropping to 300 feet, we looked for tents. Suddenly Bud veered to the ocean. There was a whaleboat with a mast and white sail unfurled, and it swept along that lonesome beautiful sea.

"Richard's People," was all Bud said. (They were more of our Eskimo friends.)

We dove down and saw other people along the shore standing like

* Technical terms for ground heaved up by frost action.

sticks upon a mighty beach. They waved. Could they guess it was us?

Further on a short ways was Oliktok Point. "There's George Woods's tent!"

George and Nanny and their boys and girls didn't recognize us when we taxied up to their beach. We were surprised to be met with what are often described by travel writers as "stolid stares." The expressionless faces exhibited no sign of curiosity or welcome. When our floats touched, George came down the beach with his face carefully composed in politeness. He looked just the same as he always had but the life, the animation we knew, was missing.

I stepped out on the front of one float then and said: "Hello, George."

It seemed a miracle, what happened then. That homely stoical old Eskimo face underwent a startled paroxysm. The expression registered bewilderment, fright, unbelief, and finally a confused and suffusing joy. George could hardly speak.

He waved his hand to his family at the tent and shouted, "They have come back. Connie and Bud. It is Bud and Connie come!"

We heard the words come tumbling out in English and Eskimo. The entire family suddenly came to life. They catapulted down the beach to grasp our outstretched hands. The lifted faces were exuberant. I felt choked. Then I was filled with remorse and a little shame. Why did our adopted Eskimo mother and father think so much of us? Whatever it was, it was too great a responsibility.

"They told me you would not come back," George said.

"Who told you?"

"Some navy fellow. They say you are rich man. They say you will not come back in Alaska any more. They kid me all the time, but I say you will come back some day. That Bud, he always come back."

"You always been just like my own kids," said George near to tears. "My big children."

"We are worry about you," said Nanny. "I think about you many time down there in United States. My tent is warm."

I had slipped from the airplane directly into my parka. Then I followed her into the little white tent.

*   *   *

I well remember the first time we saw George and Nanny in their tent beside the Arctic Ocean when we came along there in our home-made canoe. There were no other white people in that part of the world then, just a few short years ago.

"It is just an old Eskimo camp," George had said in good English, as he held back the flap of the wall tent for us to enter. Inside the tent sat Nanny at her sewing.

Nanny's other name is *Oinjak*, as nearly as I can spell it, which in Eskimo language means "Open-Water-Between-the-Ice-Floes." Nanny the mother; Martha, a young girl of about sixteen with a crippled back; Lydia age 5, and Oolak, a boy of about thirteen, composed the family as we first saw them. There was, of course, no furniture in the tent, as the custom was to live on the floor, but the bed skins were neat and well laid. The little sheet iron stove sent a warm glow over the snug interior, while on a legless table prepared for us in the middle of the tent floor sat two cups of steaming tea. While the wild waves of the Arctic Ocean beat before the door, from the tent came the fragrance of baking biscuits.

Nanny said grace in Eskimo, and as we ate George talked about the arctic coast life.

"The biscuits are hard," he apologized. "Nanny can make fine bread, but we have no supplies for two years now. We are out of everything except a little flour. No salt, nothing. But I have a few cartridge yet and the fish net, and we will get by. My oldest boy Apiak, he is gone hunting caribou now."

George hadn't been born here, although he was an Eskimo. He had come, just as we had, from what is called the "other side," meaning across the Brooks Range of Alaska from the timbered interior four hundred miles away by air. It had taken him a year to make the trip and he explained that he had expected to go right back. He always missed the forest.

"But well, I was young man then, and I met Nanny over here."

He smiled toward the woman, who with her black braids falling over her ample bosom, continued to sew, using a glover's needle and sinew thread.

She spoke no English. George explained he had learned what English he knew from the old-time gold rush miners of the "other side" around the towns of Bettles and Wiseman, and he had gone to the mission school at Alatna.

"I was pretty cold fellow on this coast when I come over here first year," he laughed softly. "You have to have the good caribou fur clothes to live here. You have to have the good woman for sew."

It was on Christmas Eve that he sledded out to Cross Island thirty miles off the shore with some other gay young blades. There were two whales killed at Cross Island that year, George said, and several families were wintering there. There was a big party at Christmas time. It was on Cross Island that he was introduced to Nanny. She was sixteen. Her people were seal hunters.

He and Nanny hadn't even spoken that first meeting. But the old folks made up their minds that the two young people would make a good match. George didn't have a chance at all, he explained to us, smiling. "The old folks just fixed it all up." A few weeks later the young man and girl met again.

"What happened?" Bud asked.

"Well, you know how young folks are," George said.

This was nearly thirty years ago. The passing seasons had dealt both kindly and harshly with the couple, and somehow George forgot to return to the "other side."

There were many children born. The parents lost more than half of them. A boy and girl nearly twenty had died just last year of a common cold that was brought by some traveler coming from Point Barrow. Now there remained a brood of four. The youngest, little Lydia, was just beginning to emerge from under her mother's skirts to peer bright-eyed at a stranger. Yet the family presented an appearance of deep contentment and fulfillment, and the longer we were to know them the more certain we were that they had happiness.

There was little in worldly goods that they possessed and little worldly knowledge, but I have never in my life known people who were such *good* people.

We were going to stay a year on this coast and we needed fur clothing like they wore; as George said, it is foolish to try to live in this treeless land where the great winds blow unless you dress in caribou. It wasn't long until we newcomers regarded the couple as our true parents, for they protected us against all the dangers which threaten rank amateurs in arctic life.

We were impatient. Why couldn't fur clothing be made quickly? Why couldn't this be done or that be done — such as the gathering of fuel for winter — and promptly? If we needed a wolf ruff for a parka hood and someone had a fine ruff on his parka, why not just buy it? Goods of any kind were scarce in this part of the world. We must have appeared fabulously wealthy with what was a scant outfit brought down river with our fourteen-foot canoe. Surely we should be able to get anything we wanted from these people! Just pay the price and get it. Get it somehow! The theory that the black market operates on, and what was wrong with it?

George never came out and told us. He set the example and we were ashamed. If a man needed a box of shells for his rifle it would be wrong to force him to pay for them with a white wolf ruff off his only parka. If a woman was busy sewing for her family it would be wrong to induce her to sew for us until she had finished her task.

Bud and I possessed the only working outboard motor, a one and one-half horse, on the North American side of the whole polar ocean at the time, I believe. It was priceless where no other means of power was available than sail, dog power, or man power. Borrowing one of the local whaleboats — Richard's boat — Bud went after a load of driftwood out to some sand reefs a few miles to sea. He and his party returned that night to our camp and piled the wood upon the beach. Somehow we figured that at least half that wood was ours, because we had the motor. It is true that a lot of people accompanied Bud upon his self-elected trip, but he didn't ask them; they just invited themselves. The men, women and children who had gone for the ride picked up wood, and everybody made a game of it.

To our surprise the Eskimos did not seem to recognize that the wood was ours. They did not seem to understand that Bud was trying to

Bud and Connie cook lunch on an island in the Arctic Ocean

Planting flowers beside our cabin

Fishing for lake trout — Takahula Lake

Richard Tukle's family at Oliktok Point, Alaska

accumulate some fuel for the winter ahead. Everyone used the wood which had been gathered and within a few days' time all of our winter's fuel was gone. Bud and I were worried about fuel because we had never lived a winter north of the timberline before and we didn't intend to freeze to death unprepared. We kind of hinted to George that maybe those people who had not gathered the wood should not use it.

To this George never said yes or no. But somehow as the days passed we began to feel foolish. There was Etta the widow with no man to haul fuel for her and her five little girls. What would Etta do for fuel? Did Bud and I mind if the poor widow used a few sticks to warm her tent? The question wasn't put to us; the situation was just gradually brought to our consciousness. We came to realize that we really owed to all these people a lot more than the few sticks they used, for many reasons not readily apparent. Later in the season when Bud and I could get no wood — for we had no dog team to start with — the people always took care of us somehow. They would bring us sledloads of wood from as much as thirty miles away, digging it out of the snow piece by piece. We paid for the wood, but money loses its value in such a land and other values take its place.

As that winter went on George and his family moved to another location along the coast where driftwood was more abundant. We came to understand why the Eskimos in primitive life didn't worry about fuel. Instead of wasting their days of summer by gathering wood for winter, they simply followed the practice common to a hunting and fishing people — of moving around periodically to different spots where wood was. Having no permanent homes, they lived all winter, as in summer, in their tents. They built a snowhouse over and around the tent and converted to igloo life in winter.

Eventually Bud and I were obliged to adopt the same kind of life in order to live in the land where the Eskimos lived, and we learned that there was a reason for everything. We hired, or you can better say adopted, a young hunter named Ook-sook and his cousin Ruth for our companions, and with their dog team took up the life of arctic wanderers. We ranged over an area generally speaking of around the size of England and Scotland put together, in which Bud and I were the only white people.

For months on end we traveled about, living in one improvised igloo after another, following the fish, following the caribou herds, the seals — but always we passed back and forth by George's place.

Inside the old tent, grown unrecognizable from the outside by its walls and roof of snowblocks supported by driftwood rafters, there was always warmth, cheer, and a glowing atmosphere of contentment. We learned to speak softly, although our voices at first were harsh with civilization's clamor. Never did we hear an angry or sharp word used among these people.

The snow lay white over a vast land and driftwood was hard to find buried beneath it along the indeterminate coastline where land met sea ice, but George worked in the twilight to keep sticks ahead, while his oldest boy hunted and trapped the white fox. Nanny sewed warm clothes for us all and the other children helped her. They rubbed the new skins soft as velvet, and talked and laughed.

The few fox skins were used to enrich the family and were regarded as family property. The one hunter Apiak who caught them never seemed to feel that he owned all the foxes or that the family depended upon him. Trapping was just his particular job, the job he did best. The whole depends upon each of its parts and no part was complete in arctic family life without the other.

There was never a sense of hurry with George's family. While explorers visiting this land have seemed, from their point of view and ours, to virtually dangle from one impending crisis of existence to another, in the viewpoint of these people there was always plenty of time to do everything that must be done. There was time for a cup of tea or time to hear what the baby wanted to say. There was time for George to read aloud from the Bible twice each week, and you may be sure that religious services held on any sandspit in this part of the world would always be held in this hospitable tent. Into their tent streamed the poor and the indigent — for many were poorer or less resourceful than they.

I hadn't paid a great deal of attention to how Nanny was making out in our conversations when one day I suddenly realized that Nanny had learned to speak English! She picked it up enough to be able to converse with me! She dressed us in the best style of the Eskimo man and wife, and we came to look just like the others. They talked to us as if we were actually their big children, and with the development of this unusual relationship we discussed many things which I do not believe teachers, missionaries, or traders usually have occasion to discuss with these people.

We were talking one day about the white men who are coming increasingly to Point Barrow as that place assumed importance in world geography. There were expeditions of learned scientists to study the ocean bottom, to study the plant and marine life, to study the sociology of the pitifully declining and diseased Eskimos living at that outpost. The arctic contractors, bent on developing oil, the navy personnel and the U.S. Weather Bureau were all cutting their slice out of the arctic. Reports of the progress they made which you could read in journals and newspapers sounded great.

"What do you think of the white men?" we asked George.

George seemed troubled and he looked away for a moment. "They have awfully poor manners," he finally told us.

But as though recalling himself and almost regretting having made this statement, he explained, "Well, you see, no one has ever taught them any better."

The troubled look remained in George's eyes when we went on to discuss the pending question of reservations for the Eskimo people in Alaska. This issue has been introduced in Congress more than once in the last few years. The Indian Service was pushing strongly for the creation of reservations with the plea that they "protect" the rights and lands of native people. Of course in doing so the reservations would paradoxically limit their rights and lands by defining them. Reservations would also coincidentally extend the jobs and holdings of Indian Service personnel.

George colored. "It is a shame," he told us. "Why should people want to treat us like that? There is no difference in people. All people have to eat and they got to have place to live. Why cannot people live in peace, and every person live where he like best?"

The troubled look passed away, and I am thankful to say, so did the reservation threat. It was voted down in Congress — at least for that time.

The creation of reservations in Alaska for Indians and Eskimos might, as a matter of fact, he found unconstitutional for the reason that when the United States bought this territory from Russia eighty years ago it was under the condition that all of its inhabitants would be treated as full United States citizens and they and their descendants were guaranteed full legal status.

That this part of the contract has never been filled by the United States Government toward Alaska's natives or toward those citizens who go there to live, is a grave breach not to be overlooked in evaluating our country's prestige among other countries.

A year passed for us on the arctic coast and another summer came. The time was at hand for Bud and me to get into our canoe when the water flowed again. We traveled along the Arctic Ocean from Alaska to Canada with a sack of Nanny's bread and a fish net. George and his family shook hands with us the day we left them, and tears were in our eyes.

"Take care of yourselves," we told each other.

And they added, "Come back and live with us again. You have friends among the Eskimos and that's the main thing."

For years I have pondered that statement. It seems to me sometimes that that is, indeed, the main thing.

We kept our promise. We did go back to the Eskimos.

Our new Cessna 140 on floats splashed to a landing on the swells of the Arctic Ocean beside Oliktok Point where we found George's ten by twelve foot tent staunchly pitched quite as usual.

Old Black, the lead dog, welcomed us with a growl, as we crawled inside the tent and took our places. The fox season was good here last year, we learned. Apiak had caught 150 white foxes. But we felt a strong wave of premonition. Fur prices were going down, down. Of all the Eskimos who once lived in this area, perhaps fifty in all, the rest had given it up and gone to Point Barrow to live on navy wages and scavenging navy garbage piles.

George and Nanny were the last of the individualists.

It wasn't that they didn't like the things Point Barrow had to offer. They would have liked to live where there was medical attention and where there was a church and especially they wanted their children to go to school. But they had observed that the Eskimos who were drawn to the city were dying of tuberculosis right beside the very doors of the church, school and hospital, and there was seemingly nothing that anyone could do about it. George and Nanny chose to remain here then, not because they didn't like progress but because here they at least had health and a living and could remain alive.

With the serenity of the world's most accomplished hostess, Nanny set before us the courses of an arctic meal. First there were boiled chunks of caribou. The most experienced meat eaters of the world do not *like* steaks, chops and roasts. In a land where fresh fruits and vegetables are unknown, in a land where agriculture can never be practiced, it is ridiculous to expect people to eat their meat in ways which have proven appetizing for us but which are adverse for them. The food pretenses of civilization are the outcome of long years of siege and famine, where a lot must be done with a little. Here the people have good meat and a family with their dogs may consume many tons of meat in a year; consequently we find the Eskimos prize different parts than we do. What these people eat almost exclusively as long as they can get them are boiled bones. Flavorless boned meat is thrown to the dogs — at least during prosperous times — and the people keep for themselves the ribs and joints that in America most usually go to Fido.

One of the things Nanny was careful about as a good housewife was that the meat must not be overcooked. Everyone present grabbed the best hunk he could see and bit into it, slicing the bites off with his knife close to his face. Those who wished to eat with their knife and fork on a tin plate held in the lap were welcome to do so, but the firm rubbery joints were almost impervious to a fork and were apt to go sailing.

For months Bud and I had talked of Nanny's boiled caribou meat when we found our strength failing on drugstore lunches.

"But this is disappointing to me," I told him as I gnawed, picking off stray caribou hairs. "Maybe I've got too civilized. It's not as I remembered. It doesn't have much flavor."

"You just can't taste anything any more," Bud whispered back. "You have to get into the caribou habit, and it takes about three weeks. This one was a poor animal anyway," he added, with the sure judgment of an expert.

Just then I happened to think of the *Arctic Tern* parked right outside on the ocean. What a situation! Here we were eating wild game out of season as guests of those who depend upon game. Yet we had an airplane now. I thought with revulsion of those airplanes I had seen in Alaska already — their interiors soaked with blood, stained dark brown with the dried blood of caribou. It was common knowledge that an aircraft was a handy vehicle for hauling caribou or moose meat for the market. A bit illegal perhaps, but some of the best people were doing it. There was a trade in caribou meat and skins around Barrow, for the "city" Eskimos working for wages there were desperate for meat, while white arctic residents felt they also had some privileges.

The caribou course finished, Nanny pulled a long roasting pan from the oven and set it before the assembled group on the floor. The pan was solid with sixteen-inch Arctic Ocean whitefish. Each fish had been scaled, split, and had its entrails removed. Then each had been rolled in flour with a sprinkle of salt and pepper and simply placed in the roasting tray, complete with head and fins left on. Now the baked fish were brown on top and floating in their own golden oil. We always used to chew the fins. They were brown and crisp like potato chips. It never occurred to Nanny in all her life that any person would take the trouble to cut fins off raw slippery fish — at some hazard to the butcher — when anybody knows that fins pull right off anyway after they have been cooked.

Our meal ended with a course of plain white bread and weak tea with which sugar was served. This was the diet upon which George and Nanny and their associates lived the year round, and they thrived, with the exuberant great health of the Eskimos, which I have not seen rivaled in any land.

We landed on an evening when gentle waves lapped and the cries of the loons from out that landlocked ocean were an arctic melody. Next day not a bird was in sight. The ocean rolled crashing against the shore, with spray and foam washing monotonously against the airplane's rocking floats. The tents on the spit trembled in the blast which was directly out of the North Pole. No fish could be caught today. George was alert to get the family's only fish net out of the ocean before it should be torn to pieces.

Inside the tent everyone sat in his furs all day. We all wore what is known as the summer parka, which has the fur turned inside, and over it a loose, washable, colored dress which protects the parka from summer dirt and rain. The small sheet-iron stove crackled and trays of delicious baked whitefish were eaten. George held a church service in which everybody sang from the hymnal: "Break thou the bread of life, Oh, Lord . . . beside the sea."

We might be here indefinitely now. In this respect the possession of an airplane made little difference at Oliktok Point. In the North you hurry and hurry only to get some place and wait and wait. I had prepared myself for these days by bringing some good books. I had even gone so far as to choose books over food. Now, here we were. Few indeed are the times in modern life when a person can truthfully say, "There isn't a single thing I can do or should do today."

Two days later we took a flight. The Arctic Ocean is free of ice in late summer all along north Alaska. George took equal advantage of the brief condition of calm by putting out his fish net again.

We wanted to find caribou on the prairie to photograph them. Caribou are not at their best in summer by any means. The gas we used was 80-octane common automobile gas bought at Oliktok from George for $1.00 the gallon.

We flew low over the prairie. We could see the ground squirrels and the fish in the lakes as we flew. Near Beechey Point thirty miles eastward, the Kuparuk River lay there just as we had left it. We could see the scars on river bars which ice had made during spring floods; every small puddle had its quota of ducks and loons and terns.

"Look, there's one of our old campsites." A pole protruded from the grassy river bank at the entrance of a small estuary of the Kuparuk.

"Look at the grayling in that pool!" The stream mouth was alive with big grayling, shimmering in the translucent water. On this river with the Eskimo name we had explored by canoe in summer and dog sled in winter. I remembered our last hunt on this river. Dressed like Eskimos, we had lived just like Eskimos, yet so vast was the country of the beautiful Kuparuk River that we had been unable to make a dent in Nature's gladness.

It was spring on the prairie with all that spring means, with its mirrored water and wild flowers. The bull caribou were putting on back fat and the marrow in their bones tasted to us like cream. There was no other food but nesting ducks and flour and man cannot live on flour alone. The staff of life is not bread but meat.

Over the winter-frozen ocean Bud and I and Ook-sook had traveled with our canoe lashed upon the sled to where the Kuparuk had melted its way through sea ice. We put the canoe into the water, paddled ashore through a great fog in the river's mouth, and let the dogs swim from the ice tongue to land. The dog sled was left abandoned, upturned on the beach. The dogs were supposed to be used as pack animals and for pulling the canoe up the river.

It ended that both Bud and Ook-sook ran off to hunt as we traveled inland into the gathering spring, and the dogs loafed and I dragged and pushed the canoe up the shallow river bed. But the exercise didn't hurt me. All day long it was my custom to pick up little dead drift willows and pile them into the canoe so that by the time we halted there would be fuel to cook a meal.

I remember the warm sun which woke us in our tent late the following day and our breakfast of king eider ducks boiled in a pot. A wind was gently blowing, bringing with it the scents of a thousand miles of early spring prairie. The warm spring wind blowing across those miles was too much for Ook-sook. He was a prairie hunter, age twenty-three.

"What is it, Ook-sook?" we asked.

"Ook-sook lots of homesick," he told us, the strong copper face clouding.

That was the day we lost Ook-sook. He had been our adopted hunter, our very own wild man, for three quarters of a year.

"Dogs strong," Bud suggested in the peculiar jargon which the two friends had invented. "Dogs pack-sacks, walk-walk, three days, Mathew."

In an hour he had all of his dogs packed and was ready to leave for the home of his father, Mathew, a hundred miles inland, west. But when he was ready to go he didn't want to go. Somehow as though sensing the finality of these brief days, he took his battered rifle, shook hands, and started over the early grass. Bud and I, two days travel up the Kuparuk River, watched him go and were powerless to stop him. From a little rise we saw that wild figure grow smaller and smaller in the distance. His dogs strung out behind him, while the pup Coaly frisked on ahead with tail high.

A little gay speck and several dots we knew were Ook-sook and his dogs moving slowly over an immense stage of limitless prairie. We had come through a winter with them. We had seen each other tired and lean. Bud and I had learned the heartbreak of supporting a dog team: the symbol of the poverty of the Eskimo, as it keeps the Eskimo always poor, yet the symbol of all his riches in life, the great heritage of his freedom to roam.

Ook-sook belonged to this vast landscape, the land of arctic prairie and sky, out of which he had sprung. As we watched those figures vanish over a land grown familiar, as the shimmering heat waves danced and the new grass swayed, we knew then that our days on the prairie were numbered. This was the last hunt.

The camp where that pole was, was where we had lost Ook-sook, and something went with him then that will never be again, possibly in all this world.

"Maybe now with our airplane we can find the head of the Kuparuk

River," we thought. We had never been able to explore it sufficiently by dog sled.

Yet what we found was that we had less fuel range with a small airplane than we had formerly with a dog team. It would take a bigger and mightier airplane than the one we had to haul enough gas to explore all of this country! An untrained observer flying over it would not dream that this river, winding sunken between its prairie banks, was the home of herds of caribou, of brown bears, wolves, wolverines, foxes and ground squirrels. All varieties of ducks, shore birds, loons, swans, geese, brant, plovers, jaegers, gulls, eagles, and many of our song sparrows nest here by summer. Ravens, owls, falcons and ptarmigan are year-round residents. Only the water birds are driven from the arctic when winter turns their pools to ice, and they must fly south as their food supply freezes up behind them. People are accustomed to asking, "Why do birds migrate north?" A resident of the arctic would be more apt to ask instead, "Why do birds go south?" and the answer is no mystery. The pitiful part is that in some seasons many thousands of birds get lost in the arctic and perish when for some reason they lack leaders or forget how to make their southern trip.

We spotted a prairie lake presently and came in for a landing. We would camp here to photograph for a few days.

In a grove of small willows we pitched the tent and soon had a fire crackling in the sheet iron stove. There were no wild flowers; it was too late in the season. There were no mosquitoes; the trillion wings were stilled. At a distance over the pastel moor we saw a single caribou. But it looked like a sheep. A mangy individual, it had been retarded in its shedding. This animal was in poor shape, as the glasses verified, for its horns were small and it limped. Grayling from the lake furnished a fine supper.

I was just tidying up from breakfast when Bud snaked into the tent door on his hands and knees. I followed him, as he grabbed movie camera, tripod and extra film, keeping my head down as I ran. All along the horizon you could see great racks of horns like a moving forest of sticks. Under the horns were five very old bulls, good ones, while the rest were young bulls — around thirty bulls in all traveling together. They were moving fast.

Although our tent was in plain sight, the caribou didn't know what it was. They saw the airplane on the lake but they didn't understand that it might be dangerous. They came right by us; then the band swung at right angles and passed some seven hundred yards below, much too far for even a good telephoto shot. As soon as we saw that they were going to swim the river we crawled away behind a slight mound and hid from them by the cut-bank.

Once hidden in the cut, we ran to intercept them at another point. Caribou travel so fast that a person is hard-pressed to get to them even when they happen to come near. With a mile or two of rapid running, ducking and crawling I became winded, and as the last of the stragglers were coming fast I flopped down upon the bare prairie with the "still" camera while Bud sprinted on another five hundred yards further to await them with movies. In this way — just as we used to do when hunting for food — we would increase our chances between us for a shot as the fleet deer passed.

The animals came over a rise. I saw their tall horns come over first. The grass was as short as a freshly mowed lawn. But the caribou never saw me there. Many hunters will try to hide behind some object as a rock or a tree. In this way they are certainly hidden, but they make the mistake of peeking around the object or over it. This small movement will panic game quicker than will the sight of a person lying down completely uncovered in the open with the whole body exposed. The system of the prairie hunter we have since tried in other climes and have learned that animals in general can be approached without cover.

It is always my luck that the least desirable animals come the closest to me regardless of whether I am after pictures or game. The gangly young bulls came trooping forward while the oldest bull in the band, the magnificent patriarch, was lagging far behind.

The caribou were passing a few yards to my right, upwind. Then, just like that, the game was up. One animal got my scent. He gave a startled spring. Instantly every caribou was staring at me. Then they turned as the wind turns. In flight they seemed to be governed by one will; every animal seemed to get the message simultaneously. Every knee was lifted in unison, heads held back, nostrils flaring and high. They poised on their prairie stage like a well-trained group of ballet dancers. Then as one animal they wheeled again, broke into a cavorting gallop as effortless as air, and strung by me two hundred yards to my right — all except the one old bull, and he ran off farther away than that.

"How did you make out?" I asked Bud at camp.

"O.K., I guess. How did you?"

"I think it's kind of fun being a hunter with a camera. It's sure different, though," I said. "I don't think I'm very good at it yet."

In the gray hours of early morning as we slept in the tent, snow began to fall. Snow may come any day of the year on Alaska's arctic coastal plain, facing the sea. We had hot tea for breakfast and Bud floundered out into the flurry of sodden snowflakes long enough to get a couple of fish. The green wet willows hated to burn in the stove.

The second day passed with closed-in fog and drizzle. Sitting inside our tent in the old days used to be a kind of luxury because we had a stout canvas tent. The porousness of canvas permits ventilation and allows a camp to "breathe." But a tight-weave nylon tent is conducive to pneumonia for the inmates because the condensation of the breath collects inside and persons become drenched in clammy dew. We missed the caribou robes for bedding and flooring to which we were formerly used.

The wind arose, making for a real blizzard out of season. The waves lashed in the prairie lake as though the lake would escape its confinement. Sitting on the little island of our sleeping bag and duffel piled high on wet willows in the middle of the tent we spent the day reading, writing, and at the laborious preparation of something to eat. I had to dry out each individual stick on top of the stove and in the oven before it could be burned. Nights were getting dark again; night came with ominous gusts which threatened to take the frail tent from its moorings. The gusts blew sheets of water, whipping the lake into muddy foam. On the north coast of Alaska the winds are steady and reliable. When a wind begins, it blows from a set direction without veering one degree on the compass. It increases in velocity for about four to six days; then, having reached its maximum, gradually the storm decreases and in three more days wears itself out. A calm may prevail for a day or two. After that the wind starts to rise and blows back all over again from the exact opposite direction. Velocities of 135 miles an hour have been registered, at which point the anemometer blew away.

The tie-down equipment you carry in a small aircraft is usually limited to three three-eighths inch ropes about twenty feet long, and your small ax. To hold any airplane with such meager equipment calls for ingenuity, and is probably the acid test of a pilot. Bud picked up his training in this from the Eskimos, who are skilled in tying down their tents, boats and sleds at all seasons.

The prime factor in successfully weathering a storm is to pick out the best area available before you even make camp in the first place. When you are flying in a storm you are far too likely to land as soon as you can in any spot that is available, but you may regret your haste if it means losing your airplane on the ground! A seaplane ranging far afield is like a boat in that you must find for it a safe harbor. No matter how hard the storm is blowing up, if you are flying over unfamiliar country and are going to land, you must study your intended area with care. Look for some sheltered bay, an island you can get behind, a slough you can taxi up. Bud had done this when choosing our camping place.

On Lake Laberge Bud had held the airplane by boxes of sand and rocks tied on its wings. A rock of about 75 pounds for each wing is what we needed now but there were no rocks and no sand here. We had her tied to the limber willows along the shore.

"I think I'd better go down and sit with the airplane," said Bud in the middle of the night.

"Do you want me to go sit with you?"

"No, go back to sleep. No use for both of us to have to sit up." Bud sat in the cockpit of the airplane drawn partly up on the grassy bank, to add his weight and keep it from being blown away. The pilot of a small plane may be called upon to do this many times in this part of the world. He may have to sit with his plane five days in succession or until the storm blows itself out.

Toward morning as the storm worsened Bud was obliged to use a device which the float pilot saves for a last resort.

The first step is to move the airplane to a spot where a gradual sloping beach permits you to work it up on land. With a light plane such as the Cessna 140 this can be done by one man. The procedure is to lift a main wing strut where it is attached to the wing. You can move the ship a few inches each time, and by lifting first on one side and then the other you gradually get it up on land. There you face it into the wind with the tail propped up and the wings tied down. When tie-downs are hard to find, you make your own. You dig a trench about 24 inches deep and four feet long. Tie your rope securely to a piece of wood, a long flat rock or even to your canoe paddle. A canoe paddle is always carried along attached to the inside of a float. Bury the toggle in the bottom of the hole and tamp the hole full of sand or earth. A modification of this principle is to pile rocks upon the toggle, but burying it is the best.

This is done at the outer end of each wing a few feet ahead of the leading wing edge. This method of tying will weather almost any storm. But there comes the infrequent gale when the sand drives like hail, the short prairie grass lays to the ground and the tent blows over. The water is no longer a mass of white caps but a caldron of boiling foam and a wind of hurricane force sweeps over all. Here the float-plane pilot takes off the inspection plates from the floats and fills the floats full of water!

Sand would do, but water is always available where a float ship is, and it is easier to dump out later. A two-place airplane can have its weight increased more than a *ton* — and right at the ground level where it will do the most good. Thus with a ton overload, tied securely, and facing into the wind, the airplane will not move, even in a tornado. The pilot can climb into the plane to add his own weight, and thus the storm eventually wears itself out. When the storm passes, an undamaged airplane, ready to go exploring again, more than repays the float-plane pilot for the trouble taken to preserve his ship.

We were beginning to get mighty hungry and damp as the blizzard continued the fourth day. In the middle of the afternoon four caribou came by, and since the wind was so violent, there was offered an excellent opportunity to photograph them without being scented or heard. From the screen of willows along the lake margin we worked our way, crawling through icy puddles. It was necessary to keep the lens shielded all the time except for the moments of actual use, for spray would freeze upon it.

Through the willow stems we saw the legs of caribou. Bud was fumbling, trying to replace the telephoto lens with the standard lens for close-range work when the grazing animal walked within six feet of us. There we were, crouched on hands and knees, almost directly under him. We could hear the soft muzzle cropping grass. Then his head was over us: wrinkled brow, antlers four feet tall, and bulging eyes. There was a snort as the caribou leapt straight into the air. On his hind legs he wheeled backward and the next time he hit the ground he was doing sixty. We shot some film. We were delighted.

On the fifth day the blizzard wore itself out and we were worn out and starved, when our tent caught on fire. Bud had cut the shavings for morning and placed them on top of the dying stove to dry. The stove was not as dead as we thought. We had been in the sack ten minutes when the shavings exploded into fierce flames and the flames caught the nylon tent in an instant. I shot out from under one side of the tent and Bud shot out from underneath the other. Handfuls of soggy snow, gathered barefooted, put the fire out but it was a pot of fish soup that finally quenched it.

"More sewing for me," groaned Bud. It was always his job to patch the tent; we had a sack of nylon patches.

"Just think," I said, "that navy oil camp, Umiat, is only about a forty- or fifty-mile flight from here. Oh, what I'd give right now for a good meal with the navy."

We thereupon broke camp and flew to Umiat that evening. We landed on the Colville River beside a Wien Cub on floats. Umiat had a large airfield and was serviced entirely by air. It was Sunday. This meant a turkey dinner with all the trimmings. We were in luck.

It was fun talking with Al West, the foreman, for he was an old-time Alaskan of wide experience. He had orders to let us have up to one hundred gallons of gas during the season, for which we would remit to the Navy Department. There were eighty men at Umiat at this time.

"We'll sleep with Mathew's People tonight," Bud announced. "I want to see Ook-sook right away."

"Do you know Mathew?" I asked the foreman and some of the others conversationally.

"No, who's that?"

"Well, they're a large Eskimo family that live right down the Colville River here fifty or a hundred miles from you," I explained. "They have lived here, of course, a long time before the Naval Petroleum Reserve was founded."

"Oh, Eskimos," one of the men said. "We have some Eskimos come by here once in a while and the cook sometimes gives them a handout. We tell them to move right on. We can't be bothered with Eskimos around here."

I was worried on the take-off as we sped out of the backwater and into the fast treacherous Colville current. But just as the violent currents met in what looked like a whirlpool our ship skimmed over the surface and made its ever-dependable climb into the sky.

"How are we going to find Mathew's People with night coming on? You know they roam over an area of hundreds of square miles."

"They're on one of these river channels. They'll be after the big river whitefish at this season."

Over the purple earth we flew in a pink sky. It was near midnight. The sun was barely sunken beneath the horizon. The tents of Mathew's People were not where we first looked for them but presently we located those little tents blooming on top of one of the great Colville cliffs some three hundred feet above the roaring river.

"Gosh, how will we land near those cliffs? Maybe there are some hidden snags in the river."

"I know the river. I could land here with my eyes shut."

Night's dark storm clouds had closed out all the world. Bud switched on the wing lights; the dull red glow of the instrument panel was reassuring. I could just barely see the great sprawling river and its scalloped cliffs winding down the horizon. Easily the *Arctic Tern* skidded onto the churning surface. I recalled some bad moments we had had on this river previously with a canoe. I was the first modern woman to see this river and explore it, and to this day its navigators could be counted on the fingers of one hand.

"You're not dealing with a canoe now," said Bud. "This airplane's got power."

The airplane walked right up the current. I didn't want to get near those crumbling cliffs but Bud was searching them for a crevice. He had already figured out that if Mathew was camping here he would have found a cleft for their whale boat. We found the cleft and pulled into it. Down through the cleft in the darkness came a trickle of sweet water from a spring back on the hill. As we switched off our engine we could hear the trickling sound. In the gloom we made out the form of old Mathew who alone came down the steep embankment. He turned, shouting back up to the others above. None of these people spoke English. Excited voices, speaking in Eskimo, cut through the night and soared above the rush of Alaska's third largest river. We could hear the words, "Bud and Connie." Then like sprites out of the night the whole family descended upon us from above, capering, jumping and shouting. I have been welcomed as a returned wayfarer in many places, but for this moment I felt as close to those people as I have ever felt to any human beings in my life.

The caribou hunting clan surrounded us and deluged us with their joy. They formed in a line as Bud handed out our camp equipment from the airplane, carrying everything for us up the tremendous bluff. Even the toddlers carried a joint of our stovepipe each. On top they pitched our tent beside their own tents and brought chopped sticks to our door for fuel. Every gnarled stick had to be gathered from the river islands, rowed to the cleft in the cliff by boat, and then carried up the three-hundred-foot bluff.

We were sorry we had not been able to bring anything to eat.

Mathew's People did not even have salt or tea. We passed out tea but that's all we could do. They were living on parka squirrels at the moment, that the children caught.

"Where's Ook-sook?"

The family pointed out over the prairie. We knew that Ook-sook was gone after caribou.

When we crawled out next day we saw three fresh caribou skins drying for clothing, stretched out on the grass. There were piles of meat nearby and Ook-sook's old rifle rested against a tent rope in its sealskin case. We knew that Ook-sook had returned with his pack dogs sometime in the night. Slabs of back fat weighing up to twenty pounds each showed that he had secured good, old bulls.

Mathew's People consisted of fifteen souls in all. There were Ook-sook and his brothers Colliak, Uke and Leffingwell: the hunters. They had some sixty dogs between them. None of the sons of Mathew and old Oliver, as we called the mother, had ever married. None of the daughters had married except Harriet and her man died several seasons ago of the flu; she came home again bringing five children.

Harriet had secured from a navy fellow at Barrow during the last year a portable phonograph and some records. Delightedly, before breakfast, she started up the music for us, the phonograph sitting on the prairie grass in the feeble sun, while a boy sharpened phonograph needles on a stone. We all wore warm caribou with the fur turned in, and our wolverine-fringed hoods danced in the wind that passed along the cliff top.

There had occurred several gradual changes in the family during the years we had known them. But a most shocking change was presented by Ook-sook when he crawled sleepily out of the bachelor's tent. Since living with us he had discarded his beautiful Eskimo dresses over caribou skins which had given to Ook-sook the dignity of the noble savage. He was dressed now — at least for arctic summer wear — in cast-off American G.I.'s. The sight his foolish face made in them was far from fetching.

"Oh, Bud!" was all I could wail, as Bud looked back at me and we both stared at Ook-sook again.

Of course Ook-sook thought he looked grand. He supposed himself to be in the finest style.

"Ook-sook white man now," old Mathew told us, nodding and clucking. Only Mathew and the mother in their ancient tattered skin clothing, seemed unchanged. Those old-fashioned innocent Eskimos with their happy-go-lucky natures and their tendency to sing all day over nothing at all, were still our same two darlings.

Little did Bud and I realize then that our airplane was destined, a season later, to save the lives of this entire family and that the old mother and the brother Colliak were to leave this world soon.

Breakfast of roast caribou ribs and tea was held in the big main tent. I've never tasted better ribs. They were rare, juicy, dripping with fat. As soon as grace was pronounced over them we grabbed fast, as the many hands shot in. Mathew's People were always fast grabbers.

I wanted to see Ook-sook's dog team. Of the dogs I had traveled with so many miles only a few individuals were left. Mathew's People had had a hard winter last year and many of the weaker dogs were eaten up as dog food. I recognized Coaly the pup with whom I once faced a polar bear at close quarters. I imagined Coaly would feel tender toward me from what we had gone through together. But Coaly seemed to have lost what few brains he had ever had. Ever since he had awakened that morning to find a great white bear cornering him in the snow alley where he slept outside my igloo door he had never been the same. Now when he saw me some chord of memory was struck and he apparently got me confused with the polar bear. He would have taken my hand off right up to the elbow.

Mathew's People proved to be delighted actors for our camera. We grabbed and gorged and smacked and belched, and our chins were greasy with fat meat. We feasted on all the leg bones of the three caribou served up in a great pile. Everybody grabbed a bone. Then there followed an enthusiastic pounding and cracking as each eater broke a bone and dug out the plugs of creamy raw marrow. Bone marrow is the greatest delicacy the Eskimo knows. What was not recorded when the camera ceased grinding was that I made off with an extra leg bone to my own tent to save for the following day.

Bud took Ook-sook for his first airplane ride. What a look on his face! I can recall his helpless fright as he clung to his safety belt on the take-off, having promised that he would not grab the controls; the astonishment, the exultation on Ook-sook's homely face as he experienced the miracle of flight.

To see this succession of expressions on any person undertaking flight for the first time is to watch the awakening of Stone Age man as he discovers that he too can fly like the birds. To fly has been the dream of centuries, the legend of every primitive tribe and every nation from the time of man's first consciousness. Man has been earth-bound so long!

Bud and Ook-sook flew to Oliktok Point and visited George and Nanny.

Another day Ook-sook flew with Bud over 250 miles, covering some of the best caribou country.

Supper the last night with Mathew's People included *agutok* for dessert, sometimes known as Eskimo ice cream.

"Look," I said, when I found out that ice cream was on their minds. "I brought something from Umiat for the agutok."

Bud hadn't known it, nobody had known it. But I had a quart of dried apricots.

You can make Eskimo ice cream without fruit, but it is better with it. Agutok is made in various ways in different sections of Alaska, depending on what materials are accessible. At Point Barrow many people like it best of all made of whale blubber and raisins. That is what is most available there. Bud and I once made agutok that we will never forget when we were starving on the Alatna River. We made it with rendered fat of grizzly bear, a pinch of sugar, and frozen sour cranberries. Superb! But on the arctic coastal plains agutok to the caribou hunters means caribou tallow, and we must say upon careful thought that it is hard to excel.

Soon the women cooked up the apricots, let the kids drink the juice off, and whipped the remaining bulk fruit into a paste. Carefully they folded in the apricot paste with pure melted pulverized caribou tallow and a little pulverized cooked meat. This was whipped until the mixture was full of air and light and fluffy as foam. The color and texture was a pink similar to chiffon pie filling.

When you start in to eat Eskimo ice cream it is so attractive looking that you heap your tin plate full. But everyone stops short about one third through the intended portion because this fare is really rich. Richer than our heaviest dessert, this cold, country dish is comparable to pure cream nutritionally.

I carried off to our own tent extra portions of agutok for breakfast.

Breakfast, before our take-off, was comprised of agutok and a boiled caribou tongue each. Colliak, Ook-sook's brother, saved it for us from a hunt. This is some of the choicest eating in the world.

The sky broke clear. "We'll travel on east and visit Barter Island to-day," Bud said. "This is the kind of weather I've been waiting for and maybe it won't happen again."

"Don't move me," I groaned, leaning back on caribou robes.

Mathew's People helped us break camp.

"You'll have to leave that leg bone," Bud firmly stipulated.

"Look," I said, "I'll just slip it in the airplane here, behind the bucket. You'll never know we have it. Maybe we won't make it to Barter Island and we'll have nothing to eat."

"I said 'no.' The airplane can't carry the load." Bud was the chief pilot and his word was final.

Before we knew it we had left the happy caribou hunters behind on their river cliff, and the treeless Colville River itself winding down the plain was only a dream.

8 BARTER ISLAND AND
THE BIG LAKES

Down the colville river we sped and over Oliktok Point we wagged our wings hello to George and Nanny and then straightened out east. Drifting ice cakes washed in the blue sea. "Right out there someplace," Bud said, "is where Johnny Tukok lost his family."

Off our left wing a thousand miles or so lay the North Pole. Off our right wing the white-mantled Shublick and Romanzof Mountains — on the mainland 200 miles away, near Barter Island — rose into the lazy sky. They were another part of the arctic Brooks Range.

Fog rolled in from the ocean, fifty miles onward. The sky was clear but the ground fog came in just like a big white cotton blanket being unrolled by invisible hands, tucking under the earth below. It was caused by the warmer air of the continent meeting the cold air of the open Arctic Ocean: an almost chronic condition along this coast in summer. Approaching it we dropped lower and commenced to fly under it, following the coast line.

Brownlow Point is always a bad place for fog. If we could just pass there probably the rest of the way would be clear. The fog hung close to the ground, although it rarely extended more than five hundred feet in thickness.

Doubting the wisdom of his daring, Bud impatiently climbed up above the fog to the sun. Presently we were flying along on top of the fog layer in brilliant sunlight. The experience was like emerging from night to walk the paved streets of heaven. Yet we would have to descend eventually to check our landmarks. Because we knew the coast from Barrow, Alaska, to Aklavik, Canada, by heart, we were venture-some. There were no weather reports in this part of the world because no people were stationed along the top of Alaska.

Near Brownlow Point we tried to come down to deliver some small packages and messages to Eskimo friends there, but when we dove down through the fog we found ourselves blind just 100 feet above the ground. Such foolishness can quickly lead to suicide. Bud switched on the instruments. When the pilot can't see, it is very easy to go into a tight spiral and crash into the ground. When the airplane is properly banked your sense of gravity is lost and it becomes impossible to tell if you are rightside up or upside down. There is no way by which sense alone can tell the pilot if he is flying level; only instruments can give him his "artificial horizon" and tell him what is happening. Luckily Bud spied a bay through the mist at that moment and plopped us down for a landing.

"Whew," was all he said as he turned off the engine and we drifted along an indistinct ocean shore. I said nothing except to suggest that now we could each eat one candy bar — our emergency rations.

We sat there drifting beneath that midnight pall, rocking back and forth monotonously on the gray waves. The fearful mystery of fog enveloped us. Everything was dripping wet.

"You know," I said, "we can be stuck here for days."

Remembering too well our last pneumatic camp, Bud set his jaw and made an almost blind take-off on the dim bay. The low land disappeared, and relying solely on instruments for our sense of reality, we stubbornly climbed the *Arctic Tern* up into the good sunlight once more.

Winging on eastward, we saw the outline of our *Arctic Tern* racing encased in a halo of spectral light. The higher we flew over the fog layer the smaller that many-colored spectral shadow became; but when we flew low near the top of the fog our shadow was immense as it doggedly traced our flight. Seventy-five miles away inland arose the peaks of the Brooks Range above the fog layer, emerging in inaccessible majesty.

Twenty minutes later we broke through the fog to see Barter Island lying in the blue ocean ahead, not far from the shore, just as a swiftly-approaching mass of inky black storm coming from an unsuspected direction blacked out the whole island. Over prairie and water we raced with the sinister mass while the halo fell away from our plane and the naked shadow kept pace.

At last this shadow caught the *Arctic Tern* as we glided safely to a landing in the lagoon on the eastward, protected side of Barter Island.

Barter Island is a flat piece of land only a couple of miles in extent and less than a half mile removed from the mainland. It has a long, slender, comma-shaped tail swinging out to sea. Built up from the ocean bottom through centuries of grinding by the ice pack, the island is important because it provides the only harbor for ships in American territory east of Point Barrow. Against one of Barter Island's barren reefs lay a ship of the "landing Barge" type, with some forty men of the Arctic Contractors living aboard. They had been here less than three weeks at this time; their purpose was to build a landing strip on the spit, and barracks for forty enlisted men which must be completed by fall, at which time the U.S. Army was taking over. So it was that in yet another spot along the farthest coast of North America surveys were to be made and communications laid out on a permanent basis, for the first time in history. A person couldn't be surprised. The only surprising thing was that it had never been done before.

We were met on the gravel beach by some fellows driving up with a Weasel. They were disappointed when they saw we were not a Wien ship with the mail.

"Come aboard and have a cup of coffee."

Accepting the invitation, we got into the vehicle, drove a quarter of a mile, and entered the belly of the visiting landing craft. We wound through black subterranean passages in its bowels and came up into the Officers Mess Room, now used for a general recreation hall, and presently had supper with the men. This old ship had been in the battle of Okinawa; the dead-gray iron hull in these seas looked unaccountably grim.

Foreman Jim Dalton, unmarried, thirty-four, was an extremely decent sort. Like Al West at Umiat, he was a long-time Alaskan, and it seemed to us that no more able man probably could have been chosen for the responsibility of deciding just where on Barter Island the new army post and airstrip should be laid out. Jim Dalton knew the arctic and he knew ice action and what it does to land strips.

Credit should also go to the Eskimos. It seems doubtful if any man now living — the race of the old independent whalers being gone — could work a ship into the uncharted channels alongside Barter Island without recourse to Eskimo counsel. The captain who had brought this ship here had done so expertly, with local help, and had departed by air, after the ship was securely boothed to freeze in.

"Why don't you sleep aboard the ship?" Jim Dalton invited us. "We've lots of bunk room. You can have a room to yourselves. And you can have a hot shower."

"Say thanks, that sounds wonderful — " I started, when Bud interrupted. "Well, thanks a lot, but we always sleep right beside our airplane. Have to watch out for it all the time, what with winds and storms, you know."

"Listen," I complained to Bud when we were alone. "Aren't you carrying this vigilance for the airplane too far sometimes? I don't see Sig Wien always sleeping on the beach, or his pilots either."

"You just haven't had your eyes open then. Wien pilots often do, when they have to. Besides, Sig has more planes to lose than we have. Do you know they say he's lost five planes, including one DC-3, in the arctic, just this summer?"

"I suppose you're right," I regretfully admitted. "We have only one airplane to lose, and we're not going to lose it."

We called next on Andrew. Our Eskimo friends at Barter Island were good friends and old friends, and possibly more permanent than the glamorous ones so recently arrived.

Andrew, the native minister — not ordained, but endowed by the Presbyterian Church — was tall, with a prominent nose, a stentorian voice and a hearty handclasp. He had a great influence over all the Eskimos east of Barrow and even the white men owed much to his intercession in many small things. When we first saw Barter Island in the old days there were only the tents of Andrew and his people to offer shelter to the traveler in a lonely part of the world.

With his people about him Andrew, of course, had been the first to reach the airplane upon our arrival, even before the Weasel could get there. The Eskimos were delighted with the *Arctic Tern* and we had broken away from them only with the promise that we would later visit them.

"Well, how have things been going, Andrew?" We sat on a packing box eating a slice of white bread and drinking tea.

Andrew was very pleased with the arrival of the white men. Already he had an A.P.O. number and so had his sons. He foresaw all kinds of prosperity for himself and his people in the future, with plenty of *tunik-tut* — white man's things — to eat and to wear. Daily he felt a growing sense of his own importance as a key figure and intermediator between the Eskimos and the whites. A certain instinctive sharp apprehension mixed with his feeling of pleasure, in that he also foresaw possible troubles and temptations into which the Eskimos could easily fall. Things like whiskey drinking and gambling with cards or dice, Andrew knew all about from the missionaries who had given instruction in the avoidance of these vices. Andrew also thought about the young girls who would be deluged with attentions from the visiting white men and for whom he saw in himself a dramatic and important role as their counselor. A true Evangelist, Andrew. He laid down the law to the Eskimos about no movies or hunting on Sundays. If he were at times somewhat confused between which were the major and which the minor sins, so are many of us, and he was nonetheless a strong and sincere man.

There was another role, however, in which Andrew might be the last to be suspected by those who were most apt to be in contact with his political talents: he was an expert arctic hunter and an original observant naturalist. It was in this field that Bud never tired of talking with him.

By perusal of our aviation map we had come to realize that there are two large lakes lying less than a hundred miles back in the middle of the mountains on the mainland adjacent to Barter Island.

"Andrew, have you ever been there? Is there game? Are there mountain sheep?"

Andrew was delighted to oblige. Yes, he had been there several
times. "My boys get eighty sheep last winter," he related proudly. To
an informed listener the words spelled tragedy, ignorance, doom.
That one family should slay eighty sheep to feed themselves and their
dog teams for a few weeks in 1949!

"That's a lot of sheep," we assented weakly, and were assured by the
innocent Eskimos that sheep are the easiest animals of all to kill, when
you once find where the bands are. Many of the sheep had been taken
with the .22 rifle. Andrew had already promised to guide some of the
army's white officers on a hunting trip, back in the mountains, for sheep
when the next freeze-up came around.

To see and photograph if possible the remnant of these last original
bands of wild mountain sheep left in Alaska, we took off next day.
Yesterday's breakfast, miles away, with Mathew's caribou hunters
had been agutok and caribou tongue. Today's breakfast in our tent
was the provision of a newly-sprouting arctic army camp: raisin pie
and stalks of celery.

I coaxed the ship's cookie into putting up some enormous slabs of
fancy pastry in a box. Bud didn't want to take off with it, but I got my
way.

The flight from Barter Island inland to the unexplored sheep mountains was like watching a painting turn to reality. Out of the mist and
dew of the coastal morning the Romanzof Mountains beckoned. One
of the twelve major groups which compose the Brooks Range, they
were named by Sir John Franklin for a captain on one of his sailing
vessels when the first exploratory expedition passed along this ocean
over a hundred years ago. The mountains were seen from the ocean.
They were never approached. In the hundred years that passed after
that few men have ever set foot on them. The one-time inland Eskimos
who used to come to trade at Barter Island in the mouth of the Hulahula River have vanished, as family by family they were lured to the
trading sites on the coasts of Alaska. No human being now inhabits
these mountains, and as to who did, history supplies little clue.

As the grassy arctic plateau climbed before us into the unexplored range we realized poignantly how lucky we were to be able to see this country, and to see it by summer: a dream made possible in the last few days because it was only just now that gasoline became available in this part of the world. Summer, the most revealing and in its way the most interesting season in the arctic, has in the past been the season in which inland arctic country has been totally inaccessible. Former explorers saw the lakes only when snow covered the ground and ice sheathed them. The Sadlerochit and Hulahula Rivers heading near the lakes were not navigable. Now for us the prairie climbed effortlessly up into the rolling hills, which were followed by verdant grassy mountainsides; here rugged 9131 foot Mount Chamberlain stood snow-etched before us, its tall sisterhood reflected in two great apple-green twin lakes connected by an arm of water in the shape of a giant hourglass.

The first, Lake Shrraeder, was very clear. The upper lake, narrow and walled-in by a canyon, was of that peculiar milky green color common to glacial waters. Set in an exquisite vast mountain bowl, the two lakes together totaled over twenty miles long and were reputed to be extremely deep, if not practically bottomless.

As the *Arctic Tern* circled the lakes at 8000 feet it seemed doubtful if even the sound of the little motor could be heard in the vast amphitheater. Below, we could see historic sheep and caribou trails winding like ribbons all over the country and about the lakes. Several small glaciers lay high and blue in the crevices of the mountains, and from each flowed some small stony river or willow-fringed creek. These are the only glaciers we know of in the American arctic. For in the arctic world generally — apart from Greenland — there is little snowfall to begin with and the snow melts away completely during the summer, while glaciers are nonexistent.

"I don't see any sheep, but let's land for now, anyway," Bud said.

The water caught in the great mountain bowl lay so still that we could see our reflection coming up to meet the airplane as we descended. When the floats touched gently, we hardly realized it. Because of the complete absence of trees, bushes or any vegetation over a foot tall, and because of the expanse of tranquil water, the whole world here assumed a distanceless aspect. A fall of fresh snow covering one shore, added an edging of white. Like a piece of fallen arctic sky the captured water lay complete and undisturbed. A person might move over it and through it, but it remained as remote and as ancient as the last Glacial Age. For eleven months out of the year Lakes Peters and Shrraeder — named for a great surveyor, who had never seen his namesake — are locked. Ours was the first airplane to our knowledge to have made a landing here on floats during the brief period of the year that this would have been possible. A summer later the army came.

"I wonder what kind of fish are around here," I mentioned, as the floats touched the rocky shore.

The schools of timid grayling we saw skirting the shores seemed to speak of doing so in order to escape the jaws of enormous, unseen, pursuing fish in the depths. I am sorry to report that we caught nothing but the familiar grayling while we lingered there.

It seemed natural to select for our campsite the arm of water just between the two lakes. Here was shelter for the airplane. It only gradually came to us that other human beings had always selected this spot, too. On the shore were what seemed to be cast caribou and sheep horns. The truth was that people had eaten the animals out from under those horns. We tied the airplane to them, and piled rocks and horns up together for anchors on the wings and tail. Where we pitched our nylon tent someone had left a small cache of sticks for fuel, carried on some dog sled from very far. We used the sticks gratefully to warm our tent and to boil our fish and tea.

We had the feeling that prehistoric people had driven caribou into the lake and speared them at this spot; in this neck of water they had trapped fish. After we had lived here for three days these deductions were confirmed. A few yards from our tent, I stumbled and was forcibly brought to my hands and knees, at which moment I recognized that we were camped upon a prehistoric village.

It came to me then that all the little mounds were laid out in even streets. There may have been forty or fifty dwellings. Since the Eskimos we know today live in canvas tents and since they are descended from people who lived in tents made of caribou skins before that, we make no effort to explain the orderly rows of former houses but simply report them.

"I'll have to make a trip to Barter Island for gas," Bud told me. "If I fly by myself I can bring back a big load. Then I will be able to have several hours for exploratory cruising around here. Do you mind?"

"Well, I guess not. But hurry back. I'll have the camp outfit with me and everything I need, I suppose."

Everything but fuel. That pile of sticks wouldn't last long.

Bud was gone into the sky and I was left alone with the ghosts of forgotten Eskimos and the blue and gold lazy day. There was some danger of Bud running into bad weather on the coast and being detained.

Alone I prowled the red-burned slopes near the frail tent, rifle in hand and pockets fairly bulging with ammunition. Alone I thrust the little twelve-inch sticks into the camp stove and made tea and ate more pastry than I should have. When Bud came buzzing back I met him with a hug on the silent shore. "It's such an immense country," I said, "I was wondering if you would ever find me again."

"Oh, I'll always find you," he reassured me blithely.

Subsequently Bud performed several flights while I stayed in the camp. He had to fly light. He would cruise up some canyon, break over the divide, and wind down another canyon back to the lake, flying low so as to be able to spot the game for which he searched, plus any other interesting material. In this way he could explore much of the unknown country. He saw occasional white sheep — although none were where we could trek to photograph them — and a few caribou, an occasional fox or wolf or a rare bear. But where were the big herds?

No one had ever hunted here but a few Eskimos and they never went far into the mountains from the lakes. Were wolves or diseases responsible for holding the game in check? Possibly, but this was not certain. True, Andrew's boys had killed eighty sheep in one hunt last winter, but these mountains should be able to support tens of thousands of sheep.

On other days we walked up the valleys to supplement Bud's aerial reconnaissance by intensive observations on foot. We fished for grayling, using foot-high ground willows tied together to make a fishing pole. We collected the parka squirrels that chirped at us for Cornell University.

It was when we came to leave that we ran into difficulty. The lakes lay at 3000 feet altitude. The *Arctic Tern* demonstrated that it simply could not take us both off together with our equipment.

"Well, I'll make two trips," Bud said. "I'll take you out to Barter Island first and then I'll return for the camp gear."

"But we'll have to fly together without any emergency equipment."

"Can't help it. I don't know any other way to get out."

When we got to Barter Island Bud led the way straight to Andrew's tent. Bread and tea were served. We talked about the new doctor who had been flown to the Island; he would help the people when they were sick, and Barter Island even had a post office now. Maybe a school would come in time, one woman suggested. Andrew hoped to build a big church.

When we spoke of the absence of sheep Andrew said, "They hear your airplane coming and they run away and hide."

Run away? The country was so open a squirrel couldn't hide. The sheep were gone.

The year following, an Alaska Game Commission airplane carrying two officials was dispatched to Barter Island; they talked with Andrew and the other Eskimos who were still hunting game to live while making fifteen dollars a day working for the army. It was the first time a game officer had seen this part of the world.

The big bands of game that were always believed to exist "over the mountain" were not there. The Eskimo mind, with its faith in the eternal fecundity of nature, was incapable of facing the facts, as were most modern people. The airplane had disclosed the sad truth that only spirit sheep and spirit caribou roam much of the northland today.

9 A GLIMPSE OF THE CANADIAN ARCTIC

Do you know," said Bud, "we might keep on flying eastward into Canada while we're at it. Maybe we can complete the entire Northwest Passage and come out the Atlantic side."

Somehow when a person gets started in an airplane he just doesn't know the place to stop. That is, as long as the gas lasts.

The way it turned out, we were not able to get all the way around the top of the continent to the eastern arctic with such a small airplane because some of the hops were too long between gas depots. What we did achieve, however, was to explore as far afield from our home at Takahula Lake as the distance from Los Angeles to New York, all in the arctic, and with only five pounds of yellow corn meal in a sack for emergency and our .22 rifle. At our farthest we were about 500 miles due north of Hudson's Bay. We never saw Hudson's Bay because we didn't get that far south.

From Barter Island it proved to be just two and a half hours' flight to Aklavik, Canada. Past Icy Reef, past Herschel Island and the mouth of the Firth, we flew easily. It was at the mouth of the Firth that we had first seen the campfire ashes of Ruth and Louis Giddings when our canoes had passed near each other in the fog a few years past. Alaskans sometimes have quite a time attempting to get together in their vast country, but their campfire ashes may be familiar to one another.

The only uncomfortable moment in our flight came when we flew out to Herschel Island eight miles offshore along our way, to look for

Connie bakes a cake while Lydia waits to lick the pan

Connie works on the manuscript of this book inside the igloo at Oliktok Point

Putting the *Arctic Tern* in the water — Oliktok Point

Connie in the garden at Takahula in September

the mounted police ship, the *St. Roche,* which was making the Northwest Passage then on a three-year cruise. Our engine sputtered – a little water in the gas, perhaps – and then it occurred to us that if we came down in the ocean an offshore wind could prove embarrassing. It is definitely best to hug the shore. It's a lonely part of the world, and as anybody knows, you can't successfully paddle an airplane against the wind.

The *St. Roche* had left Herschel two days before, after wintering in the ice there.

Aklavik is a hundred miles south of Alaska, as well as east. We didn't need our parkas. Our clothes felt hot and dirty.

Things were quiet at Aklavik. The Hudson's Bay Company had discontinued all tourist travel on their Mackenzie River boats as they did not find it a paying proposition, and yet since they held the franchise on the entire river nobody else could run boats in competition. The Mackenzie, draining three thousand miles of America and emptying into the Arctic Ocean here, is comparable to the Mississippi in size and volume. There should have been tourists now that the new automobile road was through as far as Hay River. There were only two airplanes a month to Aklavik and they carried few tourists. Canadian Pacific Airlines held the franchise on all air travel in and out of Aklavik, and they charged as much to fly to Edmonton, a matter of 1500 miles' flight, as it would cost to travel around the world. The airstrip at Aklavik, really the baseball field, is a navigational hazard; nobody can build a new field without government permission.

The native Indians, and the Eskimos, called "Huskies" here, were as diseased and run down as our native people at villages on the American side, only they lacked American prosperity. The first new public health doctor who had ever been appointed for this region had arrived but last week. He was young and energetic and so was his wife. His work would supplement the work of the Evangelical mission which was the only agency to whom the natives could look for help with their health or educational problems. Even the mounted police had no airplane of their own, but only a visiting police plane from headquarters once each summer. Most of the personnel had changed since we were here before with our canoe. The town numbered something under ninety Caucasians in all.

Aklavik, Canada's largest arctic outpost, is different in many ways from Point Barrow, Alaska's largest arctic outpost. It is in a timbered region and has the great advantage of freighting possibilities on the Mackenzie, downriver into the arctic all the way, whereas Barrow is icebound and isolated — the activity going on, on the American side, bears no comparison.

"Things are really quiet here," I mentioned conversationally to our old friend Sergeant Bean. "I wish you fellows could see Barter Island or Barrow now over on the American side. The Eskimo kids ride around on jeeps all day long, eating oranges, with orange juice running down their faces into their parkas, and the men are making all the Eskimos into pets. The Eskimos are getting real wages there, too. Fifteen dollars a day for washing dishes for the army."

"That's the trouble with the Americans. That's the trouble every place today," said the mountie who himself made a very modest monthly salary. "The natives are getting so they expect to make the same wages as a white man does." The conservative old mountie was shocked to the bottom of his soul.

The old Aklavik Hotel held us for two days as we waited for a wind for take-off. The hotel bed was dressed out in blankets only; the room was starkly bare — no closet, only hooks on the walls. The furniture consisted of one high stool. There was no screen on the window, and the mosquitoes came filtering in. No facilities were available for bathing in the hotel — only a community wash basin on its public stand in the hall, with a tarnished yellow mirror, the water to be poured with a pitcher which you carried upstairs from the kitchen and then dumped into the community slop bucket. No towels: you wiped your hands on your trousers or your shirt tail if you cared to use this wash basin with other people. As we had not brushed our teeth in some time I brought up glasses of water for us and we spit into the bucket, although the poor Eskimo scrub woman told me that she had never known of anyone brushing his teeth at the hotel before.

To get into the toilet each hotel guest was tendered a key attached by a greasy string to a much-used wooden tag. You went out through the shambles of the kitchen, waded through slop and mire, and unlocked the outhouse out back. There were no toilets in the town so that this one had to be kept locked "to keep the natives out" of the one seat reserved for the elect. Opening the lock and the door, one was confronted by a tin tubular affair, much spattered, which descended down six feet into an open barrel beneath. Periodically when the barrel got full it was hauled away by some benighted Eskimo and its contents were dumped by him into the river! A public toilet, mercifully left unlocked, stood beside, with only a thin partition separating the two cubicles. While I was there a man came in next door, unbuttoned, grunted and said, "Is that you, Harry?" When I didn't answer he said a little louder, "Is that you, Harry?" Presently I fled.

At the new North Star Inn we picked up with an old fellow who told us some tall stories of the north. He told us about the arctic to the eastward, and a legend of rich oyster beds and pearl fisheries on the Arctic Ocean's bottom. Soon we were surrounded by his cronies, a roaring bewhiskered lot. Gradually the booth where we were having lunch was full of them, and other passers-by, ranging from the age of sixty-five to eighty-five, came to join the crowd. Old ones departed; new ones were introduced, and finally we were with an entirely different bunch than those we had started talking with. It was all because we had said we were going into the arctic, east. These were men such as one seldom sees today. In Alaska we call them sourdoughs. Their type is almost gone from the earth. On the riverbank when we left they all loyally waved us a roaring and bewhiskered farewell.

Yet again the plane would not rise. Encouraged by the roars of our audience, Bud decided to leave me and take off with our outfit. He returned for me later, and we then embarked together in the empty plane. The missionaries whose charitable noonday board I shared, not for the first time, waved us off this time. It was only a twenty minute flight across the forested Mackenzie Delta to an unnamed breezy lake where Bud had cached our duffle on the bank. Yet to fly even this far with no emergency gear was taking a chance. The delta of the Mackenzie is ninety miles broad and a maze of forested islands.

The lake where we landed to repack was just to the east of the timber belt at 400 feet altitude in the Caribou Hills. It was curious to find firm walking there, warm breezes, no mosquitoes and yellow salmon berries ripening on the edge of Canada's famed Barren Grounds.

We had discovered already that when we opened the airplane door following a flight it was desirable to use extreme caution. Often pots and pans and the most conglomerate assortment of items fell out, for usually we were packed pretty solid. This time I forgot for a moment. I opened the door with a hearty exuberance — or perhaps just opened it — and plunk! went Bud's "plotter" down into the depths of the lake. This is the ruler and protractor by which the pilot makes his calculations on his map; it is usually considered an absolutely necessary instrument for navigation.

Yet Bud was always curiously detached in such contingencies. I suppose his leisurely philosophy only goes to prove to most of us how many of our alarms in this life are false ones. "Oh well," he said, as he saw the silver plotter slither into the depths, "I suppose I can navigate without it somehow." Ever afterward we were to refer to that lake as Plotter Lake.

The Americans were establishing a station similar to the one at Skull Cliff, Alaska, at Kittigaguit on a long bay. We flew over Kittigaguit's radio tower and wagged our wings, but did not stop there. A glance downward disclosed a Canso flying boat stranded in the bay in which a pilot had drowned in a crash the day before. We had been warned against trying a landing there unless urgent.

We went on to Port Barbrant, known to local people as Tuk, an Eskimo whaling station beyond the timber east of the Mackenzie. Its distance from Aklavik was 200 miles by winding waterways and treacherous shallow ocean front. By air it was but a few minutes. An Anglican mission school was maintained there where I was made most welcome by two old friends Miss Rothwell and Miss Jones. Bud wanted to go right on, after getting gas, because high winds and an exposed beach might detain an unlucky seaplane pilot. Yet once again we could not rise. After several unsuccessful attempts to get off, we reluctantly taxied back to the shore and put up for the night. This time we were met by Mike Matwichuk of Edmonton, Alberta, and 30-year-old blond Gordon Nelson of the same city, who took us into their Hudson's Bay Transport Division headquarters. The two men were stationed here summers to redistribute cargoes to the few barges and ships plying the remote Arctic Ocean eastward — to the last outposts of the world.

We stayed overnight in the comfortable home of these two expert housekeepers. I never washed a dish while I was there. I did wash my long-handled underwear and socks for Bud and me, and I had a bath in a washtub set upon the floor of our private bedroom.

In the evening a ping pong match took place; my partner was Father Raymond, the first of the many little French priests who were to be our contacts going eastward.

"Some places in the eastern arctic have no game," Father Raymond warned us in his pleasant Latin voice. "Some years even the Eskimos die," he said. "Last year we did rescue work for the people of King William Island. They were living only on the ling cod, and as you know, a man cannot live on ling cod. A man dies slowly of nephritis, the kidney poisoning, if he does not have fats. There is no fat on the ling cod. Yet the King William Island people refuse to leave their historic home for better hunting grounds."

"Yes," I said, "I know about nephritis. You can live on meat alone and it is an ideal diet, but it must be fat meat."

"There is no wood over east, you know. All our wood goes on the drift to Alaska."

"I suppose Bud and I have burned your wood in Alaska many years," I apologized. "It is tough country you have. How long have the R.C. missions had outposts along here?" I learned that only since 1928 had this part of the world been penetrated. Of the agencies now established — the Hudson's Bay Trading Company, the mounted police, the Anglican church — the Catholics arrived the earliest and penetrated the farthest. The little priests from Paris with their long beards and soft accents, strange to us and hard to understand, were to make an arctic that was quite different in its culture from that which we knew. I was convinced from the sincerity of the first one I met, who told me of how his teeth fell out from scurvy, of how he traveled on *seven hundred mile trips* by dog sled across the arctic world — that here was a group that know the arctic of Canada today probably more intimately than any other people know it. The priests learned the Eskimo language and they lived like Eskimos in all but unlivable areas.

Next day we made a 700 mile flight all the way from the edge of the Mackenzie Delta to the outpost of Coppermine at the mouth of the Coppermine River, on the western end of Coronation Gulf. The day was a beauty all the way, with only occasional wisps of fog from the sea to keep the pilot on the alert.

I recall I wanted terribly to come down on the water and have a try at photographing the 50-mile-long chain of Smoking Mountains which ring Amundsen Gulf. These mountains have been on fire for as long as any man knows. Bud decreed we had not enough gas to make the detour from our line of flight. I then begged to land in the delta of the Anderson River where Sergeant Bean said there were many geese and swans. But all these temptations were resisted. There were only three weeks of what one could call summer left.

Brief stops were made for gas at two Catholic missions: Stanton, having one 25-year-old priest in residence, and Pauletuk having two.

The priests hadn't seen any outside contacts in months. The Eskimos visited the mission only occasionally in their wanderings, scrabbling for driftwood on naked beaches, and ending by burning mostly seal blubber; gasoline is $1.50 a gallon and kerosene $2.00 a gallon here. Canadian Eskimos can afford fuel even less readily than Alaskan Eskimos, for their earnings are almost nil.

Coming down at Coppermine through a rain shower we found that town in flood stage as there had been several days of successive storms. This whole region, as may be suspected by the name, is one of the world's richest in undeveloped copper. The Eskimos are the Copper Eskimos.

Pulling up before the Anglican mission there we met Canon Webster and his wife Edie and family. It was customary for most visitors to stay the night in this home. They had one little girl of nine, Margarite, who is probably the best living interpreter of Eskimo that we have known. She had no one to play with but Eskimos since her early childhood and was brought up with their language. Never having been to school, she took her work by correspondence with her mother acting as teacher. There was also Ann who was getting her schooling similarly. Seventeen at the time, with slightly slanted dark eyes and eyebrows like wings, clean-limbed with a fragile beauty reminiscent of the wild arctic primrose, Ann was of half Eskimo blood, an orphan who was taken in by the mission family when she was six. Four years past the family had taken legal steps to adopt her and Ann was now their own. Ann accompanied the family to England last year on the *Queen Elizabeth* when they took their furlough. Quiet, grateful and very efficient, the girl did much of the work about the house.

It was interesting to us that these missionaries in the Canadian arctic, more isolated than missionaries are in Alaska today, retained a culture that was redolent with past tradition. Like us, they enjoyed raw frozen caribou marrow and they wore real Eskimo-type parkas such as few moderns in Alaska today condescend to wear. Resident here since 1923 they were true arctic dwellers. Yet we heard in the same breath that eating caribou leaves a man weak, that it does not have the strength in it that beef does!

"The law does not permit us to hunt our own meat," Canon Webster explained. "There are no hunting licenses issued to white people now in the Northwest Territories. But we buy our meat from the Eskimos, and that is legal."

"What kind of meat are the Eskimos bringing you?" Bud asked. "Is it fat meat? You always want to look for that, you know."

"Oh, no," said Mrs. Webster. "Caribou meat is always lean. I've never seen caribou meat that was fat, have you, dear?" she asked her husband.

"Well, I think if you will look you will find that there's your trouble," said Bud. "Good caribou should be fat, just as good as farm beef. But your Eskimos know that you don't know meat. They are either selling you only the poor animals or they are carefully trimming off every bit of fat before they sell it to you."

Laws of the territories allow missions all the caribou they need for

meat but they must buy it from natives. Each division of mounted police — usually two men — is allowed five caribou for their ration.
Hudson's Bay personnel are not permitted any game whatsoever under
any circumstances. They live on canned meat, supposedly. No new
hunting or trapping licenses for white men have been issued since
1938. This is Canada's effort to save the diminishing game for the
Eskimos.

It is awkward, however, for no other provision for fresh meat is
made for these people by the organizations which support them. Often
they never taste store meat for years; their salaries are not only too
lean to afford it but the part of the world where they live is too remote to obtain imported meat, due to the backward communications.

The mission headquarters under Archdeacon Marsh at Aklavik,
having some 75 or more natives in its school and hospital, had no
provision for meat aside from the mission fish nets and a stringently
limited number of reindeer from the herd which the government
managed. This herd, the one which was sold to Canada from Alaska,
has not increased in its adopted country under government management since 1936. The Aklavik mission takes from 35 to 85 wild caribou
yearly to supplement its meat supply and never has enough. Thus in
many ways are the caribou which are shared by Canada and Alaska
being decimated in spite of all.

Since 1938 Canada has quietly turned all of her territories into a huge
reservation where whites may venture only by special permit and in
which no modern enterprise can be started. Yet at the same time the
natives use modern firearms and they kill females and young of all
kinds of game in any numbers at any time. It is a fatal policy for any
country that wants its people to improve their standard of living or
that wants to prevent itself from being eventually decimated. Another name for a human reservation is "concentration camp"; the
people are denied their citizenship, cheated out of all their rights, and
ultimately it means that they will have complete poverty on their
hunted-out or grazed-out lands. In the United States it has meant almost total land destruction. For it is not possible to make a decent living by hunting and fishing or grazing *if the primitive is limited to any*

restricted area. The very nature of primitive life is such that, to be successful, it must be nomadic. It takes an immense amount of land, perhaps 100 square miles to each family, to support these people on a sustained yield basis, north of the trees, in the standard to which they have been these many centuries accustomed. Reservations can't work, then; that they could have been expected to work in the United States or Alaska, shows the ignorance of our legislators in the natural sciences.

However, Canada has for her experiment a unique situation. It may work due to the size of the lands involved, that is, so long as she can afford to set those lands aside and out of circulation.

It may not be generally realized, but Canada has set aside four tremendous reserves for her native Indian and Eskimo people (totaling perhaps merely 1800 people in all). The largest of these includes the District of Franklin and is called the Arctic Islands Reserve. The extent of this reserve is all but inconceivable. Bounded only by the North Pole, its boundaries run down the meridians of the frozen ocean to the continent and include all of the Arctic Islands known. It is a piece of the world blocked off which we can only estimate as larger than the United States. Few Eskimos use the southerly fringe of it, and even they go no farther than Banks Land and southern Victoria Island. Eskimos do not live as far as explorers have gone — no trace has yet been found of man ever having existed on the more northerly islands.

A provision bars all people except Eskimos from the Arctic Islands Reserve. Missionaries, mounted police, and Hudson's Bay Company personnel administer to them on the southern fringes. Under the law no Eskimo may use a chartered airplane to gain passage to and from his hunting grounds, thus insuring that a primitive people shall remain as primitive as possible in the years to come. This is what the British did in Africa and what the Danes did with the whole of Greenland — gave it back to the natives forthright and marked it out-of-bounds for all others except a few explorers, scientists and the missionaries. Canada's colossal experiment has both its good and its bad points — too many to argue here. However, we feel that the interesting status of our polar world should be of concern to the general public.

We fooled around all day visiting with the eight or nine white people of the community. The ship *Fort Ross* unloaded all day at Coppermine and the minister didn't even attempt to hold Sunday services inasmuch as he was busy stevedoring and checking his year's supplies.

The ship could not remain many hours. We made friends with the captain and chief engineer and our party was invited aboard, where the cook served us all coffee and pie in the galley.

The mosquito season had passed, yet the sun was warm and glorious. We took our long-handled underwear off. We were told that Bathurst Inlet, our next stop on east — southward still and barely on the edge of the Arctic Circle — was warmer yet.

Forty-five minutes after take-off from Coppermine, Bud got a notion we were losing gas. Down we plopped on a lake to check. It was a false alarm. All was well. But how to take off again?

As a sheet of thin fog veiled the turquoise ocean front and swells were running, we landed on an adjacent lake. The lake actually lay in cliffs of 700 feet altitude above the sea level and some distance from the sea. Three attempts to take off convinced Bud that we could not rise.

"You'll just have to walk over to the ocean," Bud said, "and I'll meet you over there."

I looked at the fog bank dubiously. Suppose it should move in? But the ocean was just about three miles away. It looked easy.

"I'll walk part way with you and get you started right." Bud offered.

The latent danger in such a situation cannot be overestimated. It was something I knew in my bones. I didn't have a gun. I didn't have matches with me. What use were they? There wasn't anything but rocks in this whole country. Would Bud and I be able to find each other again? What if the fog came in, blotting our landmarks out? This was surely a pretty land, but it was as uninhabited as the moon.

It was absolutely impossible to walk out either to Coppermine or to Bathurst Inlet, each of which lay over 75 air miles away in either direction. The great rivers which drained this country would be un- crossable by summer. Words fail me in describing these rivers. We had flown over some that wound through canyons comparable to the Grand Canyon of the Colorado. They were crystal rivers of tremendous volume, curling over majestic thundering waterfalls. A person on foot in the summer would be stuck. The vast rock pile through which the rivers cut would wear out your boots; in a day or two of walking you would be barefoot.

In Alaska our arctic coastal plain is not rocky. A rocky arctic was new to me. Much of it was of a stringently limited grazing capacity. Yet the trails of spirit caribou and presumably musk oxen wound through little verdant valleys between the red rocks. All those valleys and all those ridges looked exactly the same.

Most of the day passed while I threaded my way three miles to the ocean 700 feet below. Strange plants, strange flowers, springing from rock crevices, were in miniature like a Japanese garden, with strange crystal brooks tinkling through their grottoes. Visibility was so limited among the rocks that I feared at any moment that I might lose sight of the distant shining sea which was my guide. Over the top of every rise I expected to see game, but I saw nothing. The sun was a warm caress; it was utterly peaceful. I was one of the first modern people ever to set foot in all this country and certainly the only one to walk over any particular spot of earth here.

I heard Bud take off from the lake. My breath stopped as he climbed out of it into my view. He circled overhead trying to spot me. I ran to the top of the next rise, and silhouetted upon a pile of boulders, let him have a good look at my bright red shirt. How could he miss seeing it? He circled again, going farther away.

At first I was only annoyed. I could see him so easily and I could hear him from miles away as he flew about. It seemed impossible that he could not see me. The futility of jumping up and down and wav- ing was soon made apparent. It was no use. If a pilot didn't have the eyes or the good luck to spot a hiker with a red shirt walking over this treeless terrrain, there was nothing a hiker could do about it. Seen from the sky, there were crevices in these rocks which would hide a man or a thousand men even if they had on shirts of every conceivable hue in the world.

For twenty-five minutes Bud flew back and forth. He would be running low on gas. Finally I saw him make a long gliding landing into a bay far down the beach. Carefully I marked the spot. Once that little silver ship came to rest in its berth it blended so perfectly into beach, sea and sky, that it would have been difficult to know it was there.

Three hours later I reached the airplane. We flew on together to Bathurst Inlet, having no trouble with a take-off on the breezy bay.

Bathurst Inlet has the reputation of being perhaps the most beautiful place in the entire North American arctic. Walls of red rock a thousand feet sheer rise in islands from its long blue channels, and the water below is as clear as a Bermuda swimming pool. When you find your way into this great sheltered arm of water that plunges deep into the body of the continent, you discover a tiny settlement called Bathurst Inlet which is itself set in luxuriant tall green grass and giant fertile meadows.

Vegetable gardens are said to flourish here with almost tropical fecundity. The summers are four months long, with day after day of almost constant sunlight twenty-four hours around, and temperatures running up to eighty and ninety degrees Fahrenheit.

There was one trader alone in residence here at the time we called. It's odd sometimes how you can pick up a person's mental attitude and personality even from a distance, just as though it emanated outward in invisible waves. Even before our plane could be taxied to shore, from the cockpit I saw that the bearded man who stood there slackly on the beach was not particularly glad to have visitors, and I knew that he was not going to be sociable by the hang of his jaw.

Introducing ourselves, we followed him into the typical Hudson's Bay Company house. The place wasn't really dirty — he had a clean floor — but something about it was repellent, and it was grim and bare. The fact that its inmate could not stand his own cooking — and to be a skilled cook is the chief prerequisite of the good life in the arctic! — was attested by the fact that he had no appetite, and ate only one meal a day, he said, direct from the can. It was not hard to deduce that he used the slop can in the kitchen for a toilet in order to save a short walk.

"How long have you been here alone, Jack?"

"Well, six months since I seen anybody," he said. "I don't miss nobody."

After we had sat on our chairs fifteen minutes trying to make conversation, it was plain he was not going to ask us to eat. I told him we were hungry. He took us over to the warehouse then and let us choose our own cans, after which I cooked up a meal for the three of us. Our meal was a fresh fish I got for a few coins from an Eskimo in the village, some leftover dehydrated potatoes, canned lima beans, and Bud requested some canned crab meat. Of course there was the inevitable tea.

Drawing our host out, I asked him how old he was and he said only twenty; it was easy to forgive a good deal from then on. From Newfoundland he came; his father was a schoolteacher. He had four sisters and was himself the only boy. That was why he left home. He loved to hunt and fish. He had killed two caribou.

He was beginning three years' apprenticeship to become a Hudson's Bay post manager. But he had found that the old days, when Hudson's Bay men were real explorers and policemen in a wild country, were gone. He wasn't even allowed a dog team but must stay right at the store and learn radio and Eskimo. To this post came the most primitive people now left on our continent, the people from inland along the Back River. Even Canon Webster and his competition, the Catholic priests, had reached few of them in their hunting grounds. Archdeacon Marsh at Aklavik had made the only films I knew of several years ago of the eastern Caribou Eskimos.

We noticed that the older women about the trading post had their faces tattooed with blue lines — something which a generation has not seen much of in Alaska.

The Eskimo people here spoke no English. Instead of furnishing schools and teaching the people English the Canadian policy was to let them stay as they are, and traders and missionaries had to learn

Eskimo to deal with them. The Eskimos were shorter and darker in appearance generally than our Eskimos in Alaska, and not so cross-bred — Stone Age men set apart in a vast human reservation. In this part of the world the Hudson's Bay Company still held a complete monopoly so that there were no other traders; the Company *did not give money to natives in exchange for furs, but only an assortment of trade goods which government policy decided upon.* Thus, any Eskimo in this area today is effectively hamstrung.

The trade list of the Hudson's Bay Company did not include radios, for instance. Prices on foods and basic articles of existence were reasonable and fair for this remote part of the world; the Company in its indulgent paternalism even claimed to take a loss on some articles. Yet here was a whole group of human beings who had no free choice as to how they might spend their earnings, and who had no communication with the outside world even though there is no reason today why communication should not be readily available.

The Hudson's Bay Company, from long tenure and ancient experience, knew how to manage the Eskimo people with the utmost efficiency. They decided in which areas a given Eskimo group would trap during certain years to obtain the maximum amount of furs and profit for everybody. If it were necessary to move the Eskimos from one area to another, the mounted police, acting on the policy of Hudson's Bay, easily moved the people by exerting forcible pressures!

The Eskimo people did not even have a choice as to where they should live, or even, in individual cases, as to whom they should marry. The police often would move a group nearer the mission for convenience' sake. For the convenience, that is, of the missionaries.

Of all the agencies — religious, mercenary and military — who control the lives of these people and profess to have their best interests at heart — there is not one who is in a position to speak objectively and give the case from the Eskimos' point of view.

The agencies live off the Eskimo as the wolf lives off the caribou. What were once an independent hunting people became servile to these institutions. Perhaps this would be all right if the Eskimos were serving their apprenticeship for what might lead to their eventual development and welfare, as is possible in Alaska. But note that of these three institutions the fourth and most vital one is missing entirely: the educational one. What can be the future of a people denied all education, all communication, all freedom of choice, conspired against by organized agencies who are determined to keep them just as innocent as they are while the world goes on ahead?

"I sure would like to get the chance to fly into the Back River country and photograph some of these people and talk with them," I said. "Jack says they still use bows and arrows and spears sometimes. He's seen them when they come out to trade."

But we both knew we would never be able to do it with our small plane. The Canada country was vast. I never realized there was such country, right on our continent.

At the trading post I went around the village with big marbles of colored bubble gum. That was one luxury I talked Bud into carrying. To chew gum is the biggest treat an Eskimo can have. The people came to the door of the trading post kitchen where I was washing dishes, and they watched every move I made very quietly. Not one set foot inside the door. Surreptitiously I slipped out our leftovers to the women, although this was expressly against rules.

One Hudson's Bay wife lived here once a few months, but aside from her I was doubtless the only white woman these people had been able to observe. I showed them my parka and told them as much as I could about Nanny. They were interested in examining Nanny's sewing. I walked through puddles of water in the village to demonstrate to them that my Alaska-made boots did not leak. Appreciating this factor they nodded and said, "Ah, ah!" Only three seals were taken here this spring, I learned, and none of these people had boots that I considered adequate. Hudson's Bay trades sealskins and caribou hides at $1.50 flat rate, at no profit and regardless of local fluctuations in demand and supply, as a service to the natives.

We made a fine take-off around 9:00 in the morning. Breakfast was simple: just mix the powdered milk for the corn flakes.

Our next flight north and east to Cambridge Bay, Victoria Island, was made easily in two hours. Victoria Island is a rock quarry about three times the size of the state of New York. It lies about fifty miles off the coast of the mainland of North America and although all of its coastline is by now defined in the geography books much of its interior is still unmapped. It was on the north shore of this forlorn island and eastward toward King William Island, apparently, that Sir John Franklin and 119 men starved to death a hundred years ago in one of the worst tragedies in the history of polar exploration.

The visit to remote Victoria Island was to be a high point in our whole season, not only because we left the continent for the only time but because of the American-Canadian base newly being erected on its south shore. The base boasted two moving picture shows every night, so went arctic gossip.

Splashing to a stop in the crystal lagoon, Bud took care to barely miss a crashed aircraft and the spars of the sunken old hull of Amundsen's famous *Maude*, here resting in its last sleep. This ship traveled around the Pole early in the twentieth century as an experiment in polar drift.

We taxied first up to the Hudson's Bay building. A respectable-looking arctic man of trim appearance, the well-known "Scotty" Gall, directed us to the neat white buildings of the mounted police nearby.

Here we met Constables Dick Mead and Andy Wilvert. As it was then noon and my corn flakes were wearing thin, I hoped to go right on for army chow, but the two young mounties were so cordial and so glad to have company that they prevailed upon us to stay for Spam.

The mounties were fine fellows, regular picture-book types. In real life we found that mounties at the remote outposts rarely wore the red dress uniform and tight leather boots with which their public associates them, for climatic conditions made the wearing of such a uniform impossible. But we induced them to dress up for the pictures. Bud gave them rides in the *Arctic Tern* and we unloaded our duffle for a good overhauling at their home. The mounties derived much entertainment from our airplane. None of them had ever been in such a small private plane and this was the farthest north, to their knowledge, that any small airplane had been. They depended entirely on boat by summer and dog sled by winter, to get around. From six months to a year at a time, they had no direct contact with headquarters and were all but forgotten men. Yet hardly a rifle shot from their barracks there now arose upon Victoria Island's shore, a modern semimilitary base with constant daily excitements of departures and arrivals by air.

One of the most memorable things I remembered about the mounties was their outdoor chic sales. To make its utility within the realm of possibility during the low temperatures of arctic winter, it was fur lined. Fur lined: a good idea. I made a mental note of it.

In the evening the mounties gladly conducted us to the base for dinner. Dinner, after some introductory moments in the officers' quarters, was a whirl for me — and all that a young woman in an isolated part of the world, with ninety-six men, might imagine.

The mounties insisted upon giving up their beds that night, and they slept on the floor, allowing us to take over their house.

Next day it was too still and sultry for a take-off and I didn't want to take off anyway, but Bud had to try six take-offs with a full load of gas and duffle. Since the take-off attempts took the whole day — gas supplied by the Canadian-American base — we had nothing to eat all day but cookies and tea. But a square meal was contrived at the base that night, gobbled down with strict attention to the business of nutrition, from whence Bud dragged me away; eventually we camped down the bay in our tent, pitched on the rocky shore.

We never got to see that movie after all. Instead we rode in a power launch along the bay with Flight Command Officer Pilkington, called "Pilky"; Major Cameron, the English doctor just out of India; young, clean-cut Lieutenant Collins of Florida, the resident doctor; and an assemblage of others. Here also we bumped into men we had seen before at other camps — Watson Lake, Fort Nelson.

"Don't you remember me? I was the fellow from the hamburger stand who made your hamburger. See, I told you I was getting transferred north."

Bud and I slept late in our tent pitched on a Victoria Island rock pile and anchored to rocks. The 750 foot red and white high-frequency tower of the base was visible just five miles away. It would be handy for future polar flights, I thought. Each year the airlines of the world are moving closer to the Pole and they may soon be routed across it.

A radar screen for the protection of the entire north coastline of North America — a distance of roughly four thousand miles — would be a good thing.

It was no longer a military secret that if there should be another war it might come over the North Pole and it might be decided there. Guided missles must be intercepted before they reach the industrial world below.

In the morning sunshine Bud heated water in a basin on our primus stove and shaved himself, using a pocket mirror. I lay back lazily applying a new coat of nail polish. Back to the simple life again: dried caribou meat from Bathurst, stewed apricots, candy bars washed down with fresh water from a trickle. A breeze stirred; clouds moved in toward the sun. I supposed it would be good-by to our rare glimpse of little-explored Victoria Island and good-by to good weather as well. Where would we go now? Back to Bathurst Inlet, I guessed. We could go no further north or east this year as we just didn't have the range between gas stations. If we could have gone on to Churchill on Hudson's Bay we could have completed the whole North American passage, from west to east — an easy trip with a little larger airplane than we had.

Bud said he didn't care too much about going on to Churchill because it took you far south, according to the criterion of Alaskans. We were about 500 miles due north of Hudson's Bay right here, and the summer was so fine that American G.I.'s were going swimming in the Arctic Ocean every day just for the fun of it. The Americans were that way. They amazed everyone.

"We've got to get out of here," said Bud, hastening with his shaving. "This good weather can't last."

"Well, you can't fly fast enough or far enough to escape bad weather," I argued. "We'll be grounded somewhere anyway when our time comes."

We taxied back, and being unable to effect a take-off, went to visit with Scotty Gall, the Hudson's Bay post manager at Cambridge Bay.

Scotty started out in 1923, serving five years first as an apprentice, according to Hudson's Bay requirements, at a salary of $240 a year! Apprentices now serve three years' apprenticeship and make $80 a month, less $25 a month for board and lodging. They pay their income tax on the full $80, too, and must pay for their passage home if they take their furlough. The incredibly low wages are a hangover from old-country standards of hundreds of years back when bonded boys were apprenticed out to far parts of the world. They were typical of the conservatism which governs the Hudson's Bay Trading Company, the mounted police, and many Canadian government departments in their policies. All of these company and government men were very loyal. They might complain bitterly among themselves, but let an outsider make any critical comments, and they were ready to fight, so strong were the ingrained traditions of colonial ways.

Scotty, for instance, an explorer in his own right, was one of the genuine old-time arctic men. It was he who opened up many of the farthest north posts — this one in 1923. The Church of England followed his steps, establishing itself on Victoria Island in 1926 and continuing until 1939, when it closed on account of lack of funds during the war. Most missions in Canada are supported, not by Canadians, but by the English abroad.

Scotty admitted that for him the kick was gone out of Hudson's Bay post life. There was no independence left to it, no adventure — just storekeeping. A fellow today was not allowed to participate in arctic life. Because he was here before the new laws were passed, Scotty himself might hunt and fish, but he did not do it much because the men at the base right beside him could not do so and such discrimination makes for hard feelings amid the group in which one lives. So he lived on the canned stuff he despised. He maintained it ruins the stomach over a course of years. No doubt he was right. Canned and condensed foods were probably the cause of the stomach complaints which we heard in the North, not game and fish.

Scotty had had two wives in the arctic. The first one, of Eskimo blood, died unexpectedly of a heart attack while she was captaining a power boat hauling supplies in the Arctic Ocean. After her death life lost its flavor for Scotty, he said; it was never the same for him again. He later married a woman in Scotland, his homeland. She spent nine years here at Cambridge Bay with him and last year gave it up and went back to Scotland. He never had children. Scotty was highly esteemed by all who knew him.

After a supper of canned spiced meat, catsup and beans, which Scotty dubbed "arctic strawberries," we left the bustling efficient Scotty in his neat quarters, and tried to get in to a PX movie. But it was too late to get a seat there. The visiting Eskimos from such places as Banks Island and Parry River had come hundreds of miles with their schooners and they crowded into the first free entertainment brought by the Americans to their part of the world. We slept once more overnight, after tea, at the mounties' house. This time we were on the floor and they took the beds.

The dreaded bad weather did not come. A stiff headwind enabling us to take off, we flew back to Bathurst Inlet, which was to be all but our undoing in a strange adventure.

Our memories of Victoria Island would be false ones: of inviting blue ocean, of hot rocks shimmering in a kind of Arabian desert at 78 degrees, and of radio and radar technicians boating and swimming. Actually the average mean temperature of this sizable arctic island is just thirteen degrees above zero.

10 LOST NEAR THE NORTH MAGNETIC POLE

At bathurst inlet the boy Jack had a new companion who had been transferred from Coppermine, and we had a big surprise waiting for us in the presence of another fellow explorer visiting there!

It was the Eskimo women of the village who first told me about her. They led me to a tent, I pushed aside the flap, and there she was inside. She was seated on a packing box, having a cigarette with several Eskimo women, and drinking their tea. Our blue-tattooed hostess waved me a seat on another box, and poured a cup for me.

The explorer was Margaret Oldenburg, a former Vassar girl, now from St. Paul, Minnesota. Edie Webster had told me about her. Margaret had sent one of our books as a gift to Coppermine, where I had been thrilled to see it in the Webster library. The woman explorer had been described to us at every post for hundreds of miles.

After the age of fifty, Margaret Oldenburg had been left a small private fortune upon the death of her mother, and had taken up an unusual hobby: arctic exploration. To her this was livelier than knitting or settling down to continuous games of contract bridge. She had been tied down for the best years of her life by obligations, but she was making up for lost time now and doing with her life exactly what she pleased; this, indeed, is a rare thing at any age. Seldom have I met a woman of more original and definite views.

Margaret had at this time been making her yearly explorations in the arctic for ten summers. She was crowding fifty-six and her only concern was that she must hurry to get everything explored that she wanted to see before the Canadian authorities or some other authorities might suddenly take it into their minds that she should be stopped. The Canadian arctic residents had for years looked forward each summer to her arrival, as to the arrival of the ducks and the geese.

A trained librarian by profession, her delvings into ancient manuscripts in the course of her work each winter in the United States provided Margaret with ample lore to inspire her trips afield. Yearly she sent her arctic people books and gifts and letters from the cities of the world below; their homes were filled with mementos of her thoughts of them — thoughts which they cherished through the lonely years.

Margaret was the first and only woman up until this time to visit Banks Island in the Arctic Ocean and remote Melville Island far out near the North Pole where the fabled musk oxen roam. Almost no one in this generation has visited these islands since their coastlines were defined by the first seafaring explorers. She gathered botanical specimens there and at the North Magnetic Pole on Boothia Felix Peninsula and donated them to the University of Minnesota — specimens from places at the top of the world so remote that few knew of their existence. To the arctic people on the fringe of the continent Margaret was a legend. It was rumored that to charter the big Norseman she used, along with its pilot, his helper and equipment weighing a gross ton, cost her almost a thousand dollars a day in this part of the world.

Her pilot was always Ernie Boffa. We had heard him mentioned, too. Ernie Boffa was to arctic Canada what Sig Wien was to Alaska, we surmised. Whenever anyone spoke of flying this country he spoke of Ernie in the same breath; probably no man living had covered more arctic miles by air for the purpose of local commerce and mail carrying. Ernie was a bush pilot who flew north of the bushes; each summer it was he who, on charter trips, had by habit become Canadian Pacific Airlines' recommended pilot for Margaret, and there was a strong sentimental attachment between the two. Margaret refused to fly with anyone else and Canadian Pacific could do naught but allow their best and favorite pilot to go vagabonding with her, whether they wholly approved of the wayward pair or not.

More than anything else in the world the pilot looked forward to his chance each year to be released from his routine contract flights to the south to take Margaret to some new place never before visited by modern white woman or man. Ernie had piloted Dr. and Mrs. Lincoln Washburn in Victoria Island, where they had named a lake for him, Boffa Lake, and he had served several expeditions, so that he had gained a reputation as an explorer. He suggested many of Margaret's trips; on her part she consulted him as full partner on the tips she dug up from her books.

Ernie Boffa was forty-three, the father of three children; his family was at Yellowknife, which most people consider a northerly place, but which arctic residents refer to as down in the "bush." He was as average-looking as probably any man you would find on the street, being under six feet, with dark nondescript hair and brown eyes. His teeth were rather uneven; his jaw jutted out, denoting stubbornness. Stubbornness was in the set of his stride. "He is the kind who would see anything through," I thought. I had learned he was famed for many rescues during his twenty-three years' flight experience.

Bud and I, Margaret and Ernie, and Ernie's mechanic, young Dick Hahn, descended upon Jack of the Hudson's Bay house, and upon Jack's companion who had been transferred there to live. We ate boiled fresh potatoes, canned frankfurters and canned diced carrots and tea, while Jack, who had never wanted any company to begin with, was forced to endure us all. Within a matter of minutes Bud and Ernie were talking aviation. Midnight would soon be settling. The shadows were long.

Ernie displayed interest in our little airplane. "I think I'm going to come up with an idea," he said. "How would you guys like to join forces with us for a few days?"

I was wondering what use our little airplane could possibly be to their larger and more magnificent expedition.

"How would you like to go into the Back River country?" Ernie asked Bud and me.

"Just show me the way," I said impulsively. "We could never do it alone with our airplane. We figured that out already. We just haven't the range and it's too big a country for one little plane to get lost in."

"I'll tell you what we're after this time," Ernie said. "The Back River or Great Fish River is just about inaccessible. It's a big land area and you see we don't have the range either. This ship burns a lot of gas. Margaret would like to get some plant specimens from that country.

"Confidentially, we would also like to try to trace down a cairn of one of Back's early expeditions. According to private sources of information it is somewhere in the Peacock Hills back of Back's River. So far as we know this country hasn't been visited for a hundred years. This man Back was with Franklin, you know. He became an explorer of considerable merit and named the Back River and wrote a book Margaret has along.

"In short," he said, "we wouldn't venture into that country alone with just the one ship, but seeing you pop up here makes me think that if we had the two ships, we might work something out. It would be uncovering history if we could find something."

Bud said, "When do we start? How do you propose that we can be of help to you?"

"It comes to me," said Ernie, "now you folks have explored before and I think it is wise to have a bigger party. What we'll do is go into that country 200 miles and make a base camp from which we can operate, see? The Norseman burns 30 gallons of gas an hour. We'll use the Norseman just to freight in a gas depot. Then we can use your little plane after we get there for most of the reconnaissance work. With the little ship we can survey hundreds of miles on the gas we'll have."

"Yet if Margaret and I flew into that country alone," he added, "we couldn't accomplish much. We could get in there, I suppose, but we would use up all our gas, and anyway I don't favor trying it unless there are two airplanes to check on each other."

"It sounds like a wonderful idea," Bud and I agreed. "Let's merge expeditions and help each other."

"Ernie always thinks of the most wonderful plans," said Margaret. She was immensely enthused.

It was tacitly agreed that Margaret would furnish all the grub. She had lots on board. In return Bud would fly Margaret around in our ship and be her personal pilot and guide.

Within an hour the two pilots had drawn their courses on their maps laid out on the kitchen table at Bathurst Inlet, while our unwashed supper dishes were pushed to one side.

We took off in the late evening glow. Bud and I left in the *Arctic Tern* first. We climbed to 3000 feet. Then the Norseman followed. Looking down on it below, we saw it make a white trail across the bay on its big floats and sail powerfully into the gloaming.

Turning, we followed the Norseman's lead.

"Can we keep up with him? How will we keep from losing him?"

At least he was big and bright. His colors were silver trimmed with big red numbers. He cruised at 110 miles per hour, while we did 95. Across the winding channels of the great inlet we trailed him and struck a course south and east into the darkening continent. At the beginning the mountains near the coast were rugged. After the first hour, however, the country flattened out into a more rolling nature. I knew from experience afoot that it was neither as rolling or as open and aboveboard as it looked from the sky. It was sneaking, deceptive country, and vast.

"Help me watch our course carefully," mentioned Bud, as the big Norseman carrying Margaret and Ernie and Dick steadily pulled away from us. "We've only got enough gas on board to make it there. If we should miss them, it's not quite clear to me how we would get back. We just can't afford to miss, that's all."

I kept my eye glued to the ship ahead. It shrank to a speck and vanished after a while in the twilight. Even after it vanished I still imagined that I saw it. I wished they had waited a little for us, what with night coming on. It was hard to trace the contours of the all but featureless landscape beneath, and after all, we were under the influence of the North Magnetic Pole area, which meant that the magnetic variation on the compass oscillated continuously between 23 and 45 degrees off. The North Magnetic Pole moves about itself and encompasses an area of around 300 square miles, requiring relocation by instruments every few years when it tends to get away. It is an elusive thing.

A man named Walter Gilbert was the first pilot to fly over the North Magnetic Pole in 1930.

Ernie landed Margaret Oldenburg there in the mid 1940's.

Fortunately Bud had learned to fly by landmarks and by the sun and wind drift rather than depending too much on the compass. Ernie was used to magnetic variation. It was nothing to him, and his course was as sure as a homing bee.

The country beneath us was unmapped and unexplored except for a few large lakes. One of these lakes on our way was named McAlpin Lake. Ernie had told us it was named for a mining engineer, Colonel McAlpin, who with a private party had become lost in this region in 1928. His plane got off course when en route from Baker Lake to Coppermine. It was said that it took a million dollars to try to find him, and they never found him. The Canadian Air Force lost three airplanes of their own during the search. McAlpin and his companions eventually turned up when they walked out after the freeze-up months later, several hundred miles distant at Cambridge Bay, Victoria Island, guided by Eskimos.

Anyway, this was the proof that at least there were Eskimos in this country in 1928. As we passed along beside McAlpin Lake I was glad to imagine the existence of Eskimos below us someplace, for reasons other than curiosity. The Eskimos meant that the country was safer for us.

Our destination was an extremely large body of water called Lakes Pelly and Garry. The map indicated that the lakes were joined together, the whole body being around a hundred miles long. Thus we had a large target to hit on a straight shot. But I wondered how Bud would ever locate Ernie when we got there.

Words can't do justice to the splendid teamwork between the two pilots, for when we were at last swallowed up in the night, I saw far ahead the welcome red and green wing lights of Ernie's ship.

The larger airplane had settled on a bay of McAlpin Lake and was waiting for us. We saw it take off and speed out and up into the black velvet sky, where it described a series of brilliant arcs. Playing "follow the leader," we circled down and down behind the Norseman, and with wing lights on, came trustfully in for a safe landing on the strange waters that Ernie had hastened to explore before daylight gave out. The two planes taxied gingerly into a cove, we tied them to rocks, and pitched our tents in black night in a world of absolute boulders.

Even though the cove sheltered the airplanes from the buffeting of the open lake, it seemed a precarious position because airplane floats are easily punctured if they are able to swing and rub against any obstacle.

On the floor of Margaret's tent, we gathered for a nightcap of an excellent imported cordial she had brought along to celebrate adventure and discovery.

Adventure was destined to come all too suddenly.

The lakes of the Barren Grounds have treacherous hidden reefs like shark's teeth down their middles, rising out of deep black water at unsuspected places, waiting for the float ship pilot to tempt fate.

After a cheerful breakfast of bacon and eggs cooked over the primus stove Bud took Margaret Oldenburg in the *Arctic Tern* early in the forenoon for a short flora-collecting jaunt about the immediate area. They did not take their caribou skin parkas with them that morning. It was such a mild day that shirtsleeves were more than sufficient. They did not take any food with them. They expected to be back for lunch. They did not return.

Ernie and Dick and I passed the day tramping around on our peninsula, and discovered that we were surrounded by seas of water. Ernie shot a ptarmigan for the pot, and we examined rock cairns and Eskimo tent rings. I found some white wool like sheep's wool trampled into the small green pastures between the rocks. It was musk ox wool from living musk oxen. Dick found a big strange fish with a fat belly, presumably a different species of whitefish, upon our shore. Turning it over with a foot, we saw that it had a large hole punched in its belly that was made a few days past with a spear.

Dick went behind a sunny rock and reappeared garbed in bathing trunks. He went swimming beside the Norseman which Ernie had given him instructions not to leave. Late in the day Ernie began to get restless. He suggested that we make a short hop over to an island which we could see rising in white sandy bluffs from the lake.

We did so and briefly explored the island. There were fresh wolf tracks in the sand, but we couldn't find the wolf. From the top of the island bluffs we saw the gleam of a little white tent on the shore farther up the lake.

"Let's go over and talk with those people," said Ernie easily.

It was exhilarating taking off in the powerful empty Norseman.

The big floats touched shore and Dick leaped off them lightly, vigilant for their safety. It was as though all of us were subconsciously waiting for something disastrous to happen. Several stalwart Eskimo figures watched our approach. They had the same look on their faces that George Woods had that time when he didn't know us.

As we walked up to them swarms of flies roared up from many bloody caribou carcasses thrown down in the sand in front of the tent. A strong odor of carrion suffused the whole atmosphere. I recalled that many Eskimos like to eat some of their meat "high."

Dick stood watchfully by the airplane while Ernie and I tried to make palaver with the Eskimos. Ernie's Eskimo was worse than mine, if that were possible. I realized that these Eskimos spoke a different jargon than I was used to in Alaska.

We could not understand each other. I took a picture of a beautiful boy with a spear, which later did not turn out well. We gave the people a little tea. So grateful, that an animal exuberance of good feeling possessed her, the woman sprang upon me and started patting my body and hair. She became so excited that she pulled my hair rather roughly. Suddenly I was almost scared. "Help!" I said, in not quite mock alarm. "Ernie, can you call her off?"

"Well, you're crazy over Eskimos, aren't you?" he said dryly. The woman desisted, and I realized sadly that Ernie himself was definitely *not* crazy over Eskimos. At the same time it came to me how delicate a situation might become in this country, requiring infinite tact. This was not our country; it was *their* country. Those Eskimos could be good friends, in case a person ever needed a friend.

"Surely Bud and Margaret will be back by now," was what we three had in mind as we flew back to our camp. But none of us mentioned our thoughts. When we were over the home bay and saw our tiny tents pitched below — they were hard to decipher in that huge stony landscape — there was definitely no *Arctic Tern* in her berth on the water. "I suppose they just got so busy collecting that they hated to come back," I said.

As night came on our ears were tuned to the sky, waiting for the sound of a little airplane. There was no sound at all. A great stillness seemed to press down from the sky. There were no cries of water birds. These lakes seemed to be too stony to possess much food for birds. Dick said it seemed to him it was even too stony to grow fish food. He said fish in the region probably grew very slowly because he had heard that studies on Great Bear Lake to the south had revealed that even there the food for fish was insufficient. Bud and Margaret had not taken our fish net with them.

We talked in the tent late that night. We discussed exactly what Bud had on board. None of us had paid great attention to how much gas he carried in the tanks; we surmised he had about four hours' fuel. The pair had no warm clothes or sleeping bag or tent. They had five pounds of yellow corn meal in a sack, for that was something that was never taken out of our airplane under any circumstances, and they had the .22 take-down rifle. The little primus stove would furnish a cooking pot from the container it came in and it burned fuel from the airplane engine.

We talked about what had probably happened. In more civilized parts of the world lost planes are usually found crashed with all occupants dead or disabled. We knew that. But, we thought, in the case of summer float flying here, it was much more likely that there had been a busted float on some reef.

A busted float could be serious enough. Bud had no equipment with which to mend a float, not even a tin plate along. And maybe it was going to be difficult for a rescue ship to locate him.

Why had they gone out from camp so ill equipped? It was a hot day and the ship wouldn't rise from the water with any load in it. Bud had planned to land and take off in tiny potholes with Margaret in order to get her into country that was otherwise inaccessible. He had to cut the load to decrease take-off distance if he were going to work in those potholes. Margaret understood that fully, and of course she was always game for anything.

We got to thinking about Margaret. She was a rugged character, thank goodness. But she was not such a young woman, and if it came to walking out of this country she would never be able to walk out. Yet neither would Bud be free to leave her to cross the country alone. We recalled the footwear they were both wearing when last seen. Bud had on his one pair of sealskin boots. There was an extra new pair carried always inside our floats. That would take care of them for a while for hunting. Margaret herself had no Eskimo-made boots, neither did Ernie nor Dick. Margaret had on a pair of woman's town shoes with Cuban heels, about two inches high. She had said, "I never could walk in low heels." Yet, she wouldn't be walking across this country with the heels she had on, by any stretch of the imagination.

While the sun passed below the horizon, for about five hours, I slept in my tent in the warm down sleeping bag. It was too cool a night for anybody to be sitting up without shelter. Ernie and Dick didn't sleep. I could hear them talking the situation over in their tent until the dawn came. At two in the morning they roused me by the sounds of gassing up the Norseman.

"We'll go out for a cruise," Ernie said. "This is a delicate situation. They've been gone 15 hours now and we know something must be wrong. Every hour counts from now on."

"How do we go about searching?" I asked.

"We've got to keep calm and not get excited," Ernie said. "We've got to be methodical. I've been on many searches and what we've got to do is fly back and forth, back and forth, covering an area of about three miles each strip."

"What about gas?" I asked.

"I see you've guessed it," he said. "Why do you think I stayed up all night thinking? It takes 30 gallons an hour to fly this thing. If we had the gas — why, I wouldn't worry about it. The trouble with rescue work is that it takes a lot of gas.

"You wouldn't realize the gas a plane burns just flying back and forth. We'll have to make every drop count, so keep your eyes glued to the ground we cover. We've only got two hours' gas to spend. Then, if we don't find them, we'll have to go back to Bathurst Inlet to get more, and a fog may come in and it may take a day or two, you never know what's what in this damned country. I don't like it. We'd better plan to find them in the next two hours."

I began to see that this was really a rescue operation, no less. The weather had been fine until now. At 4 A.M. we took off at first daylight and until 6 A.M. we searched. Then we saw the fog rolling up from the ground, collecting in little wisps in the gulleys. We were racing against time, and all of a sudden the race accelerated. It was approaching winter when snow might cover the ground any night, I realized. A slight delay in finding our ill-equipped companions, and anything might happen.

The country was so vast that the sound of the airplane itself was hushed and muted. Through the puffs of treacherous unearthly fog we flew, watching the gray sameness of the hills and rocks and endless waterways below. Bud and Margaret had said they would probably visit some of the small lakes in the vicinity. How far away yesterday seemed! Pelly and Garry Lakes were drawn with firm regular outlines on our aviation maps, but the maps meant absolutely nothing. The whole region was a series of scrambled winding arms of water which were so intricate that it would be impossible to draw them, I thought. Through a part of Lake Pelly ran legendary Back's River, some 580 miles long, with 83 waterfalls and innumerable mighty rapids, only once traced by man a hundred years ago. Perhaps Bud and Margaret were somewhere in the intricacy of Lake Pelly trying to paddle the unwieldy airplane toward camp but separated from it by rapids. We hoped that at least they might be somewhere on the main body of water.

I find it hard to describe the forebodings and the mental depression which settled over the three of us when our short cruising time was up to no avail. Formerly so friendly, this land, it seemed, had set itself to conspire against us. As Ernie said once:

"It's always lying there waiting for you. I always tell myself, 'Keep at it long enough and it will get you someday.' "

Whether he was speaking of the arctic or just of flying in general was not clear. The strange fact was that we were possibly not in the Arctic Zone at all. We had explored so far south that we were in the Temperate Zone. If the Barrens are hostile the reason is not merely because of their northerliness.

We were pretty blue when we pulled out for Bathurst Inlet, 200 miles away. It seemed like gross desertion of our comrades. I offered to stay at the camp, but even as I made the gesture we knew that there would be no useful purpose in that. We left plenty of food, and a note of explanation, hoping that by some miracle our comrades would return in the meanwhile. All we could do was that, and make sure, while we were at it, that nothing happened to us during our searching!

For nobody in the world knew our whereabouts. We were the only people who knew that country at all or who could give even a clue to the location of the missing ones.

Ernie watched the weather with an eye I could read without any trouble, and cursed under his breath; we took a sip of Margaret Oldenburg's good cordial as we took off through the cold, gathering fog for Bathurst Inlet. The fog got thicker as we went on. I wondered how Ernie could keep going. Banking low and sharply over a fog-shrouded lake, Ernie flew by the seat of his pants, and suddenly recognizing the game was up, let the Norseman drop like a bullet, just as fog blotted the world out. We could hear the slow clunking of its big engine turning over, and we held our breaths for an almost blind landing. The engine popped from unburned gas blown back into the red-hot exhaust stacks; we hit unknown water with an expert swish, and there we were.

"Where in hell are we now?"

Nobody knew. Nobody will ever know until earth's last picture is painted. "Well, I know what I'm going to do," I said, and dragging my sleeping bag and the greasy engine tarpaulin up on the shore, I was fast asleep in five minutes. This was just the beginning. I was going to get rest where I could.

Ernie caught a few winks. Dick stayed by his vigil inside the airplane and dozed, glad to borrow my long woman's parka of caribou skins because everything was so clammy and damp that our teeth began to rattle like castanets as soon as the airplane stopped.

At 10 A.M. the fog cleared enough so that we were able to take off; we reached Bathurst Inlet at noon. Ernie had been trying to contact Yellowknife with his radio operator's "key" during the flight. It was too far to get through with voice and so in desperation he tried the Morse code. He couldn't figure out why he could get no response until he recalled it was a Sunday.

At Bathurst Inlet the gassing up of the Norseman, lashing of several great barrels of gas inside it, and the initial steps to start an organized search, took six more precious hours. Ernie was at his wit's end to make a decision as to what kind of wires or messages should be sent.

He hated to have to notify Canadian Pacific Airlines, his employer, that his passenger was missing. It meant that they would call the Canadian Air Force out. The complications and embarrassments that such a step would mean both for him and for me cannot be overestimated. I hated to think what anguish this would mean to Bud's family and my family, too, who would be hearing the worst by press and radio.

In the end, we decided to wait before spreading a general alarm, and to make one more trip inland to give it another try. Ernie directed Jack at the Hudson's Bay post to alert all the arctic radio stations to stand by for a possible emergency.

It is a tribute to Ernie that he never once blamed Bud for getting lost with his passenger nor did he become bitter over it. "I'm going to borrow this pile of gas drums here. They belong to the air force, but I'm taking them," was all he said at Bathurst. "I'll probably catch hell for it, but it is my judgment that this warrants an emergency. We can't afford to wait for permission."

"I hate to think of risking other lives in that country," I added truthfully. I remembered how in 1928 the Canadian Air Force themselves got lost.

"The trouble is," Ernie assisted my observations, "there isn't a great deal of gas in this whole part of the world. Even if the air forces of two countries are called in on the deal, it will take them a week to haul enough gas here to even begin to put their rescue operations to work. By the way," he added, "I hope you carry rescue insurance."

"Rescue insurance?" I quavered. "Never heard of it."

I learned then that search and rescue service in Canada and her territories is not furnished free by the government as it is in Alaska. Ernie, for instance, had search and rescue insurance carried on him by his company, and he said that carrying this type of insurance is standard practice for bush pilots in the vastness of Canada.

We left Bathurst Inlet at six in the evening and flew back to our camp at Lake Pelly, hoping that by some miracle Bud and Margaret would be there. Of course they weren't. At my suggestion we had brought an interpreter back with us: Steve, age eighteen, a nice Eskimo boy who had had some mission education. We were going to check systematically with all the local Eskimos we could find. Two people simply couldn't disappear with no clue in a country so bare that you could see a billiard ball a mile distant. "The Eskimos of the country must know something," we thought.

Ernie had located the position of our camp and given it to Bathurst. As nearly as he could figure it in unmapped country, it was approximately 65 degrees, 50 minutes north latitude and 101 degrees west longitude. We were east of Victoria Island, and although 500 miles north of Hudson's Bay, not in the arctic at all.

The Barrens are a strange place. The willows start dropping off south and inland as you proceed eastward toward Hudson's Bay, and coincidentally many species which depend upon the willows. The reason for this occurrence in the eastern part of our continent is not clear. Here arctic conditions extend hundreds of miles south down even into the Temperate Zone. While the summers on the Barrens are exceedingly warm, the winds and cold of winter are severe.

The temperature had been ranging from around 55 to 75 degrees.

Time, for us, had merged into a half existence of labor and physical exhaustion. Search and rescue is exhausting work.

Ernie had to fly and worry. I knew it was a rare privilege to fly off the air routes with Ernie Boffa at his best, but I couldn't enjoy it. Dick had the exhausting task of loading and unloading eternal gas drums, in which Ernie assisted him. We never dreamed just how worried he was until one day it came out:

"Gosh, I never thought I'd end up here," he said. "You see, they sent me on an assignment out of Edmonton north to Yellowknife. I'm supposed to be married at the end of this month! I didn't want to go but they were shorthanded at Yellowknife.

"When I got several hundred miles north to Yellowknife they said I should go north on this exploration trip. I didn't ask for this assignment. They said I'd be back in a week. Gosh, my girl will be wondering what's happened to me. No word, nothing. I keep wondering every day when I'm going to get back and have a chance to explain to her."

Dick was a tireless and eternally vigilant worker. On those take-offs and landings we often carried more than 3400 pounds gross load that the ship was licensed to carry. Dick lashed the heavy drums solid to the top of the cabin. During a take-off Ernie was in the cockpit at the throttle with Dick in the seat beside him, and I as the uneasy passenger lay across the tops of the 375 pound drums of gas just behind their necks.

"Get your weight far forward on the take-off and hang on to me," said Ernie, and then I only hoped Dick's good ropes on those drums wouldn't break. They never did.

Now we had three pairs of binoculars to use from Bathurst and our bright Eskimo boy, Steve, to help.

Steve had never been in an airplane before. He was frightened but brave. Steve and I had to crouch upon the gas drums in a tight-lipped comradery of fear and nausea as Ernie endeavored to coax our tail-heavy bare old crate off the water, and succeeded at last only by his skill in "porpoising" it. When you have "porpoised" in an overloaded Norseman you've had it. After the take-off for some time either wing tip threatened momentarily to touch the water. Slowly then we climbed and saw wicked rocks and reefs falling below.

There is quite a lot in learning how to interpret what you see on the ground below you from a moving aircraft. Ernie was excellent at it, Dick was fair, I was negligent, and Steve proved to be nil.

We dumped most of our gas at our camp at Pelly Lake, and cruised out from there. Ernie figured Bud couldn't possibly be more than 125 miles away in a radius; this would be Bud's maximum range when he left that day. But what you wouldn't realize unless you stopped to figure it out was that this meant 49,062 square miles in which Bud and Margaret must be located!

We stopped at several Eskimo tents that we found and Steve seemed to make a fine interpreter. We learned that the Eskimo families living on the south side of the lake heard the little airplane go northeasterly early Saturday morning but they never heard it return.

The people were noble specimens of humanity to look at, dignified and proud in carriage, lovely in their skin clothing; there was a fierceness about them. They were all quite smelly, like lions you visit at the zoo, because of eating meat in the carrion stage.

It seemed wonderful that people could find a living here. While the Barrens seemed devoid of life to us, they obviously weren't if they supported these wandering families.

"If there are Eskimos there are caribou," I thought. "And if Eskimos are here — and they are here — they'll eventually find Bud and Margaret." It was all a chain reaction.

I wondered how the Eskimos cooked their meat in this land without fuel, and what they did for heat in winter. We saw that they were grass burners. I had read about grass burners but had never seen them in action, for they were before our day in Alaska. It wasn't a true grass they burned but a kind of heather or lichen: the same strange pasturage which the caribou and musk oxen depended on when, and if, all else failed. It was almost the only growth of any sort covering much of this area. Ernie, experimenting, showed me how quickly and easily handfuls of this crisp plant could be gathered and how readily it burned in dry weather, giving a brief, bright flame.

"Do you suppose Bud and Margaret will learn how to burn this for fuel?" Dick asked.

"Sure," Ernie grinned gamely. "They're not so dumb. They'll find it out. I think Margaret knows it already." It was never mentioned by any of us that Bud and Margaret might have been in a crash and that they might be lying still or critically injured some place and unable to burn heather or do anything.

Ernie believed that the Eskimos stored mounds of this heather during the summer and kept it dry for winter fuel. I believed myself from what I had seen of Eskimos in Alaska that it was more likely that they made no provision for winter whatsoever. The great winds which sweep the prairie country north of timberline keep much of the snow blown off, and it would not be hard to get fuel even in darkest, coldest winter if you knew how. Bud and Margaret should have no trouble building a fire in this veritable carpet of fuel. Margaret was a botanist skilled in arctic lore, and one of the many nice things about her was that she was an extremely adaptable person who could eat anything.

But, if they were alive — it was a terrible "if" to put into words mentally — why weren't they giving us a little help in finding them? Why didn't they start a big prairie fire? Such a smoke would be visible ten miles. Why didn't they use a mirror or reflector to attract our gaze? We looked in vain for all these signs, first in the safe harbors a pilot would logically choose for landing. Now we began to scrutinize with a more morbid interest the stony edges of lakes and the bare ground about. Each of us began to look closer, and we kept our thoughts to ourselves.

We began to look for just pieces of a wing foil or fuselage — the smallest clue from the heartless and unanswering country. Often a rock splashed with spray would lure the weary Norseman from its course for a close study of it. But the suggestions and specks which caught our eyes were always just only another rock. We looked for pieces of half-submerged wreckage sticking out of a pond. The dread, the nervous tension with which we examined each site left each of us feeling limp and sick in the pit of the stomach.

"Well, I'm going to try a little trick I've been keeping up my sleeve," Ernie announced cheerfully.

"It's something I've used before now and this should really rouse them. We'll take off and fly by night," he said. "If they're alive, they'll build a fire, and we'll be bound to see it after dark."

"But you can't do it," I said. "How can we find our own camp again and not get lost ourselves?"

"I can do it," he said.

All day long as we flew Ernie had his earphones on, listening. He was listening for any faint signal from Bud who might be calling on the radio of the *Arctic Tern*, if it weren't knocked out.

I now had two Eskimos with me in the back seats: Steve, and a delightful old fellow in fringed buckskin and oiled caribou wading boots, whom we had picked up at one of the Eskimo camps we had visited. The old fellow was frightened almost to death. He was a brave man to consent to lend his assistance to these aerial maneuvers — braver even than he knew. Yet his face, frozen into lines set by a lifetime of honest and dignified living, scarcely revealed the agonies he endured in flight. I merely saw it grow whiter and whiter. My job was to teach the two Eskimos to use their seat belts and to "pop" their ears when losing altitude fast. The old man gave me little clue as to what was happening inside him, when suddenly it happened. I grabbed for a burp cup, thrust it under his face. Then I grabbed for another and thrust it to Steve. Then suddenly I grabbed for a third burp cup for me.

The Eskimos were good sports, such good sports that they would have died without saying a word, but they were no good for searching. They couldn't tell their own hunting grounds from the air or their own tent from Timbuktu.

Ernie said every single day so far had been bad for radio. "Sun spots" caused the radio to go dead on some days and this was intensified by our extreme nearness to the North Magnetic Pole. We had promised ourselves we would radio out the go-ahead signal to Yellowknife for a rescue operation to organize by ten in the morning today if the missing airplane was not found. But the radio couldn't get through. We were cut off from the world as though in the land of the dead. In imminent peril of a crack-up ourselves if we persisted in fooling around these lakes interviewing Eskimos, we could feel in our bones a superstitious intuition of impending doom as every hour and every day the trail of our comrades grew colder, and we could not find the slightest clue.

Late that night we flew out again to Bathurst Inlet, arriving in darkness in a state of frayed nerves and exhaustion, only to learn that the radio there had not yet got any of the "alert" messages through which they should have relayed to other stations.

What was the reason that no message had gone out from Bathurst? Well, the wind-charger was down. Ernie's temper snapped. He was like a nest of hornets.

"Why in hell can't you guys do something besides set on your fat cans? Good God, I'll fix the wind-charger myself."

It is true that no move had been made to get out a message in a situation which meant the lives of two people. I couldn't believe it. That fellow Jack was really more indifferent than I had even given him credit for. Ernie set off a bomb under the two Hudson's Bay traders and personally saw to the wind-charger and the sending off of the message himself in the course of the next several hours that we were there.

I looked around the place, tottering on sea legs. Jack's new companion was in the midst of baking bread. His oven wouldn't heat in his bum coal range so he put a primus stove under the bottom of it. Jack himself looked as usual, with a ragged beard and slothful posture, slopping around the house in run-down house slippers. Suddenly, like Ernie, I truthfully wanted to kick him where it would do the most good.

Sid cooked supper for the whole bunch; Jack didn't care if anybody lived or died, literally. The house was in complete confusion, dirty, unkept, the slop bucket and the coal bucket full of garbage and egg shells. There was no hot water to wash with.

That day at our camp at Lake Pelly we had been given a gift of fifteen young ptarmigan. An Eskimo man and woman with their two .

small children had arrived via rowboat to make a call. The rowboat must have been brought into the Barrens by dog sled in the wintertime, perhaps many years ago. It was a family possession of prime importance.

"How did you get the ptarmigan?" I asked the woman, through Steve, as she and I and the children together dressed the birds on the grass. Lacking a knife, the children used their teeth to twist off the birds' joints.

"The children get them, throwing stones," was the reply. I learned that although these people had rifles they were for the most part always out of ammunition. Yet they lived well. It was enough to make civilized people feel pretty foolish.

I told Steve to explain that my husband was lost. She knew it. The woman told her children and they all looked very sadly and curiously at me. I could read in their glances that they already considered me a widow.

Now at Bathurst Inlet we all could enjoy the ptarmigan which the woman had traveled far to give me in my bereavement. It would be good to eat some fresh meat again. Our party was doubly out of sorts from living on poor irregular food, while under such a strain. Ernie opened up a bottle of whiskey and said we would all have a drink. A person had to relax, he said. The situation was so painful to him he had to forget it for a moment. I took a short sip with the assembled men, as the drama of the situation seemed to call for something. Then suddenly my nerves snapped. I believe I gave no evidence of it externally, but suddenly I saw the situation very keenly: all these men were going to do was drink and talk all night, when poor Bud and Margaret were waiting to be rescued, shivering out their third night of exposure somewhere, perhaps fatally injured. Thinking of that, I couldn't drink whiskey. It was something I never drank in my good moments and now I found I couldn't in my bad. The others drank and perhaps found the relaxation which they deserved. There was nothing else to do. The cold rain poured down in the black night.

They insisted I shouldn't cook or lift my little finger. Everybody was heroic. When 1 A.M. came and there was still no ptarmigan supper in sight I went into the only bedroom, stripped, and threw myself down into Jack's unmade bed amidst a welter of trousers and discarded socks. The men slept on the floor of the sitting room in assorted sleeping bags. I only hoped they would be fit on the morrow to be able to continue the search. They were.

The household awoke late, as might be expected. Around 11 A.M. from my bedroom I heard Jack heavily tapping out a message on his key, having nearly missed his schedule. Ernie got going and cranked up the post's auxiliary generator to get more power; he sent an SOS over the hundreds of miles south to the Canadian Pacific Airlines offices in Yellowknife.

This was it: the go-ahead signal for an organized search to begin. I sent wires collect to my family, to Bud's family, to our literary agent and to Cessna Aircraft. I had only $15.00 on me and wondered if I would need immediate cash. Ernie said he would remain to head the search and he would never give up until that plane was found. He was in a way quite happy because he could miss his mail run. Although, strictly speaking, he wasn't supposed to further risk his company's plane in more searching before assistance could arrive, he felt that in the name of humanity he could not stand on formalities.

At two on the afternoon of the fourth day we left again, Dick and I closely co-operating as crew with whatever our tireless and faithful leader planned next. Everything else would have to wait, even a wedding.

We had one more lead. Yesterday on the north side of the lake we had landed on a small rocky pond to interview the residents of an Eskimo camp. It had seemed too risky after we landed to put into the shore. Too many rocks. Ernie had given the word to take off again. So we never talked with this group of people.

Ernie wanted to find them again, and this time he was determined to contact them even if it meant half a day's walk from the nearest reasonable landing water. Ernie had one of his hunches. "Hey," he said, "do you remember all the smoke that boiled out of that tent and the people waving? You know, I got to thinking last night maybe those people wanted to tell us something."

"That did seem an awful lot of smoke just to cook caribou meat," Dick agreed.

"You know," Ernie kept musing, "what I still can't understand is why Bud doesn't get busy on his radio. His radio must be out." I knew that Ernie had been trying to contact the *Arctic Tern* continuously at all hours for four days, that he had never given up trying. It didn't look good. It didn't seem possible that the missing pair could be well and alive.

Just as we had pulled out for Bathurst the night before Ernie had heard a very faint call in his earphones at the 31.05 frequency used by Bud. Now as we headed back inland he mentioned this to me for the first time. It meant that at least Bud was alive somewhere. But the picture was not a good one by inference: it meant that Bud could be injured so badly somewhere that he couldn't get out of the cockpit. And of course his battery would be run down by days of futile calling.

We wondered if Bud had got off course and run out of gas. That was a better picture. But it had been such a clear day. Neither would he burn up all his gas, said Ernie. He would come down and save some gas for charging his battery or save enough so that he could fly up and meet us when we came near to show us where he was. It was the fourth day.

Margaret Oldenburg hadn't even had any breakfast the morning that they left. She had passed up the bacon and eggs.

The Eskimo tent belched forth smoke again as we circled it and then flew on to our base camp to dump our gas drums. No time to eat. It was even now approaching darkness again, the fourth night. Eskimos had been here with a rowboat and left a note written in hieroglyphics on a piece of bleached caribou hide that we couldn't read. Steve said it was the same code language used by the Crees and all the tribes. But even without reading it Ernie knew that those people, whichever ones they were, had taken food from our cache against his explicit orders. My mistake for accepting the ptarmigan perhaps. They had borrowed the food or traded, as they saw it, and left in exchange a fawn skin and tongue. Although it could not at once be ascertained what food they had taken, Ernie flew into a rage, and threw the fawn skin and the tongue down in the sand, swearing that all Eskimos should be treated like dogs and horsewhipped. "That's the only way to deal with them. That's the way they like it," he said brutally.

It stung me because my nerves, too, were wearing thin. Of course he was not responsible for what he said, and I said nothing. Ernie could not understand that they were valuable articles in this land — the best the people had. Think of the temptation to the poor Eskimos to "borrow" some of this abundant food!

People dealing with Eskimos or other nature people think they understand them and usually find out that they don't.

We tend to make judgments of a race as a group, not as individuals. We refuse to see the inherent kindness and goodness of the many, in a group that is foreign to us, but we easily remember the errors of the few — errors according to our lights, that is; we point these errors out as "proof" of the alien badness of the whole group of people ever afterward.

We went up to Eskimo groups here and loudly told them, as though they were deaf, that they would get all kinds of food from us if they would only find our missing party. Yet these people would have done all in their power to help just as a decent gesture, without bribes. In Alaska Bud and I had never known people so quick to help, so intuitive of understanding in matters of rescue, as our Eskimos.

At Bathurst the rhythmic beating of a drum at the door became annoying to the civilized inmates. It was plain that the Eskimos at Bathurst Inlet knew. When I stepped out of the plane the sympathetic women took my luggage, children of five years were solemn-eyed. I was amazed to look into their eyes and see such understanding of trouble in small children. The women took my boots to mend.

We stopped at the smoky tent, this making eight tents in all that we had visited. It was nothing. These people had made a smoke just because they wanted us to come down and visit them. They enjoyed the excitement of it. Ernie was burned up! Playing around with us, when such a landing was a hazard to his ship and all our lives! "Damned Eskimos," he really raved. Then he began to imagine things. "You can bet they know more than they're telling," he said.

We flew back to our camp. I cooked supper for the tired men. They were finicky and didn't seem to want anything to eat from our generous grub box. It was an ordeal to select complicated menus that would suit everyone after the simple camps Bud and I were used to where salt and tea were the only things you had to worry about, and you were glad to get them.

We had by now flown four thousand miles about the Barrens searching. We would now make that night flight as a last resort to spot a possible campfire. I was to stay at camp and keep a fire to guide Ernie and Dick in their return.

We were just finishing our supper in the tent, when a canoe was seen approaching on the darkening lake. Our spirits were at their lowest. It was near midnight. Even I paid but slight attention to the approaching craft. It was just the carefree Eskimos again, hoping for a handout. Even I didn't want to see them now. I was exhausted.

Then the tent flap was pulled open and a head stuck in. I thought of giving the head a good bat, but of course refrained. The person was wrapped up in a fresh caribou hide, with the bloody skin side out and the warm fur turned in toward his body. The rump skin of the animal encased the face, with the stump of a tail sticking straight up on his head. Not one of us recognized him for a moment, for in our minds he was far away. It was Bud, and he grinned.

11 VAGABONDS' RETURN

GOT ANY SUPPER LEFT?" was the first thing Bud said.

"Bud, where under heaven have you been? I've never spent such a five days in my life."

Bud was in fine health, although very hungry; he had walked forty miles this day. He had left Margaret Oldenburg in the airplane. Was she all right? Our questions came tumbling out.

The *Arctic Tern* was out of gas. Bud had miscalculated and run dry. He had flown about 115 miles out from camp in a northeasterly direction, where he and Margaret had landed on water, making several stops to gather plant specimens. Because the wind was a headwind going out, Bud counted on a tailwind to come home. The wind changed. He found he had a headwind to battle going back. He had taken only a little gas because he had to operate with a light ship. Realizing that he was running out of gas he decided it would be futile to try to follow up the winding Back's River to reach camp, as he had planned; instead, he attempted to make a straight shot for it. He missed camp, his gas was gone, and he was lost. He landed somewhere on the margin of Lake Pelly.

The two adventurers had put in some shivery nights sitting up together in the tiny cockpit of the *Arctic Tern*. Since the weather continued to be mild, they had managed to sleep some during the days; Margaret had continued making a fine collection of the botanical specimens of the area which were just crying out to be grabbed and uprooted. She was having a wonderful time out of the experience.

"But how could she enjoy it? You must be crazy. She must be half dead."

"You don't know Margaret," said Bud. "She's tougher than an old army mule."

"But what did you two eat all this time?"

"Caribou."

Bud related that they had roasted the meat on hot rocks, using moss for fuel. He had had no trouble killing a nice caribou the first day with one shot from the .22 rifle. "But these are the dumbest caribou I've ever seen," he related to our astounded party. "I could have killed a hundred caribou today. They even follow you. But they are a lot smaller than our Alaska caribou and just about the size of white tail deer; their fat cycle is later in the season so they are not in really good shape yet. But they will be later on."

"Later on," I said. "You and I aren't going to be here later on."

With Bud were three Eskimos, whom he hastened to introduce. "Cook up something nice for them," he advised me aside. "Especially tea. They're good fellows. They've come a long way with me today."

"As soon as it gets light," said Ernie, "we'll fly with the Norseman and get Margaret."

"She's waiting in the airplane," Bud said. "Had a big day picking flowers."

"Come now, let's hear what happened when you got lost," we cajoled him, as we all began at last to relax from the previous terrible tensions.

"It's pretty easy to get lost in this country," Bud began, admitting what we all knew. "I had no idea where camp lay, except every day we could see you come from this direction to search for us and then return in the same direction again. We did everything in the book to try to attract your attention."

"Did you build fires?"

"Build fires? We must have had ten acres all burning at once. Incidentally I looked that moss up in Margaret's book. It was called *tripe de roche,* and George Back and twenty men ate that stuff when they were starving in 1840. I guess they didn't discover that it could be used for fuel because they burned their canoes."

"You say Margaret is all right?" we kept asking anxiously, trying to visualize it. "She's not angry or anything?"

"I'd say she's better than she ever was," Bud reported thoughtfully. "The diet of caribou meat seemed to agree with her, and as she always said, she had no relatives to worry over her if she got lost. The battery ran down on her earphone, that's the only thing; she's anxious to get a fresh battery from camp."

"Could you charge her battery from the airplane engine?" I asked naïvely.

"No, you can't do that. But you know that cough she had when she left? Well, maybe life in the open did it some good because she's all over that now."

Bud enlarged upon this by relating that she had been obliged to ration herself to one cigarette a day and in his opinion this was good for her.

"She's the best sport, bar none, I've ever been with," Bud concluded his detailed report. We sat in our tent visualizing Margaret sitting in the airplane confidently waiting for the rescuers to come at dawn.

"When did you pick up these Eskimos?" we then asked.

"I noted their camp not far away when I picked out our forced landing," Bud replied. "I knew they would come over, and in about a half day they arrived, two of them. They couldn't talk with us, but they understood something was wrong, and they just attached themselves to us and stayed. They lay down and slept all night right beside us in the rocks. Next day this fellow, kind of like our Ook-sook, Connie, only this fellow's name is Kook-sook, he and I went hunting right off, and he showed me how easy it is. The only meal Margaret would never eat was breakfast. She never eats anything at all until about 2 P.M. each day."

"That's right," said Ernie. "She never does."

"Well, every time you guys in the Norseman would fly by we would all hustle and set the prairie on fire and I would get on the airplane radio. I couldn't get you on my radio but I could figure no reason why you couldn't hear me. I was sending on 31.05."

"I was listening on 31.05 but I couldn't hear you," said Ernie. "We'll have to check the radios again."

"How did you make the Eskimos understand that you wanted to be guided home to camp?"

"I saw about the first day that you were never going to find us in this country," said Bud.

"Every day in your flights you got farther afield. So I just started paddling the *Arctic Tern* around the shoreline in the general direction you came from. Kook-sook stuck with us and followed along the shore. The other fellow went home. Probably his family was hungry. Anyway, Kook-sook stuck.

"It took about six hours of paddling to work the airplane down the lake to where I was sure the water we were in joined Pelly Lake proper, along with a part of the Back River. Kook-sook cooked lunch, and Margaret went off looking for specimens when the wind turned unfavorable for crossing the bay.

"When the wind changed back I went to find Margaret. I found an old tent ring where people once camped, and a half-mile farther on was a human skull, just lying there on top of the ground. Maybe it was one of Kook-sook's relations. Most of the teeth were missing and a vole had once made a nest inside the skull. This led me to Margaret collecting specimens nearby and she took some of the teeth as a present for her dentist.

"We drifted again across the water, and Kook-sook rode along on a float. He spelled me as paddler. We paddled for hours; finally, we heard the Norseman again. You were flying low, about three miles to the north of us. I turned on the blinker lights and got busy on the radio, but on you went, and soon you began to climb and I knew you were heading out for Bathurst Inlet again. I got scared you were going to call out a rescue. As we were used to seeing you fly by all the time, we just settled back to paddle as fast as we could.

"Finally we got into a shallow bay. It was sure pretty country, but the bottom of the bay was so covered with rocks we couldn't get closer than fifty feet to shore. Darkness caught us there and we anchored. That's where we might have lost the airplane."

"What happened then?"

"Well, Kook-sook saw a good bull caribou on shore, a lot fatter than the one we were eating, and he wanted to get it, so I went with him. It was near midnight and a storm was blowing up. We couldn't see the barrel of the rifle, let alone the sights. Kook-sook had a .22 Remington. We could only hear the caribou running. It ran in circles around us and Kook-sook emptied his rifle at it without a hit. Finally we went back to the airplane, and do you know the caribou followed us back to the plane! So we loaded up Kook-sook's .22 again and this time he hit the bull in the rump. The caribou limped about and lay down on the shore. Kook-sook shot a few more times and hit him in the back, and he died.

"Then I realized a fierce storm was progressing, with streaks of lightning as bright as day. I hurried to get more rock anchors onto the ropes which were holding the *Arctic Tern* which was holding Margaret. I had to carry the rocks out from shore. This sounds easy, but to save my boots I went barefooted, and to save my clothes from the rain I was nearly naked, stumbling in the dark across uneven slipping rocks, while wind and rain about laid me down. The *Arctic Tern* was banging against rocks as waves rolled it about. Margaret kept my spirits up by shouting encouragement."

"I am sure she must have had an exciting adventure with you," I said.

"Oh, she did. Well, all night the storm blew us back and forth on the ropes while the airplane pitched, and I kept watch. Finally, Margaret kept watch while I slept. Kook-sook slept, apparently without discomfort, rolled up among the rocks in the most recent caribou hide.

"You know the people here kill a caribou if they just want a tongue for supper or a skin to sleep in that night. A hunter will kill one for breakfast and then he will kill another one for supper, just wandering on and leaving the remains. The people believe the supply is unlimited, I guess. And I suppose it is as far as they are concerned. So it goes here. People too poor to even keep in tobacco destroy more meat here in a week than a bank president in our cities can buy in five years."

"How did you finally get home?" we asked, impatiently.

"The wind got too high to paddle the airplane, so I made several hikes across the prairie in various directions. I roused a flock of about 300 geese, a lot of ptarmigan, three caribou, some plovers, eleven gulls, three terns, some Lapland longspurs and ground sparrows. There were a lot of bays and arms of water to detour around. I knew there were some people nearby but I couldn't find their tent. Later I learned they were in the process of moving camp when I was looking for them.

"I tried to explain to Kook-sook by drawing with a stick in the sand that I wanted a boat or kayak to use to hunt for the big airplane. He told me there was a boat back where I had just walked. He would go get it, and bring along another fellow to help paddle. It was about six hours before we came to this understanding. Then he started off.

"Margaret and I took our time at a good big supper of meat and marrow and boiled cornmeal mush, and I slept for a while in the airplane. When Kook-sook came back without his rifle I knew he had something in mind. He said there were three white people and lots of gasoline a little ways away.

"I had prepared myself a parka by crawling inside the green caribou skin, fur side in, and I set off with Kook-sook. Margaret said she would wait with the airplane. I didn't realize that Kook-sook was leading me right here to our regular camp. What I understood from him was that there was a gasoline cache, and I thought it must be some gasoline you were leaving around the country for your search.

"We walked back to where I was that morning, a little ways below the rapids. Here the people had just finished setting up their new camp. Their possessions were still wrapped up in caribou skin rolls. A heather fire burned and the kettle was on. They greeted us gaily and the women quickly set dried meat before us. I was eating away when the hum of the Norseman broke the solitude again. So I got the men to hurry with a boat so we could get to the airplane before you could take off once more. You see, I thought you were landing only at a gasoline depot.

"First the canoe had to be patched. We had to chew caribou tallow and rub it into the holes on the canoe's bottom. I chewed and rubbed like mad. Finally, we got on our way. The man of the family paddled with a new factory-made canoe paddle that looked strange with the dilapidated set of oars Kook-sook pulled. A little boy sat in the bow and I rode shivering upon the back thwart. For over an hour we traveled fast down the Back River. Records say it has 580 rapids and waterfalls in it, you know. It was a wild trip that I hope never to make again. A thousand times I thought of my parka left behind in camp. At last a light gleamed and the Norseman came into view on the water.

"I know it seems odd," Bud concluded, "but still I didn't recognize that it was our camp. I thought it was a strange place where you had stopped temporarily, even after I opened the tent flap just now. That's what it means to get lost. Now, everything has come back into focus and suddenly I can see it is the same old place. That's all there is, I guess."

Probably Ernie would have quickly found the *Arctic Tern* had he not been given wrong information by the Eskimos. One Eskimo camp that Bud and Margaret flew over so low that the people scattered had told Ernie and me that they had never seen them.

Why did the Eskimos lie? Perhaps it resulted from a misunderstanding of the interpreter. Or perhaps, not appreciating the seriousness of the situation, this family hoped by a little prevarication to keep the visitors in their country longer for reasons of food and entertainment. To them it was doubtless all just one big free show.

Asked on the sixth morning of her outing if she would not have something to eat from the ample meal set before her, Margaret Oldenburg said:

"No indeed, but thank you. You know I never eat breakfast."

I just took some tea myself. And promptly threw up on the ground.

The mystery of the airplane radios was soon cleared up. Bud had been sending on 31.05 and Ernie thought he was receiving on 31.05 but he was really receiving on 31.18. One of the radios had wandered off course. Had the two pilots taken pains to synchronize their radios before starting out, all this trouble could have been avoided.

A few hours' sleep, and Ernie and the indefatigable Margaret were hatching plots to be off again. Their time was running out. They announced that they would dash off a few hundred miles yet that day down the rugged unmapped course of the Back River, tracing it to the coast, and over to Garry River. Bud and I willingly voted to remain in our sleeping bag and keep camp until they got back.

We marveled at the endurance of that pair. It was rough weather to beat across the skies. Ernie had to get to Bathurst Inlet without delay to call off the search. Suddenly, too, he realized, in two days he had to be back on the job at Yellowknife southward to make his regular mail run.

"You'll never know what I went through worrying over you the last five days," I told Bud when the others had gone. "I guess I even got downright superstitious," I confessed. "I shan't forget what a privilege it was to travel with those others, yet somehow it was a spooky country without you, do you know it?"

We were just wishing we had a couple of caribou tongues to eat when two Eskimo hunters came right to camp with four choice tongues. We entertained them in our tent for a good many hours. They found all of the strange food I cooked for them unacceptable and could eat only meat, without salt. They consumed buckets of tea but could not endure sugar in it; they ate with relish the slices of plain white bread.

"You know," I mused, after our guests had abruptly and silently departed, "I enjoy these people. They're good sports to be with. Did you ever read Collier's book, *The Indians of the Americas?* He makes some awfully thoughtful remarks in it. I remember especially that he observed, from his quarter of a century as Indian agent, that the nature people, as he calls them, have a great deal of poise and a sense of inner security and peace. He observed that the more insecure man's environment is — that is, when man has to contend with nature daily to survive — the more secure the man feels. Then he noted that contrarily, the more man searches for physical security in civilization, bulwarking himself against the slightest risk or hardship, the less security he seems to find within himself."

"I've often wished," Bud remarked, "that I could help some other people to acquire that sense of their own dignity and inner security that I see in the most primitive Eskimos."

This set us to talking, as we often did, about the social problems of our times, by comparing primitive and modern cultures.

Roused by the thunder of the returning Norseman we staggered out of bed to grab its lines and maneuver it tenderly into its harbor of boulders. Margaret, Ernie, Dick and Steve had been gone all night. It was already nine o'clock the next night.

They didn't pitch their tent but poured into ours. I hastened to make tea and boil potatoes and more tongues. But before I could get well started they announced that they would just gas up and we would all leave now for Bathurst Inlet. They couldn't bother to wait for a bite, despite the fact that none of them, including Steve who rode along as a kind of confused and hungry mascot, had tasted cooked food in twenty-four hours.

The darkening night with its stormy sky looked like unlikely flying weather. I began gathering up our camp gear. But even as Dick and Ernie and the obedient Steve gassed the Norseman, Bud said that he and I would not fly with our ship this night. It was too late. We had better wait for dawn to at least give us a sporting chance when making an approach to those 2000-foot ridges which guarded Bathurst Inlet.

Ernie conceded the point then. He crawled wet and bedraggled into our tent once more; I reversed my first labors and gave such impetus to the lagging stew as I could.

Presently, I got all four of them to eating in relays from our two pie pans. They were famished. Relief registered on the Eskimo boy's face. "Small wonder," I thought, "that people like Eskimos, around the world, think us crazy sometimes."

Our companions sat upright in the tiny tent all night long and talked. I dozed off in a sitting position.

With dawn Margaret and Ernie were ready to go. When we took off with the two airplanes, not more than a few yards of visibility lay ahead on the lashing waves. Fog banks enshrouded us at intervals along the way. Bud and I were blown off course over dismal McAlpin Lake, battling a headwind. We never saw the Norseman after the take-off until Bathurst, and the Norseman had our load, even to the life-saving sleeping bag.

But with familiarity we had come to know somewhat, and to really love, the strange Barrens. While many Canadians maintained it had no fuel, our party knew that it had perforce. While people at the outposts said it was not livable and even the mounted police seldom ventured there, there were actually as many people living in it as the country could support. There were lots of caribou, at least at the moment. Some years, according to the tales, the caribou disappear completely. Although small wildlife seemed totally absent to the stranger, and even the rocky lakes barren of fish, yet Eskimo children, because they felt sorry for us, had given me a bag of ptarmigan all killed by throwing stones; and grown Eskimos had nonchalantly helped us out, not comprehending the exact nature of our distress, just for the lark of it.

We said good-by to Ernie and Margaret and Dick at Bathurst Inlet. We flew to Coppermine after that, where we expected to meet them later. At Coppermine, Bud and I were ushered up the bank to the Anglican mission by the whole town. The good radio boys, who had been on a sleepless, twenty-four-hour alert on our behalf, wired notice of our safe arrival there to the outside world, while I wired our families and friends. Canon Webster advised that he had been in a similar position one time when he was lost with his dog sled for several days; he recommended that we spare no words to explain to our families, because he said the press and radio always made much of such things. It would be a great anguish to those who cared for us.

Meanwhile, the Associated Press had not been idle. News of our predicament, labeled as a "crash," was dispatched quickly throughout the United States and Canada. The official teletype upon which this news was based was as follows:

EDMONTON, ALBERTA — THE ROYAL CANADIAN AIR FORCE SAYS IT HAS LEARNED THAT A PARTY OF THREE WAS FOUND AFTER BEING MISSING A WEEK ON A FLIGHT IN THE CANADIAN ARCTIC.

THE RCAF SAYS VETERAN PILOT ERNIE BOFFA SENT WORD HE HAS FOUND A WOMAN IDENTIFIED AS MISS OLDENBURG, A UNIVERSITY OF MINNESOTA GEOLOGIST. WITH HER IS THE PILOT, IDENTIFIED AS BUD HELMERICKS, AND HIS WIFE.

MEANWHILE, A CIVILIAN PLANE IS SEARCHING 200 MILES NORTH OF EDMONTON TO REPORT THAT A PLANE WITH ENGINE TROUBLE WAS HEADING FOR THE KENSHUN HILLS LAST SATURDAY. IT IS BELIEVED THE PLANE MAY HAVE BEEN PILOTED BY DR. VANCE MURRY OF WASHINGTON, D.C. HE HAS BEEN MISSING A WEEK.

There is scarcely a day or a week that a small airplane isn't missing someplace in Canada or her territories. It is an education to know the facts behind one of these alarms as an object lesson in how completely distorted much news becomes by the time the public gets it.

News is like that game, Telephone, that we used to play at children's parties. We used to sit around in a ring and somebody whispered some words which were passed on by whisper around the group. The result always was that what came out at last to be spoken aloud by the original starter was so ludicrous that it set us all to laughing heartily. I do not believe there is a conspiracy of the press, or of the government, or big business to keep us, the public, from getting accurate news. I just think that accuracy is difficult for human nature to attain.

A dispatch to newspapers in Minnesota alerted them and they carried Margaret's picture in her Eskimo parka with this caption: WOMAN SAVED IN AIR CRASH. MARGARET OLDENBURG AMONG SURVIVORS.

One of our home town papers stated that we were rescued by the Anglican mission at Coppermine and were doing well, although still recuperating at the mission and in a weakened state. Another report had it that Bud and I were lost and that our airplane had been found but "there was no sign of life about the airplane."

Our families heard several garbled versions over the radio, from which nobody in his right mind could have made sense. Later, back in Alaska, we heard the best of them. A government agency there had relayed word out to the world that Bud and Margaret Oldenburg were lost in a crash with a small *baby!*

At Coppermine, Canon and Edie Webster were just starting their day. It was noon and breakfast time in the arctic; we sat down at their table for corn flakes, toast, fried eggs and sausage, and strong boiled English tea. Kind, motherly Edie Webster arranged that I could wash our dirty clothes in her hand-pump washing machine. Bud and I took hot baths in an unwieldy tin tub carried into their bedroom and fell into their bed and slept until we were called for supper. Friends of the frontier are real friends.

Life as lived by the Websters at this season was one of cheerful and total disorder. While the canary in his cage screeched, family prayers were held kneeling, sometimes on the right day and sometimes on just any day at all. A part of the prayer always went: "Bless all the missions in the foreign field, bless Margarite and Mummie at her work too . . . and please fill our nets soon so that the dogs may have fish."

Everyone in the village was concerned with this last down-to-earth entreaty. The village dogs were in peril of starvation year by year, and the Eskimo people as well. For the salmon were mysteriously diminishing or changing in their runs up the Coppermine River, perhaps because of some change in the ocean currents. But more likely it was due to the river being fished out by successive generations of people living near the mission, leaving no breeding stock. The nature of any land, not only the arctic, is that it cannot indefinitely support a growing and concentrated number of people off old resources.

"It was right there in that house," the Websters told us taking us along the mud street, "that Dick Finnie spent a winter and wrote his first book."

"Oh, we know him. We met the Finnies in Ottawa."

"We heard the other day in a letter that they've gone to Arabia."

"Is that so?" I said. "I hadn't heard."

Little Margarite, nine years old, played games that would seem strange to most of us. She had her own tent, not a child's toy but a real man-sized tent, and she played at pitching it morning, night and noon. Once, her mother told me, Margarite was seen pitching the tent with one of the most primitive of the old Eskimo hunters in the village to help her.

"Pity that Eskimo!" her mother told us. "What we didn't know is that this had been going on for weeks. Margarite got him to move her boxes and her dolls around in her tent all day long, and then she got him to move the tent around from one spot to another. You see, with her complete command of the Eskimo language and having no other children to play with, she had to invent her own games, and she discovered her ability to dominate. We heard her abusing him in the roughest language, calling him "slow," "stupid" and "dumb," and I don't know what else in Eskimo. The poor old man was a veritable slave under her, and he didn't resist at all. Fortunately, we discovered it and put a stop to it."

Dinner was fresh baked whitefish from the mission nets, boiled potatoes, canned string beans and a terrifically wonderful fresh lemon pie.

After a night on the new Webster convertible couch, we arose near noon, according to the arctic custom, had the usual breakfast and later a real dinner of rare roast prime ribs of caribou, browned potatoes, English Yorkshire pudding, apple pie and tea. During the afternoon Margarite and I prowled around the village and found a few cupfuls of the only blueberries possibly ever to be gathered in the stunted moss of that town's outskirts. It had been a very warm summer. Edie Webster then made blueberry tea muffins.

Ernie and Margaret Oldenburg were expected on the mail run from Yellowknife. We waited for them, intending to get the last of our things which they still carried aboard the Norseman. But the radio boys indicated the mail plane would be late, and meanwhile the sky cleared and there was an excellent tailwind going westward toward Alaska.

"Well," Bud said, "I think we'd better be off. We'll meet them later over at Aklavik."

The way it turned out, we never saw them again. Part of our camp outfit — some old cooking pots and a decrepit jacket — are probably still on board some Canadian Pacific Norseman making its mail flights back and forth into the Canadian arctic, for all I know.

As for Margaret, she went to Tierra del Fuego at the tip of South America. Later in 1950 we heard of Ernie in one of our volumes of *Arctic,* the official journal put out by the scientific organization known as the Arctic Institute of North America, of which we all became charter members. The journal said:

> Ernie Boffa landed Dr. Lincoln and Mrs. Washburn at Holman Island Post, Hudson's Bay most northerly new post on Victoria Island, to explore.
>
> It was on the return from this flight that Ernie Boffa had a forced landing some fifty miles north of Coppermine (on the sea ice of early spring), when his aircraft became a total wreck. Fortunately, owing to expert handling, neither Ernie Boffa nor his mechanic was hurt, and both were rescued a few days later as the result of a most successful RCAF search directed by W/C D. R. Miller.

So went the fortunes of one of the greatest arctic pilots of our time.*

* *Arctic;* Vol. 3, No. 1; pp. 45–46; April 1950.

12 TO AND FROM OLIKTOK POINT

WE FLEW TOWARDS ALASKA, arriving at the little Catholic mission of Pauletuk at eleven that night. The ocean was wild. Bud picked out a short cove and plunked down in the friendly gleam of a light which came on for us in the upstairs window of the church steeple, somewhat as the lighthouse beacon gleams for the sailor at sea.

Arctic missionaries live under the same roof in which they have their church services with an improvised take-down altar. We have reported that there are no landing fields any place in the Canadian arctic. Pauletuk got its mail and its only contact with the outside world once a year with the visit of the R.C. mission ship, *Our Lady of Lourdes*. The two French priests in their bare sticky house made us wonderfully welcome; they put us to sleep on the upstairs floor of the sanctuary in our sleeping bag on caribou hides. A pile of hides was stacked near the wall beside the pews. Midnight mass was held while we slept. We saw the mukluk-clad feet of the faithful walking past our faces.

Strong winds held us there over Sunday. Fathers Metier and Lemeur, both of them little more than boys, were gallant and gay when their duties as hosts happily necessitated that they must entertain visitors. We saw them don their long black gowns at intervals throughout the holy day, over grimy shirts and work pants. We heard them tiptoeing upstairs into the tiny chapel, carrying with them cracked enamel cups of water and ringing little bells.

The hymns drifting down into the warm kitchen below, were sung in minor keys in Latin. They were oriental love songs, songs of adoration.

They could not help but have an emotional effect upon the listener as they brought to mind vividly the countless ages unrolled, in which man has sought God.

The modest fathers adapted themselves to this arctic land in a way that was more than surprising. They ate *quak* — raw frozen meat and fish — in great quantity when fuel was short in winter. They did their own hunting for caribou and seal, often sharing the proceeds of a hunt communally with an Eskimo family with whom they would affiliate. Living off the country in oblivion to the game laws, two priests would consume from twenty to fifty caribou a year with their dog teams. The French arctic culture was at once practical and astute — but absolutely parasitic and unprogressive.

Yet there were several possible infant industries which might be developed in Canada and Alaska, in the arctic: reindeer herding, the fur clothing and souvenir business, possibly limited commercial fisheries in the Arctic Ocean, coal and copper mining, and conceivably oil and uranium production.

Our flight back to Alaska from Aklavik, Canada, was a foggy run. Blown to Barter Island on a tailwind, we got there on our last drop of gas and were relieved to make it to the lagoon. Old Andrew met us with a crowd of Eskimos. Night was coming on.

"We have lots of airplane every day now," he told us, right off. "But I get up from my sleep when I hear *Arctic Tern*." Looking around we saw that a whole prefabricated orderly army city had sprung up.

An army truck rolled up and we were taken in it up the graveled road to the mess hall, in hopes of a late meal. We hung our parkas on a hook in the empty hall and leaned over the counter with the corporal who accompanied us, to attract the cookie. All the personnel we knew there before had completely changed.

Then I heard a decisive military tread behind me and suddenly trouble came in person. He was the new commanding officer of the post. We knew by his posture that he was not going to shake hands, but Bud held out his hand and the captain had to shake it. Before the captain could say anything, I held out my hand, too, and he had to shake it while I made cordial opening remarks. However, the captain was not to be deterred.

"Just who are you," he began belligerently, "and who gave you permission to come to Barter Island?"

We explained deferentially that we had been coming to Barter Island for some years, and although we had our Scientists and Explorers Permits and permission from Washington to fly over the petroleum reserve of the navy in Alaska, we had not known that any further permission was required.

"The navy?" said the captain. "Well, this is the army."

The captain knew perfectly well who we were. He had learned of our passing eastward into Canada, and he had not approved.

"Is it a new rule?" asked Bud. "You say civilians can't come to Barter Island any more?"

"No, it's not a new rule," said the captain. "I have been in the army nine years and never have civilians been allowed to come onto any military reservation without permission. You will have to get permission from General Gaffney at Fairbanks."

"Just how would you propose that we return from Canada to Alaska, where we live, if we did not stop here on the way?" I asked.

He had no countersuggestion. I continued: "We will have to buy gas from you. We're all out of gas. You know that there is no other gas in this part of the world. So you will have to let us have gas in order to be rid of us, unless you want us on your hands for the rest of the winter."

"No, ma'am," retorted the captain spiritedly. "I don't have to let you have gas. I am not committed to let you have anything at all. If I were Andrew the Eskimo there, I would be glad to give you anything myself, but as an officer of the United States Army I am here to protect Uncle Sam's interests, and I will not tolerate civilians running around here."

Thus the ungracious captain stood there and continued to abuse us — civilians who were worn from a flight along a totally uninhabited and hostile coast in a tiny plane. While this harangue was going on, we could see the Eskimos walking in and out of the Polar Bear Bar across the street where they were enjoying the hospitality of the army in considerable abundance.

"You could at least offer us a cup of tea before you begin to bully us," I told him.

"Madam, that has nothing to do with the point," reiterated the harassed officer. "But you simply have not permission from the army to be here. Rest assured that if there were any doubt about your character, I would not permit you to leave except in chains, accompanied by an armed guard."

"Threats now!" I fairly howled in such incredulous anger that Bud had to pinch me very hard. Through this ridiculous argument Bud had maintained his poise. He asked the captain then, what were the boundaries of this "military reservation."

"Why, the island," replied the captain, with increased mood. "Barter Island."

"Well, if that's the case," offered Bud, "we are sorry if we have caused you any embarrassment. But you can explain to your superior that we never landed on your airstrip. You see, we are on floats. We landed on the water adjacent to the island, and only the tails of our floats are touching the military reservation."

The captain didn't like it, but he had to be satisfied with that, things being what they were. "And I don't mind you having your cup of tea, ma'am," he growled at last.

"Oh, we'll go over to Andrew's place and he'll give us tea."

We walked out of the building. The captain was furious. Perhaps no rules in his book covered this.

All of us in Alaska had seen the military grow and expand to distasteful proportions. They came with their installations during the last war and they had never withdrawn. Public feeling in the United States endorsed preparedness. Businessmen in Alaska endorsed it because it helped business. Doubtless it was right to be prepared. Yet the hopelessness of trying to maintain old-fashioned conventional army posts along the tremendous arctic coastline of North America must be apparent to all. Certainly it was a great problem to know just what to do. Yet two results of the military occupation were clear enough: their destructiveness — for there is no group on earth more destructive to the earth's resources than military groups — and their acquisition of increasing tracts in Alaska upon which they seemed to do much of nothing, but where no civilian could set foot.

At the house of Andrew we had bread and tea. It was there that an Eskimo messenger reached me with a letter. It was from a Mrs. Vella Altree, and it said: "As far as I know I am the only white woman on the island. Won't you come visit me soon?"

I hadn't dreamed that there was a woman here. She had come down to the beach to meet our airplane but had just missed us.

In a short time we were having supper with her and her husband, who was chief of the Coast and Geodetic Survey Group, in another mess hall which was but a short walk from the army barracks. In Hank and Vella Altree's "wannigan," a movable Quonset on sleigh runners, we slept that night on one of the extra cots let down from its wall.

Vella Altree and her husband were farmers from the state of Washington. He was also a surveyor and she had a job measuring the tides of the Arctic Ocean. Vella was a practical, clear-thinking farm woman.

She was applying her energetic ideas to the welfare of the Eskimos at Barter Island. Both she and her husband were aroused by their discovery that there was no public school at Barter Island, and that the American people were not concerned over the Eskimos dying of tuberculosis.

"Why, these are some of the finest people I've ever met," said Hank. "They're just as smart as any white person if they are given a chance to learn."

Vella and Hank were doing something about this in their own small way, as Americans. They wrote letters home by air mail, amply illustrated with snapshots, and got their local minister interested. Their church at home told everyone who would listen about the plight of the Alaska Eskimos, urging that there should be more investigations.

It seems probable that thousands of such letters have been written home from Alaska by the pioneers at many outposts during the last ten years. Investigations, medical and social, have been made. Yet the problems increase and multiply. I remember the fervor I felt in my first book when I told about how cruelly the Indians along the Yukon treated their dogs. As a result the first Humane Society was started in Alaska to do something about the dogs. But as for the human beings — well, their problems, it seems, are just not easy to solve; actually when you get right down to it, even the dogs are about the same as they were.

As for the unmannerly captain, who can keep a grudge long on an island? We shook hands the next day and got our gas from Andrew. Thus Bud's prophecy, that the Eskimos were more dependable than the new glamorous arrivals, was fulfilled.

I flew the course to Oliktok Point while Bud counted off landmarks at an altitude of 700 feet all the way. We could only see dimly the line where land met sea, but that was all we needed.

To our Eskimo mother and father we related our adventures with the strange people to the eastward with many a hearty laugh. Bud and George began together to rig one of the new fish nets which we had brought for him and for us from Aklavik, where nets were plentiful and cheap. It snowed during the night. Bud and I slept in George's still-empty tin warehouse on a pile of hides.

Old Samuel, whom we had known several years, arrived with his furry party out of the foggy night on a launch from Barter Island. The party was looking, they said, for a box of misplaced Bibles.

We lounged inside the hospitable tent beside the Arctic Ocean: not a thing to do but lie back on skins, eat fresh roasted whitefish and sea trout, and listen to the wash of the sea, to soft Eskimo voices and to the idle strumming of the guitar we had sent Martha the crippled girl, from the U.S.A. The strumming was in minor chords and the guitar was converted to the strictly Eskimo message.

Bud, in complete Eskimo costume, with sixteen-year-old Oo-lak, squatted on the point for hours behind a two-foot mound, waiting for the geese and brant. When the birds were brought in, I helped Nanny and Martha and seven-year-old Lydia pick them, and I swept Nanny's floor, not for the first time, with a gull's wing.

"Have the people around here ever thought of wearing porcupine

We cut a window in the Takahula Lake cabin

A grizzly did this damage to the inside of our cabin

Connie feeds Bud marshmallows

Bud and Connie have supper at their nook table

skins for parkas?" Bud asked Nanny seriously, as she sewed away with sinew thread on a new parka for me. My old one was wearing out.

She thought a moment. "No," she said. "They never do that." Belatedly the Eskimos burst into guffaws of laughter. They were getting more used to that Bud, whom they adored, each year.

It was overcast right to the ground. Bud said he absolutely would not start to fly over the mountains to home until a really clear day came. Our load was so large that it must be taken in two trips.

A day came which permitted him to take off. I didn't mind staying with Nanny. "Its' just 350 miles straight home," Bud told me. "Don't worry. I'll stay overnight and I'll be back tomorrow. Next trip we'll both go together to stay."

I stood on the polar shore with Nanny while the men pushed the float ship with Bud in it out into deep water. Bud took off his bulky parka inside the crowded cockpit. He was packed solid to the roof. He made a long run for the take-off, dodged incoming ice cakes and waggled his wings over the point in flight. The rest of us crawled back into the tent.

Over the low coastal plain sped the *Arctic Tern,* heading inland. Umiat came and went, the first and last radio contact. The water in the Colville River had fallen so low by fall that Bud couldn't have landed there.

Bud thought about a story concerning Umiat which he heard from several Eskimos. Right on the very top of the 1000-foot hill called Umiat Mountain, from time immemorial there had lain the skull of a whale. The Eskimos are expert observers, and when it comes to bones, they don't make mistakes. No Eskimo could explain how a whale skull got there one hundred miles from the sea, air distance. As a whale's skull is the size of a house trailer and weighs hundreds of pounds, it didn't seem likely that anyone carried it there. Relating the object to what they had learned of Christianity the Eskimos decided in their logical fashion that probably this whale skull was lodged there at the time of Noah and the Great Flood. It was always regarded by them as a piece of Old Testament evidence.

Recently word had got around that the historic whale skull was gone.

We asked our friends where it could have gone to. "Maybe the navy took it," the people said. Now just for curiosity Bud flew right over the top of Umiat Mountain on his way, to check on local gossip. Sure enough, the whale skull was gone. The navy must have taken it.

We had long talked about a place called Chandler Lake. This is a large body of water on the north, treeless side of the Brooks Range. Sig Wien and a couple of his pilots were among the few people ever to have visited this place which was the summer home of a group of Eskimos believed to be the last of the inland caribou hunters left in Alaska. Simon Paneak was the name of their leader.

"I believe I'll drop over to Chandler Lake on my way and see how they all are," thought Bud. "I'll see if they want anything."

Chandler Lake, immense and cold cobalt blue, lay between mountain walls, facing the arctic plain. It had the same features of Lakes Peters and Schrraeder, except that it was windy all the time and Eskimo people still lived there today.

Beneath the flashing silver wings there stood revealed a group of half a dozen perfectly round, skin dwellings standing on a mound beside an arm of the blue lake. They were the last of the old-fashioned caribou skin tents to be found today.

Simon Paneak was an intelligent man; a self-made man who in his maturity had taught himself to speak fluent English and to read and write. But he preferred the old-type tent made of caribou skins stretched over a bent willow frame to the commercial white canvas tent simply because in the arctic the former is infinitely more comfortable. Here Bud was privileged to see in actual use the kind of dwellings that prehistoric man lived in. People and dogs clustered around the staunch skin tents and came running to greet the rare airplane as it landed.

There were Eskimos of all sizes. Two walked out into the water in their oiled boots of bull caribou hide, turned fur in, and Bud, wading in his coastal sealskin boots, shook hands all around, even while holding the bouncing plane off the rocks. He ran hastily back to slip into his parka.

"Everybody fine here?" There were nods and fur-ringed smiles.

"I can haul you fifty pounds of stuff on my return from Hughes. How much have you been paying freight?"

Simon replied they paid fifty cents a pound for freight. A one-hundred-pound sack of flour cost $70.00 delivered here!

These people scarcely tasted any food but game and fish. They made what money they got by hunting wolves along the divide, for which they received $50.00 bounty and a maximum of $30.00 on each pelt. To get this trade a Wien pilot serviced them in the summertime. By winter the group wandering with their sleds along the divide, were inaccessible. Because they lived north of the trees, each small stick to burn was a precious commodity, and they carried the willow frames for their skin houses with them on their sleds as they went.

"How much would you charge?" asked Simon about the freighting.

"I'll haul this fifty pounds for nothing. But hurry and make up your list."

Bud took down the orders in his logbook.

One family's order ran:

tobacco	2 pounds
tea	2 pounds
cigarette papers	2 packages

Another family's order was the same with the addition of a carton of chewing gum and one wolf trap. To Bud's amazement half or two thirds of each of the orders consisted of demands for popular brand nostrums, such as cough drops, muscle linaments, cathartics and headache tablets. Apparently, Simon's people, exuberant and healthy as they seemed to be, were going through the patent medicine stage. The possession of these things in their camp would bring them a certain degree of entertainment or self-mollification to alleviate the barrenness of their existence. Hypochrondria is not peculiar to civilized people alone. These people preferred tobacco, coffee, tea and patent medicines to salt, flour, or any kind of food.

Bud tried to divide the poundage fairly equally between families. But two men held back; they wanted things badly but they had no money.

"Can your wife sew?"

"Sure. My wife is good sew."

"All right. I'll buy your headache pills for you if your wife will make me some mittens and fur stockings."

It was agreed. Although Nanny always did our sewing for us, we could use an extra supply. The Chandler Lake garments did not turn out to be "good sew" as was promised.

"Oh, well," as Bud put it later, "we can always use them for company."

The people told Bud how to follow up the canyon that heads Chandler Lake to get through the pass to hit the John River which goes down into the Koyukuk. Then Bud planned to fly through a second pass by the John into the upper Alatna. The pass into the Alatna was a new one that hadn't been flown, so far as we knew, by anyone.

Following the Eskimos' directions Bud was soon winding among the peaks and down the John River southward. Although the arctic side of the Brooks Range was whitened under early snow, the southerly side, carpeted with its stands of regal spruce forest, was still a land in which summer lingered. Cottonwoods and birches stood out in bold orange and gold groves. Bud wove through mountain valleys, following cascading crystal streams while the side hills above burned dull red and purple with dead blueberry leaves. Reindeer moss added a velvety gray carpet to the scene while the setting sun splashed its fire, and the rock walls, like miles of standing organ pipes, threw back the staccato bark of the small airplane in their midst.

Slowly the sun sank. Bud recognized the towering rocks of the Arrigetch Peaks and thought: "Almost home now." Black rain clouds gathered and as Takahula Lake came into sight the rain beat suddenly onto the windshield, turning to sloppy snow as it hit. High over our cabin Bud sped, then spiraled down and down. He landed on the darkened lake in the midst of the flurry of white flakes, taxied into Airplane Cove, and tied up.

There the cabin stood, and Bud saw that the birches leaning over the porch were a paradise of color. The air smelled of fall leaves. It was good to see trees again. The wild cranberries were bright red underfoot all along our path.

Bud had left the sleeping bag with me on the north coast. No bedding, no stove, and a depleted house combined for him to reach Hughes early next morning. It was necessary to change oil in the travel-weary airplane there.

By 4 P.M. Bud returned to Takahula Lake where he cached some supplies for the cabin, including a small iron cook stove, and was on his way toward Chandler Lake over the arctic divide again. There were heavy thunderstorms scattered about the mountains.

As he neared the pass he was flying at 6000 feet. The outside temperature was 38 degrees. The peaks on either hand became veiled from sight but there was still plenty of ceiling to get over the pass provided he did not miss the proper turn.

Should he turn back? This question is the hardest of all for the pilot to answer. Every situation is different and nonrepeatable. And it is changing every minute. The question comes as to just when does a situation become actually, rather than merely potentially, dangerous? Shall I go ahead or shall I turn back? The question can come on the take-off when you don't know if there is enough room. The question can come on landing when you think perhaps you had better give her the gun at the last moment and go around again. The question can be asked under a thousand different guises. But it is really always the same question — the one Hamlet couldn't answer. Unfortunate, indecisive Hamlet would not have made a good flyer.

"It's only about ten miles further on to Chandler Lake. If I turn back now I'll have to go clear to Hughes again for gas. This could mean days of delay. Connie is waiting. Besides, maybe clear weather lies just over the top on the other side," Bud thought.

Reaching the head of the John where three creeks join, Bud turned onto the extreme left one.

Rain spurted in rivers over the windshield of the laboring airplane as the sheer rock walls of a canyon drew closer on either side. Fog pressed in. A few minutes later Bud was flying as low in the canyon as he could get, following a narrow ribbon of white water. The ground from here on seemed to rise up and just vanish. The rain turned to snow, sticking to the windshield outside, from whence it could not be removed.

"This is it!" he knew suddenly in a sweat of fear. "Turn back — if it isn't already too late!"

Here is where the tight maneuvers that a pilot learns in training come in handy. Banking sharply against the wall on the left as far as he dared and using full power, he swung the little ship into a sharp climbing turn and headed back out of the canyon the way he had come into it.

He flew back to where the river forked. He circled about for half an hour more, hoping the fog would lift. It didn't.

Three times Bud stubbornly tried to get through the pass. There must have been an angel riding on his shoulder. For that canyon was a blind one that ended in a wall of cliffs 2000 feet above. It was the wrong canyon.

He then set off, following another canyon. Dropping down onto its floor he again followed a stream upward into the mist. The air was smooth, the fog solid. Bud spotted a high mountain lake to one hand. "If this pass is another phony I'll return to this lake and camp," he thought.

Over the divide the valley broadened out even as the fog came closer. There was nothing to see in all the world but the thin winding ribbon of a stream which must lead somewhere. The water flowed north! The fog was blowing in from the unseen Arctic Ocean out in front. At last a gray heaving mass loomed below with whitecaps rolling on it — Chandler Lake.

Watching the lay of the waves, Bud flew just a few feet above the wild water of the lake, blinded in fog. After a few moments he gradually cut the throttle and managed to make a landing in the big lake. After taxiing a few minutes he cut the engine and climbed out on a float in his parka and listened.

Faintly from upwind there came the sound of dogs howling. Starting up the engine he cautiously taxied toward the sound.

The Eskimos were waiting on their rock-bound shore. They were ready with ropes and a boat. Then followed stevedoring and transporting the freight to shore. Gradually the good, round skin tents took shape through the night as Bud strode, a tall rangy figure, up the path with the people to the mounds.

Supper was raw dried caribou meat thrown down on a board on the willow-laid floor. Bud got out his pocket knife and ate.

"We never expect to see airplane today," the Eskimos simply said.

Tobacco, tea, chewing gum. These were quickly pressed into service as Simon Paneak lit the single-mantle gasoline lantern. Outside the wind moaned and the night was black.

Bud sat observing the tent in which he was a guest. The skins of old bull caribou had been used to make it, as they are the toughest and are not considered useful for much else. The long winter hair, turned out to the weather, provided excellent insulation, while the hide side turned in to the inmates was not unpleasant. Right now extra canvas sheeting was additionally lashed on the outside to protect the hides from rotting in the fall rains.

The skins, numbering twenty to thirty to a house, were laced over a frame of mountain willows to form a beehive-shaped structure. A Barren Grounds grizzly hide hung untanned over the doorway, which must be entered on the hands and knees. Erected on rocks in the center of the floor, a little sheet iron stove just like ours burned sticks and roots which must be carried long distances. A cupboard made out of a packing box stood behind the stove, and a battery radio set upon it, its antenna protruding from the housetop!

There were thirty-three people in the group, including several children. One family said they had lived in Fairbanks for several years working for wages but had joined the group by chartered airplane this past spring. Simon wanted to bring a school here to Chandler Lake for the children, a couple of months each summer. He had written the Native Service at Juneau about it, and he had agreed to furnish a tent for a school and another to take care of the teacher.

For two days the fog held. These people, Bud realized, led a strange half life at variance with their modern ideals and aspirations. They wanted a school. They wanted and had radios, blue-flame gasoline stoves, high-powered rifles and airplane trips. Yet they still wanted to live — and were forced to live, by reasons of geography — completely off the country the year round by hunting and fishing.

Around Chandler Lake Bud saw lines of stones tilted on end and recognized that a prehistoric method of hunting caribou was still being practiced to advantage. We had seen the same thing in Canada's Barrens. The lines of upturned stones stretching for miles along the contours of the prairie were used for driving caribou towards the lake. The Eskimos have a word for these lines of stones, *inuksiut,* translated by Dr. Stefansson as "likenesses of men." Caribou are timid, foolish creatures, and once frightened by a few people, they imagine every object along their line of flight to be a man. Hence, rocks only two feet tall in this bare country are all that is necessary to guide the animals into a trap. Whenever a herd came wandering through this valley they were pointed automatically into the lake. Once they were in the water, boats were launched and the caribou were overtaken and speared — a great saving of ammunition. The spears Bud saw were contrived from half of a steel trap spring sharpened and tied onto the end of a pole. The Eskimos knew that a slight puncture in the front of the chest of a swimming caribou collapses the lungs almost instantly. Kills of fifty animals at a time were made in summer. The bulls were killed for back fat, principally. The cows and fawns were usually fed to the dogs while their skins were sought for clothing.

If the band of animals was a small one the hunters would often just lie in wait along their route on the skyline. Because .22 shells and .25–20 shells were cheap, these were the highest caliber used, along with the cruel .22 Hornet. All these guns are good for playing around with but are unfit to use upon big game. They make an explosive shallow surface wound, and in practically all states are illegal to use against big game, as are all .22's, except in Alaska. Bud got a chance to see the theory put into action.

A band of caribou came along the rock markers, trotting nimbly. A hunter from the encampment walked out to ambush them with a .25–20. As the deer passed, the hunter fired perhaps a dozen shots while everybody in camp watched the sport. He was careless and shot at long range, probably because there was plenty of meat in camp.

Bud watched with binoculars. He saw two caribou fall. Three others staggered with broken hips. Two more fell but they got up and followed the other animals, although they lagged behind. At last the pitiful procession vanished up a "draw" with its five staggering cripples. "Hard to tell," as Bud told me later, "how many others in that mass were struck in the abdomen."

When reminded of these cripples the modern Eskimos, unlike all we have supposed true of Hiawatha, replied: "It is no matter. There is plenty of meat."

Stefansson always warned: "Primitive man, armed with high-powered rifles, will consistently kill off his own food supply."

Jack O'Connor, for twenty-five years the chief of the Alaska Game Commission, said:

"Generations of living off the country have taught the natives to kill today, for tomorrow game may be gone. *Kill anything that moves,* as tomorrow it may move out of reach is the natural reaction of such limited intelligence as they possess."

"It is a waste," Bud tried to tell the Eskimos. "The animals that are hit will die."

"They will not die," stated the Eskimos confidently. "They are very strong."

It was explained to Bud in perfectly good English that those animals which did not fall from being shot were always simply "stronger" than the bullet. Such an animal may "throw off" the bullet. Thus the people privately believed that the animals that they crippled would recover in some magical way, or some of them might be spirit animals.

Bud's second experience with the age-old attitudes of the people at Chandler Lake came in regard to death and the disposal of the aged.

"Old man is want to die there," the people told Bud, pointing to a small tent set aside.

Another black night was setting in. "Do you mean an old man is dying right now inside that tent?"

"Yah, he try to die for long time now. He is very old man — my father."

Cautiously Bud peeked into the isolated tent. Dressed in tattered skins (for it is the custom for the old people to be quite unpretentious), an ancient hunter lay in his bedding on the floor. *There was no stove in his tent and no food.*

The old man's mind was wandering some place in the nether regions; he had lost his memory of where he was. He did not know nor recognize the white man, who withdrew at his feeble invectives. Clearly Bud was not wanted here and there seemed nothing to do but get out.

"I am living too long," the old man had said a week before, and according to the story, he had specified that he be put here alone. "I hope I can die now before the ground freezes, so that it will be easy for you," was his main practical concern. He was aware that the season was upon them when the group would soon be on the move, and his old bones ached at the thought of making the long trek again.

Back in Simon's tent the explorer-pilot sat uneasily with the village hunters, playing cards, calling each card by its Eskimo name. As they played they discussed the dying man as they might have discussed the weather.

All of the old man's possessions had long been given away, aside from a small pocket knife he had carried many years. "Bury it with me," he had instructed. "I may not need it when I am dead," he reasoned, "but it is of little value to you anyway. Then, a man can always get along any place with such a good knife if need be."

According to what the people told Bud, the old man must have been around a hundred years old. He was about the age of thirty when he had traveled far, far to the coast and met white men for the first time. He had traded furs and received in return his first rifle. The rifle was a muzzle-loader and these people told Bud that the old man had met explorers coming from the east. Those first white men were Russians! It would have been a wonderful thing if some person could have questioned this old man about his impressions of the first Russian explorers of Alaska.

The old hunter's son and daughter sat in the card game and everybody discussed the problem of making a coffin for him. It was decided that a coffin could be contrived from some of Sig Wien's discarded gasoline boxes.

"I hope the old man can die this time," said his son. "He try once before this time last year, but he could not die."

All present agreed that probably he would die tonight. The wind was dropping, the night broke clear, and the mysterious northern lights came out. "There will be the mark on my tent when I am gone," the old man had promised.

The next morning came clear as a bell. When Bud stepped out of Simon's tent and made ready to depart with the *Arctic Tern* the wild night which had preceded seemed unreal. There were the group of skin tents on their mounds. There were the smiling faces of his Eskimo friends. Everything seemed as usual.

Then, embarrassingly and unavoidably his eyes were drawn to the tent of the outcast old man. Bud started.

There *was* a mark on that tent. Just as the old man had said there would be. A snowshirt was hanging over the tent door as though it were a signal.

Bud strode to the tent purposefully in the bright daylight. He lifted the flap over the doorway. Inside, the tired old hunter lay dead.

13 FALL FREEZE–UP

At OLIKTOK POINT the fall wind howled, all day and all night, and all day and all night again. I slept in my own little nylon tent but I spent the days with Nanny while that blessed woman sewed for me and gave me her big Eskimo smile. Lack of conversational ability was no embarrassment between us. "I know why Nanny is the world's perfect hostess," I thought. "She doesn't expect you to talk."

My nylon tent blew down and then blew down again. Only a windbreak of extra heavy canvas which George provided succeeded in keeping it in this part of the world at all. At night, Nanny's tent seemed awfully far away. In the pale moon's glow I might have been seen (I hoped I wasn't) crawling out of my warm down bed and reaching out the tent on hands and knees to drag in the ax and lay it beside me. It was just an afterthought, a foolish one. I got to thinking about that crazy old Eskimo Cyrus who with his family, lived nearby. Cyrus was queer. Nobody liked him. We had had trouble with him before.

Thinking this, I further improved my defenses by adding to the ax a booby trap of pots and pans placed on precarious balance at the tent entrance as I slept.

Bright, windy morning came. I walked along the ocean front and the drenched sea grasses and over the prairie, warm in my caribou skins, wading pools in boots which bore the imprint of Nanny's strong teeth where she had crimped them. Evenings I stepped out of Nanny's tent and I was enchanted by the romance of the scene before me. I looked out to the North Pole and the sunken sun across that burnished expanse of ice-spotted sea, and I saw for a few minutes that never-never land where the clouds form into bright arrows pointing the way to eternity beyond the realm of mortal man.

The tinkling of the guitar coming faintly from the last primitive human habitation at land's end, the muttered squawks as a flock of black brant came out of the gathering night, veering with a magical rush of wings; the smell of burning driftwood emitted from a camp stove. "When this way of life near nature passes from the earth never to return," I thought, "will not the earth itself and the soul of man find routine artificial existence a dull disappointment?"

Out of the cold gray foggy sea early in the morning came Dave Brower's 30-foot cabin launch from Barrow with the long-awaited provisions for the store. I heard the slow chugging of the boat making its approach, heard people getting up sleepy-eyed. I slept on until 7:15 when, at an hour far earlier than usual, Nanny came to my boudoir to announce that breakfast was ready, and fell into my booby trap of pots and pans.

Now the men were stevedoring and everybody was chewing gum with happy vigor. Martha, Nanny's oldest living daughter with the twisted back, had returned from her first visit away from home, with her lips and cheeks red and in a state of almost hysterical happiness. She related to her family excitedly in the Eskimo language her times in the big city. You would think that big cities had never been discovered by a seventeen-year-old girl before!

Nanny observed her adolescent daughter calmly with wise eyes in which there always lurked a hint of wonder and pain when she looked at this one.

At three one afternoon we heard the sound of an airplane. But presently its droning grew fainter and was lost altogether as it bypassed our camp on Oliktok Point by a distance of some three to five miles inland.

"It might be Sig Wien," Dave said. "He may be going to Barter Island."

Yet we all thought the engine sounded like the *Tern*. If Bud had come straight on to camp there happened to be a hole in the fog at that moment, directly overhead, and he could have come down through it. As it was, the fog closed in right away after that, and day went right on into night without a break. After supper with our tired crew, I crawled into my own tent and sat there in my parka, and put curlers in my hair to sleep, using ice water. There was nothing else to do.

My usually sound repose was much broken by involuntary visions of Bud flying out to sea lost in the fog, or crashing in a spin. Whatever happened, if that was him we heard, he would be out of gas by now.

His boat unloaded of its cargo, it was time for Dave and his crew to pull out. Alice, who was sick, her husband Cyrus, and all their family and all their dogs were loaded aboard; Alice was bound for the hospital at Barrow. Their tent was going along too; they would set it up when they got there.

I hated to see Dave's boat leave before I got word of Bud. It was the last and only contact before freeze-up on the Arctic Ocean.

A few hours after Dave left, Bud came in safely. He had visited Mathew's People as he followed the Colville River down to the coast on his way. From Chandler Lake he had secured choice fawn skins for his own new parka. He had some sheep leg skins for Nanny as a gift from Simon's wife, a bale of *sik-riks,* ground squirrels, which Mathew wanted to trade at the store for tea, and part of which were going to Cornell University's zoological department, and he brought me the fanciest wolf ruff in all Alaska.

It is very important that an Eskimo woman has a fancy wolf ruff. The piece must be cut from a white wolf's mane and only about one wolf in a hundred has the coloration and the thickness of hair that are considered really first class. Finally, Bud unloaded from the *Arctic Tern* six wolverine skins which we caught in the Alatna Valley previously. We wanted Nanny to use the best one for trimming our parka cuffs and hems. The other skins would go for $50.00 each at the trading post, the standard price on the north coast. The people were overjoyed to get wolverine.

Bud meanwhile had traded four white foxes for George to Mrs. James at Hughes in return for special things. Last of all, he pulled out presents for the children. Little Lydia almost cried when she thought Bud had forgotten her, she the child who had once been so afraid of the white people that the very sight of us had sent her weeping under her mother's parka. For Lydia: gaily-colored, hard candy and a box of crayons with a book to color in.

Bud showed signs of hard travel but his enthusiasm seemed to give everyone more lift than they had got out of the whole fifteen tons of supplies delivered here a few hours past.

"When you come here, Bud," as George put it, "it is like a thousand men come for me."

"Oh, Bud, did you get the mail at Hughes?"

"Nope, too heavy to bring." He got a book but it got dropped in Chandler Lake.

"Oh, for heaven's sake. Did you get me some writing paper then?"

No, he forgot it. Was there any world news he had learned? He couldn't think of any.

"You should have a good permanent igloo to live in here now that you are manager of the trading post," Bud told George. Up until this time George and Nanny had for their home only a tent the year round; it had never occurred to them that a house might be nice.

Bud convinced me that we should linger a few days longer to help George build an igloo.

"What if we get caught by freeze-up on the Arctic Ocean?" I asked.

"The freeze-up can't come as long as the fog holds," he replied.

The foggy windy days passed with Bud happy as a lark helping George and the boys to build George's first real house. Bud looked enormous and boyishly gay in his new big furry parka.

A typical igloo is made by erecting a frame of driftwood poles about five or six feet high and about ten feet by twelve feet at the base. All the walls are made to slant in so that the split drift logs will lie tight when they are stacked vertically around the frame. A ridgepole down the center of the roof holds up the roof and slabs. The material used is usually cottonwood, one of the most northerly trees. It drifts down the larger rivers of the world, most of which have cottonwood at their heads, and lodges on the polar beaches where the Eskimos of many lands pick it up, one scattered stick at a time.

Sods stacked against the slanting walls complete the igloo; a skylight is cut in the middle of the roof about two feet square, over which is fitted a pane of translucent stitched sea animal intestine. The Eskimo window is thus not in the wall of the house, but in the roof. The door, small and low to conserve heat, and a very important ventilator shaft in the roof near the stovepipe, go to finish the house.

The floor may be of hand-hewn planks, or of willow twigs over which caribou skins are laid. People live on the floor.

Such a dwelling, when properly made, is so completely weatherproof that a stove only a few inches square, set close to the floor, can heat it. By winter the igloo is, of course, buried in snow blocks cut from the hard-beaten drifts with a saw. A snow alleyway, preferably one with a turn in it if you are located on the windy coast, along with any number of snow "wings" may be added during the winter to accommodate tools, extra clothing, dog harness, frozen meat and unexpected overnight guests.

Such a house is the warmest, the easiest to heat, and the most comfortable to live in of any yet devised for people living an arctic life of hunting and fishing. When Bud helped George as advisory architect on his new igloo there were a few modifications. They used some planks brought by Dave Brower for part of the structure, which helped out on the driftwood, and they had real glass for a windowpane. They put the window in the side of the house, modern style; for day by day living this did not prove to be an asset since snow continually drifted over the window and had to be shoveled away, and the violent coastal winds caused the house to lose heat on the side where the window was.

When George's igloo was done, Bud and I thought the family would move into it right away, for winter was all but here. We were disappointed when George said that it was really better living in a tent until after the snow came, and he had only wanted to get the igloo finished before the ground froze and you couldn't cut sods any more.

During these operations and many others I was usually the photographer. Photography was rendered complicated due to the fact that even momentary exposure of the lens from its own "parka" sheathed it with particles of driving frozen mist. The hard job of arctic photography must be done bare-handed!

The brant and ducks and shore birds were nearly all gone. Only the gulls were happy because shrimps were washed up on the reefs. They were foolish gulls to linger too long. We had seen their fate before. They would wait until the water was closed on all sides, securing their livelihood from some puddle. Finally when the puddle closed they were lost in a frozen arctic world and didn't know where to go. Their feet would freeze first and then their bills. We would see them on the ice-bound shore awaiting a slow end. Freezing to death is not a fast business or an easy death. Sections of the body will freeze days before the whole body itself freezes.

"Bud, George says that a hard freeze will come any time now if we get a clear night with no wind. Today is September 12. George predicts that the deadline is probably the fifteenth."

"I know it," said Bud. "But we haven't had one day yet that I would cross the divide."

We had to get our float ship out of this ocean or it, too, would be like the gulls.

The very next day our chance came to leave. It was our only chance, for even as we took off on that one clear day, the Arctic Ocean was freezing behind us.

Incredibly the *Arctic Tern* carried everything, probably because a stiff wind assisted in the take-off inside the point. The tiny figures of our Eskimo family on the brink sank below the horizon behind us. Over Mathew's Camp on the Colville we dipped our wings and the people knew it was good-by as we headed south.

We flew to Chandler Lake. Because it lay at 2900 feet, Bud explained he would have to make two trips from here to get both us and our remaining stuff home.

For years I, too, had wanted to see Chandler Lake and its group who were supported by a caribou and sheep economy in the arctic interior mountains. The people came from their skin tents as we landed.

About forty-eight years old and in the prime of his vigor, Simon

Paneak made me think, oddly enough, of the popular concept of a Chinese military man. The strong mountain men who stood beside him might be Turks, or Greek guerrillas, or Russians or anything. None looked particularly like what we think of as Eskimo, and I was struck again with the exotic possibilities of their ancestral mixed blood. Like hill people the world over these men, while hospitable, were clannish, rude, vigorous and outspoken. Strange that the most picturesque Eskimos left in Alaska should be at once the most astute, foxy and sophisticated! Simon told me that during the past summer some exploring vacationists from New York City had been brought in here by Sig Wien, where they had camped for several days, participating in the killing of some caribou and taking home-movies.

As we crawled into the headman's residence for our supper, and a side of raw dried caribou ribs and a slab of back fat were thrown down before us, we reflected, getting out our knives, that we were seeing a type of human existence of a passing day in America. Just as our grandfathers saw the last of the old ocher-painted parchment tepees of the Cheyennes, we who lived today were seeing the last of the hunting people of all North America.

"How many caribou do these 33 people and their dogs eat?"

"I would estimate from 600 to 800 a year," Bud told me from his large experience.

Originally, primitive people were not so destructive as they are today because they had not the means to be. Today, it is fashionable among them to support large dog teams which the white man had taught them to use.

Simon Paneak was interested in our cameras, and in return he showed us his. For years he had taken and developed his own pictures. In his family album he showed us films he had taken when he guided the first geologists to the oil seep at Umiat. Here was a broad rear view of a geologist skimming oil. Here were line-ups of many Eskimos we knew, dressed in their best furs, years gone by.

Welcome to me were some ancient *Time* and *Life* magazines, but best of all was the wonderful sleep — a pile of people all lying on the floor together, wrapped in soft caribou robes. The air, creeping gradu-

ally inside the house as the fire died down, was like cold nectar while
we slept; Chandler Lake, lying in a draft which comes down the
canyon, is, as Simon said, in the "hole of the winds." In the night the
loose dogs pushed aside the bearskin door flap and sneaked into the
house to crowd up close to us. They were gorgeous large fat dogs,
and reminded me of luxurious upholstery. One of them was a dappled
green calico dog and it had green eyes. In the night I reached out to
pull my caribou pillow closer about my neck and it let out a yip.

"If you want to stay with Simon you could probably get some fine
pictures here while I make the first trip home," Bud urged.

"No, take me home first." Suddenly I wanted to be in my own home
and I could hardly wait.

In no civilized land would you dare leave valuable cameras and other
equipment stacked on the beach under a canvas to pick up on a return
trip. But in the arctic not only will you be safe from pilfering and
vandalism but the people will inconvenience themselves to see that the
things are cared for. The experience of leaving our things here made
me philosophize.

People can't get away with anything here. But even more than this,
perhaps the main reason is that people living under circumstances
where they feel they have plenty of elbow room do not have as much
of a psychological drive to build up the hostility which would cause
them to harm or cheat their fellow human beings. But in closely packed
masses of humanity the destructive urge smolders dangerously beneath
the surface, where individuals are crowded and frustrated beyond endurance.

It is clear that people in North America can't just go on hunting
buffalo or caribou. But they can try to keep a crowded situation from
becoming worse. They can seek voluntarily to have reasonably small
families, rather than the large old-fashioned family which used to be
the ideal, in order to preserve the necessary resources and the elbow
room.

Spray cascaded over the tail of the airplane as we took off from
Chandler Lake. We were winding up the canyon of the "hole of the

winds," heading for the pass. Outside, the temperature today was nearly zero.

I didn't think there was anything strange about flying a float ship in zero weather. We were warm inside with our cabin heater. It came as a shock when suddenly Bud mentioned, "Say, I can't move the tail rudder. I guess the spray thrown back from the take-off must have frozen the controls."

"You mean we can only fly straight ahead? You can't turn either to the right or to the left?"

"That's what I mean," he said.

It was just as if the rudder pedals had been welded solid. Spray had frozen in the under parts of the tail and on the water rudder which was attached to the tail of one float.

I just sat tight for a few minutes. There was no time to waste in questions and answers, although I felt mighty peeved at Bud.

Bud had to think. I believed he would figure out something. I tried to think, myself, but it wasn't much use.

"Well, can't you force the tail loose?"

"I don't dare stomp hard on the pedals to try to break the ice," he said, "because I might break a control cable, and that would really be terrible. Anyway," he consoled me, "we're heading south. When we get into the warmer climate it will probably thaw out."

As we flew the canyon toward the pass all I thought about was climbing high. We had a heavy load, and the ship was slow to gain altitude.

I saw the canyon wall draw nearer, nearer, and realized that it turned up ahead.

"It's all right," Bud chided, as I involuntarily crowded closer to him for protection. "Now don't work yourself into a tizzy. There's plenty of room to turn and I've still got aileron control."

He demonstrated it nicely. "We used to have to do this in training class," he explained. "I never expected to have to use it, though."

Leaning the airplane partly on its side in a shallow bank by a turn of the wheel in his hands, he let it just have its head, and of its own accord the airplane made a wide gradual turn in its course. We were through the canyon bend.

Bud straightened the airplane out in level flight again. I let out my breath. The slow turn was so smooth that no passenger in the plane would have suspected that it was executed entirely without a rudder.

"See how easily it's done," Bud said. "You looked for a minute as though I told you we had lost the entire tail. Don't worry so. The controls overlap. The only delicate part about doing these maneuvers," he explained, "is that you have to be careful not to slip out of your turn. But modern airplanes won't spin unless forced to."

I shivered. "Now move over to your own side and don't crowd me." I had pushed Bud's large bulk into his own far corner.

Slowly and methodically Bud turned and twisted the ship through the walled canyon. We gained altitude over the pass and flew above the peaks.

Still in a frozen condition we reached the timbered south side of the Brooks Range, where the dropped leaves of the birches were scattered as if some careless artist had spilled his paint.

The snow was left behind; the thermometer slowly climbed as Bud let the airplane glide downward. An airplane permits one to change quickly from one environment to another. Yet that two hours' flight from Chandler Lake was the longest of intense concentration I ever endured. Before we reached home the ice melted from the tail and Bud had full use of the controls as we circled for a landing on Takahula Lake.

I glanced toward our house as we landed on the smooth pane of water, and it was then that I received a considerable setback. The door was wide open! Cautiously we stepped ashore and made our way forward. The story was clear even at a glance. During our absence a grizzly bear had come to call!

Before leaving the lake the last time Bud had taken precautions to barricade the house. Yet the great bear, coming along and discovering the abode, had taken the tin sheathing off the boarded door with one rip of his claws and walked right in.

First we noticed that the bear had torn up the logs that composed our front porch, biting a few right in two. We reconstructed his motives. Discovering some cans of sweet condensed milk inside the house, he had carried them out on the porch and punctured them with big canine teeth. The trickles of sweet milk running from the punctured can went down between the cracks of the porch, eluding him, and that was why he took the porch apart to get at it.

As we stepped into the door, startled tears sprang into my eyes. Our beautiful house was a shambles. Breaking all of my new hand-painted china in the cupboard, the bear had eaten every provision we had stored. Jam, canned milk, catsup, window cleaning fluid, soap chips, boxes of oatmeal, dried meat, a hundred pounds of sugar: all went down his throat mixed with the detergent I used for washing dishes. Flour and beans covered the floor, mixed with broken glass from the shattered mirror in which he must have had the astonishment of seeing himself. The fly sprayer was punctured, the skillet and pots and pans were bitten through. Our relatives' pictures on the walls were ringed with angry claw marks. The water tank lay on the floor where it had been walloped from the wall. He found our clothes underneath the bunk and pulled them out and ripped them. And for dessert he had apparently eaten a box of shotgun shells.

As to the ill-fated yellow canoe which had been left inside the house for safety, he had just stepped over that craft which had been demolished once before in its career. Tipping over the gas lamp on the table, he broke its glass chimney. Our library of books lay as they fell with the stamp of big grizzly feet imprinted on their pages, muzzled with dried saliva. Yet he carried my spectacles carefully out into the yard, where we found them cast miraculously unharmed, their case lying a few yards away.

It was exactly as though a cyclone had struck. But the real damage done only amounted to $50.00. That the bear had suffered some indigestion from his holiday was shown by the huge piles of manure surrounding our house and the near vicinity.

"Get the shovel," Bud instructed, even while I threw up my hands in dismay. "The garden can use that for fertilizer."

A wonderful thing was that while we had been gone our garden on the terraces in front of the house had grown by leaps and bounds.

There were lettuce, turnips, and radishes as big as golf balls, crisp and firm and as sweet as apples.

We started cleaning up the mess and hastened to set the fish net out at once to get something to eat.

"Now you'll never be able to get back and pick up our cameras!" I lamented as night came all too swiftly. "What will we ever do?"

"Oh, I'll get them in a day or two," Bud said, unconcerned with this problem for the moment. It never occurred to him not to get them.

"I know the mountains pretty well by now," he added in explanation. "Next time I'll just climb high and shoot straight for home. If the tail freezes I won't worry. It will thaw out by the time I get south. First, though, I'll have to go down to Hughes for gas, and then Simon wants an order put up, so I'll make a load both ways. It will mean a lot to those people to get a last order before winter."

"Just don't forget my things at Chandler Lake," I urged. "And I left my brassière over there somehow."

The airplane could be flown during only two or three hours each day around noon because its rudder would freeze from splashing spray. The days were clear with the thermometer on the porch rising to as high as 55 degrees, to sink to ten degrees above zero each night. It was time to get a moose. We were mighty hungry for meat. If we hadn't been trying so hard to photograph moose all fall we would have had one three times over.

On his last flight to Hughes, Bud arranged with Johnny James that Johnny would fly up here with skis if we did not appear by November 21 after the freeze-up. We planned to remain and photograph up until the last minute for the lecture tour. On Bud's last trip out on October 7, he found that the Koyukuk River was running ice cakes and he could not land when he got there. He dropped a bullet with a message on it for the Jameses by their door. Then he returned to Takahula Lake for the freeze-up. The main thing now was to get a moose or we would starve.

Our landscape that fall was a riot of mice. They were big red-brown, plump seed-eaters called voles, and everywhere you looked they rustled.

Our Linkanoe had been freighted into the lake before freeze-up period began and was very useful. From picking blueberries which were soft and sticky and burst between your fingers, I went on to pick cranberries which were crisp and mahogany brown on the hill. Crops might fail and the domestic flowers I had planted by summer might never bloom, but nature's harvest of the wild berries, fish and game were our real living. There were not hours enough in the day to gather all our harvest at this season.

Bud set traps all over the place and caught the voles for Dr. Bill Hamilton of Cornell, and together we took their measurements, prepared the tiny skeletons and hides, and listed all pertinent information. It was thrilling to think that here might be some previously undiscovered species that made our lakeshores their abode.

I hastened to finish chinking between all the logs of the cabin with moss for winter; meanwhile we lived as the occupants of a sieve. I contrived lunches of boiled dried lima beans, greens from the garden, gingerbread and tea. "Greens" to start with meant boiled radish tops; then, boiled turnip tops. Both were soon gone. After that greens meant three or four of our individual cabbage plants boiled for a meal; they had never matured. Eating the whole plant or any part of it you can get is the foregone conclusion if you will insist on trying to grow the farthest north garden on the continent. Evenings we read books like *Peace of Mind, Civilization on Trial,* and *War and Peace.*

There were many meatless days when the fish net got nothing. Breakfast was bowls of fresh blueberries with a few corn flakes, powdered milk and sugar, followed by the comforting hot tea and pancakes with cranberry syrup. Lunch was baked corn bread, tea, and individual apple-cranberry pies. All fine, except that you soon get weak on such a diet, and where was the meat?

Where Takahula Valley joins the Alatna Valley below the lake there are many small potholes and vast swamps and forest. At two in the afternoon one day we flew down there, where, carefully estimating wind and distance, Bud effected a landing on the largest of the ponds. We were gathering the last berries of the season when to our great delight, an immense bull moose was sighted across the swamp. Here was an opportunity to get our moose, to photograph the kill, and to freight the meat home with the airplane.

The long evening shadows of the mountains were already cutting across the valley. It was late in the day. But it might be our last chance to get a good specimen, for the moose had reached their maximum condition of fat in preparation for the rut. Once the rut started the moose would wander far and shed fat rapidly, and we might lose out altogether.

Both of us were wet through. Fall gnats whirled about our heads as we staggered across the swamp toward the moose with our bulky photographic and butchering paraphernalia. I got bitten right between the eyes by a gnat, where the swelling grew to baseball size. Bud started off ahead, leading a fast pace over the niggerheads, despite the packboard weighing some forty pounds on his back. All I had to worry about was getting myself up to the moose with the rifle. It was my fifth moose and I knew what to do, but as usual when that right day comes along in the fall, haste was utterly imperative.

I followed desperately, while Bud cast stern glances rearward whenever the willows would slap my boots. At almost every plunge forward we would sink into some crack two feet below the general surface of vegetation, as we traversed the miles of blueberries dangling like long pears and frozen on the bushes.

By nice calculation we reached the proper lake where the moose was, although he had disappeared from sight. Bud pointed to the moss. There were slight dents in it as the moss tried to spring up again from where our quarry had freshly walked. I sighted the moose nearby on the lake margin. You must never shoot big game in water, for not only is it illegal in most places, but you can't get it out of the water after you have shot it. We were lucky to catch the moose on shore. While I shot at 70 yards, Bud photographed. The moose plunged into the brush but he was shot near the heart by the way he acted. Thrusting a special light bullet into my rifle barrel, Bud urged me to advance with care. The light bullet was not supposed to "ruin the meat."

Protesting, I found myself creeping into the brush, although a wounded moose can be dangerous. Fortunately, the great antlers and shoulders were visible, a moment later, where the giant lay prostrate, and the eyes were glazed. We advanced from the rear, threw some sticks, and finally poked. For several minutes we stood back before approaching those powerful legs and hoofs.

It was a tremendous moose! The antlers weren't special, some 58 inches across, but the size of the body underneath them was surprising. We didn't realize how big it was until we tried to roll it over. We tugged and pulled, but could not budge it. Yet we had to hurry. Darkness was falling. The splendid fat animal, whose eye looked belligerent even in death, would spoil if it were not skinned and opened at once to cool off.

Bud was able, with my help, to pull one of the hind legs up on one side and lash it to a tree with a piece of rope, then he tied the front leg to an opposite tree, so that he could get at the belly. With great difficulty we got the insides out and the hind quarters disjointed from the carcass.

Then we began to realize the lateness of the hour, the enormity of the animal and its distance from home. We expected all the time to use the airplane to transport the meat in several flights. It was merely a matter of taking off and then setting one's wings for a landing glide onto the home lake. Just a hop from one puddle to another by air. But it was twenty miles of detouring creeks and ponds and half-frozen swamps if you had to make it on foot from the house and back in a day. What if the freeze-up caught us before the job could be finished? During the time we butchered, we saw the lake in which the moose had just been feeding, glaze over beside us in the sunset, freezing for winter.

Then only did our thoughts turn to our airplane. "We've got to get out of here and get that plane home," said Bud. "These little lakes are all going to freeze tonight and they'll never open up again until next year."

When we killed the moose we never dreamed that the freeze-up was going to occur that very night. Bud led me in the darkness toward the lake nearby which held our dear *Arctic Tern*. Across the swamp we plunged recklessly under a full harvest moon which rose over all.

"We're lucky to have that moon," said Bud, "for I certainly don't relish flying home by night."

We had a hard choice to make. It was either fly by night to our home lake or the airplane would freeze into the ice and be lost!

But even given a moon, how could we dare fly in these remote mountains? To add to the darkness was the complication that we knew that our rudder would freeze solid immediately after take-off.

Still, as Bud said, he could maneuver the ship by aileron control. He could turn by holding her on her side as he had done on the Chandler Lake trips. Yet our valley, surrounded by mountain peaks rising up to six thousand feet, was pretty narrow!

All these factors were being weighed in the pilot's mind as we raced for our airplane, leaving our cameras behind and bringing only the moose tongue with us. Reaching the airplane a few yards ahead of me, Bud turned on the master switch and the red and green wing lights to urge me on. Only then could I see the dim outline of the stranded craft lying there on the freezing lake under the moon.

"Hurry up!" was all Bud had time to say. Should I let him try it alone and wait all night in the swamp to hike home later? Bud wanted me to make up my own mind. It was already made up. I was going on this ride, much as I dreaded it.

I hopped in, fastened my seat belt, and slammed the metal door. Bud checked instruments and controls. It took several minutes to get her started, as she was cold, and he had to whip the propeller by hand. Coughing, she reluctantly moved forward, plowing a swath through the half inch shale ice, acting as an icebreaker.

"Take over while I warm my hands," requested Bud, and I taxied the length of the little pond while ice showered every way. It was necessary to keep the window open so that fresh air could disperse the fast-gathering steam from our breaths which threatened to obscure the windshield.

All too soon for me, we reached the place and moment for the take-off. The wind which had been blowing all day, and upon which we had counted to get out of the little pond, had slackened to a mere night breeze. Could the airplane possibly lift from the short run with the two of us in it? We would try a run. If it wouldn't lift, Bud would be obliged to leave me in order to try to save the plane himself.

If the plane would not take me I planned to go to a certain good stand of timber which we had decided upon, and sit by a big fire until, with first morning light, I could return to the moose to guard it from the birds and squirrels which awake at dawn; there I would wait, eating meat roasted on sticks, until Bud could work his way to me down the Alatna River with the Linkanoe. We only hoped now to be able to use the canoe on the river to get the meat home. At the moment of the take-off I would have been willing to sit out all night, when I thought of the hazards of that ride.

"All set?" Bud asked.

I replied that I was.

"All right. Water rudder, up."

At that moment as Bud pushed forward on the throttle it was too late to inform him that the water rudder was frozen and I couldn't get it all the way up. No need to worry him about that; he had other worries. The water rudder meant an extra drag. But counterbalancing this was the cold of the night. An airplane operates much more efficiently in the cold temperatures.

Because the lake was half-moon-shaped, being in reality a part of the old river bed, we had to take off in a curve. Lickety-lick, up the moonlit lake we skipped nimbly, and before we had covered two thirds of our allotted narrow run, we found ourselves in the air. Flying into the blackness, soaring above swamp and trees, we headed straight ahead up the Alatna Valley, gaining altitude as fast as Bud dared push it. As we left the water the rudder froze into concrete.

Now, heading up the Alatna Valley meant two things. It meant that we were going straight into the mountains northward and it meant that our valley rapidly narrowed, so that a full turn, even with the use of all controls, would scarcely be possible. Bud climbed high and we soared in the night, with controls frozen.

How could we turn aside for Takahula Lake? Could we maneuver between those mountain walls — which took close maneuvering at any time — and make a safe landing upon our home waters?

Bud had made his calculations. He knew perfectly what he was going to do before he took off.

There is a pass between the high ridge which separates the Alatna Valley proper from Takahula Lake. That is, it is more or less of a pass. Bud planned to climb high enough from the take-off point to nicely make this thousand-foot cleft and to gradually turn through it. A short distance beyond — say, two miles away — stood 4000 foot Takahula Peak, guarding the head of the lake. Bud intended to fly through this pass on the ridge, make a big gentle turn to the left, and come back down around the ponds where we started, at a higher altitude; then turn once more in a big arc where the valley was wide, straighten out and glide straight in to the lower end of our home lake.

This is what we did. We cleared the pass by a good two hundred feet, if one can judge by moonlight; made our wide circle, and then made a straight shot for a blind landing on our own lake. This was the only way it could have been done. It was quite a trick to figure out enough space for a wide turn between the mountain walls. With a long, sloppy approach we sank into the darkness upon Takahula Lake.

Landing on familiar water in the night gave little alarm, although we did not hit the water quite right for the wind there. All we cared about was to hit the middle of the lake somewhere. There was just a little squeak of protest and a mild bump from our ice-shrouded undercarriage as we landed. Our landing light — kept off in making the contact, because its beam would only confuse the pilot over water — picked up the little yellow canoe and the big yellow Linkanoe lying side by side on our new dock.

When I got ashore I unashamedly kissed the airplane, cold as that metal was.

"She's a good little *Tern*," said Bud huskily. "She saw us through once again, didn't she? We couldn't have abandoned her."

Bud towed the airplane out to its anchorage using the Linkanoe, and soon it was resting safely on the water, out of the reach of bears, and we were snug in our cabin with a moose tongue and thankful to be alive. Surely, we almost lost the airplane that time.

*   *   *

There is no more bitter day than when you get a high wind and low temperature early in the fall and the ground is still bare of softening snow.

"Better wear your new caribou parka today," said Bud. "I'm wearing mine."

"Better take our sleeping bag with us," said I. "Heaven only knows when this job will be done."

Other provisions were tea, sugar and salt in little glass jars, a boiling pot and some forks, cups and spoons, an ax and a berry sack. Leaving home garbed as Eskimos, we paddled the big yellow canoe to the head of the lake and portaged over to the Alatna with one rifle and one packboard. At the Alatna we were met by an arctic mountain river crowded with slush ice and drifting ice pans.

"Oh, well," we thought, "we can navigate downstream all right through this stuff. Of course getting back home with the canoe and the moose will be tough. But we've got to get that moose at all costs."

As we made our way down the river the whole Alatna Valley was the object of a sand blast. Sand hung 200 feet in the air. The wintry sun in our faces, reflected on ice cakes and water, burned rings around our sunglasses. We were cozy in our furs, handling our paddles with waterproof sealskin mittens. The river was low and in some places we would scrape bottom and would have to get out and wade with the canoe. In other places the river perversely turned backwards and we had to thrash water for our lives in the stiffening wind to make an inch of progress. There were five ice jams spanning the river, some caused by ice cakes becoming piled up in a bend, others caused by still water freezing over in a thin glaze. The first we portaged around by successive packs along the long exposed beaches. The second kind Bud scooted the empty canoe over, using it as a sled, pushing it ahead of him while he plunged through shale ice like a long-legged moose following the shore.

At noon we sat on a beach with our backs to the wind, and while the wind ruffled our parka hoods, Bud munched frozen corn bread, in an Eskimo dress of yellow, and I munched in strawberry pink, fringed with white wolf.

After fifteen miles of this travel we reached the moose kill. We were able to beach our canoe nearby. There was only time to roast a side of good ribs, chop ice for tea water, and gather a cup of blueberries which had turned to raisins. Thus we had a complete menu for supper. Using our nylon former tent floor, which was also the airplane engine cover, Bud rigged a windbreak beside the moose; we slept under this open-air awning in our down bag on spruce boughs and chunks of the moose robe.

Never had I seen a more beautiful animal when it was dressed out. The back fat alone must have weighed a hundred pounds. The live animal was probably nearly a ton. All was safe, despite the fact that a marten had been by to investigate and a very familiar grizzly track covered our own footprints of the day before. A strong adverse wind blowing had prevented the big bear from discovering the prize.

The same strong wind blew next day. After a breakfast of dripping ribs and one lower leg bone of raw frozen marrow, we finished the butchering quickly. I picked over the frozen stomach and intestines, stuffing the handfuls of fat into my sack. Then we hauled the meat trip by trip on our backs through the brush, down the cutbank, and out on the beach to the canoe. Each load had to be wrapped in the nylon sheet to protect it from the sand blast, else in a few careless moments all the meat would be ruined. Next came the ferrying of each load across the river to the shore on the homeward side. When one of the canoe thwarts cracked from a load, Bud lashed a log pole across it to hold it together. With the completion of the delicate ferry command through wind and shifting ice cakes, Bud cached all the meat upon a nearby frozen pond where the ermines and shrews would not be likely to find it. He covered the meat with brush to guard it from the eyes of birds, set traps around it, and hung white rags on the bushes to scare the wolves, foxes and wolverines away.

It took Bud a month to carry the moose home. He made eighteen trips altogether from the cabin, totaling a distance of twenty miles to the trip, and brought it home in ninety pound packs. Because the river froze, he even had to carry the canoe home!

But those twenty-five pound prime rib roasts we ate in the cabin were a just reward, and as Bud queried, where else in the world today can a man work a month and pay for what amounted to two thousand dollars worth of meat? We always considered in the arctic that we consumed around $8000 worth of meat and fish a year, which is a diet few people can afford because the earth cannot maintain it for many.

We believed this high protein diet to be responsible for the prodigious health and strength in which we flourished. Even our pet, Easy-Weasel, ate more meat a year around our cabin than the average American family. We easily disposed of the whole moose that fall, including its fifty-pound liver and its big gelatinous nose (an Alaskan delicacy), before we left Alaska for the lecture tour. Before going on tour each year we were usually fortified by our yearly moose.

I dried some of the meat and fat for next season's trail rations. I put all the extra tallow through the meat grinder and rendered it out into cans for storage. Boiling the head bones, I added smoke flavoring and cooked cornmeal mush and poured this into long pans for breakfast scrapple, which is an old Philadelphia dish. We had suet puddings made with molasses and dried fruit and tallow, and we had steaks and ribs and hamburgers, which if you make them from a moose you call moo-burgers and if you make them from a caribou you call booburgers. We wallowed in blueberry pies, and after the first snow I contrived a wide variety of snow ice creams and sherbets for dessert. As if this weren't enough, the trout which refused to bite all summer long, struck eagerly on the surface at our lures as soon as fall weather came. You could select the individual fish you wanted in the lake by casting to it just as though it lay on display behind a pane of glass. These were the junior trout, all of a uniform two pound size. Their flavor, which was relatively indifferent during the summer, improved steadily into winter, for it is during the winter months that fish, like game, at

Bud and Connie and a nice bull moose

Bud carrying the moose antlers

Bud sleds meat home over the frozen slough

Hanging moose meat up to dry

the opposite season of their rut (or spawning) tend to put on fat again toward the next summer.

Takahula Lake always freezes last in the fall after all adjacent bodies of water have long since frozen. It is a deep, sizable lake and there is a considerable lag because of the radiant heat it has stored during the summer, which it takes time to disperse. The fact that it has no inlet and an insigificant outlet isolates it. Some days I worked with Bud packing moose meat, and of course photographed the whole process. We would come home so starved that we could eat practically all we carried. Bud wrote in his diary:

> Tonight we are nearly starved and a real feeding is in preparation. There is a great roast, fig pudding, gravy, mashed potatoes, and I don't know what other surprises Connie has in store for me.

During the fall we were obliged, on several occasions, to sweep the airplane with the household broom, when wet snow and frost crystals commenced to freeze on it. We had to wash all the salt water spray off it from the summer's work. Bud had to flip its propeller periodically to keep it in working order during those weeks that it stood outdoors unused. This lubricated the inner parts of the engine with oil so that they would not rust or corrode. Just before the lake was due to freeze we hauled the airplane out of the water and up on the bank, by contriving a series of ropes and pulleys.

I made a fruit salad of cooked rice, chopped marshmallows, apples, fresh frozen cranberries and cream (powdered milk), and we sewed window curtains. Bud fried rare moose steaks larger than any cow's over the coals in the big rock fireplace and I made French fries and a tapioca pudding. It is amazing what a high life you can live if you just have a good moose. At that time I had only two cans of food, which lay untouched upon the shelves. In the United States if I went to market I would spend $20.00, and the refrigerator would be empty within three days. Here the refrigeration was furnished by nature and $20.00 worth of powdered milk, powdered eggs, sugar and flour, would last all fall.

Bud asked that I step out on the porch and bring in the birds' feeding can to thaw out. It was full of frozen food that they couldn't get at and so it needed a cleaning. I went out and to my surprise I found a large bar of sweet milk chocolate in the birds' feeding can! How did that ever get there? The answer was written on the wrapper of the chocolate bar:

> TO CONNIE: From the Chickadees, the Camp Robbers and Easy-Weasel. The days are lonely when you are gone, and cheer follows your return. This is a slight token of our love.
>
> SIGNED BY ALL WITH AN X

Wasn't that nice of all my forest friends?

The time of 4 P.M. on October 21 can be given as the official freeze-up of Takahula Lake that year. Trapped as it was between its mountain walls and unable to escape, the sullen ice began to bellow and groan as cracks by the pressure ripped down its diamond-studded length. A succession of clear days were followed by frosty nights, lit by a never-setting moon which drifted around and around the horizon, while the northern lights — the Valkyries of arctic Norway — came out riding again on their white chargers across the heavens.

At felling timber Bud slipped and cut his thigh with the ax. Nothing serious; about a half inch deep through his trousers. It scarcely bled. Repairs in the house with a Band-Aid. Then he put on a display of running, leaping and jumping to demonstrate to me that he was all right.

We took movies of felling a giant tree on the hill. Bud performed beautifully, hoisting the tree on his back.

Bud took time-exposure movies of the arc of the sun with the camera mounted firmly on the tripod. This kept him running up and down the path from the dock for four hours, bursting in and out of the house where we were reading intermittently from *Human Fertility the Modern Dilemma*. Bud was dressed all in fur, in his fanciest white wolf pants. I made chocolate fudge set with nuts and raisins, and we began fishing under the ice with the new 150 foot net.

It meant quite a change in living habits when, on November 14,

Bud said the ice on Takahula Lake was thick enough for a take-off, and we left to fly out of Alaska back to the United States.

To thaw out the *Arctic Tern* from its sleep, the following method was put into effect: At the time the lake ice was four inches thick Bud cut several big panes and stood them on end for this occasion. With these panes we built a little shelter for the nose of the airplane, using snow and water mixed to a slush, in my dishpan, for cement. On the morning set for our departure we easily pushed the airplane from its berth on the sloping bank down onto the ice into its ice shelter. Erecting the little camp stove on logs inside the ice house, we fired it up, placing the tent over the top with the stovepipe sticking out.

My job was to fire the stove and watch that it did not set the airplane on fire. Many airplanes are burned up in the north each winter in the process of "fire-potting" them.

Bud finished the last chores of packing supplies and closing the house. When the propeller bounced against compression Bud knew that the engine was ready to start. Pouring in warm oil which I had heated on the stove, Bud flipped the propeller while I held the tail. We broke down the ice house quickly.

By this time it was 11 A.M. and we had been going since six.

A snow storm started blowing in, and it began to look like a bad day. But the storm was coming from the north and we were going south.

We had found that storms usually came with warm weather. It was the warm temperature we wanted and if the storm came with it, no matter. It is not advisable to try to take an airplane off ice with floats at any time; if you must do so, it is best to pick a day that is not colder than ten below zero because the metal bracing on the floats gets brittle, and there would be a likelihood of breaking one of the parts on take-off.

Bud hadn't flown for several weeks while the plane was confined to the ground during the freeze-up. He had never tried to use a float plane on ice before, although we heard that northern bush pilots occasionally did it.

First, Bud made a trial taxi run out on the lake. As the wind had made drifts of snow alternating with glare ice, the *Arctic Tern* bucked like a wild horse even in taxiing.

Bud came back to our shore for me and I got in. We shot over the glare ice, sprang and fell over the drifts, and finally jumped into the air. It was a scary take-off, wondering if some part of the landing gear might break at the series of impacts. An airplane on floats is not equipped with any springs in its landing gear. Ordinarily the water is expected to furnish the cushion.

Through heavily falling snow we made it to Hughes by flying just 300 feet above the winding riverways all the way. We had barely enough gas to get there. Bud's planning on gas was not carelessness but precision. We could not have got off with a full load. We must have a light plane with practically empty tanks to make the landing on the Hughes field with floats.

There was absolutely no snow on the ground when we got to Hughes! We circled forlornly while the gauges said empty on both gas tanks and our friends below came out to wave encouragement. As we circled the field I expected to hear the engine stop; when you turn an airplane on its side with the gas low, what little gas is left is pulled to one side of the tank by gravity and by centrifugal force.

There were a few snowflakes in the air. From where I sat I could see one big float sticking out ahead, as we settled over broken river ice and sank toward the Hughes field. The big floats seemed to be searching for water but there was none. In slow motion I saw the bare field come up to meet us, and then suddenly it was shooting by. Bud brought the nose of the ship up so the keels of the floats would contact the ground evenly.

There was a slight jar. We rocked forward against our seat belts. I heard the engine roar as Bud applied full throttle to keep the ship from nosing over, and then we were standing still on the runway.

We had skidded but forty feet. We climbed out and down off the floats. The *Arctic Tern* towered above us, standing there on her big floats on the bare field.

It was to be a quick flight back to the United States on wheels, using the regular landing fields all the way.

It was always our custom to stay up most of the night when we visited Hughes and have homemade ice cream and talk.

"You two worry the life out of folks, staying up there at that damned lake," the Jameses would always say.

While the snow fell next day all over Alaska, Johnny James helped Bud take off the floats from the *Arctic Tern,* and store them under the fish cache at Hughes for next summer's return.

14 WINTER PHOTOGRAPHY OF THE ARCTIC

THE LIFE of the well-fed lecturer is one of indolent physical ease but great nervous debilitation. Five months of lecturing is enough to pack the lecturer off to a sanitarium if he doesn't take care. We tried five once. Three months usually was all our health could take and the close of that period found us yearning once more for arctic air and the weak tea of the explorer.

We flew our first *Arctic Tern* back to the United States straight to the Cessna Aircraft factory at Wichita, Kansas. Strangers, we just walked in there and introduced ourselves one day. The officials were much impressed with the exploits of the little ship and agreed to give us a profitable exchange on a brand new one, thereafter selling it to a South Seas mission where it went to spend its days. The second *Arctic Tern* we flew to Alaska the next spring direct from the factory on wheels. Having completed a season's work with it, after seven months we sold it in Alaska to a private individual who neglected to funnel the water and dirt out of his gas with a chamois cloth — as we all had to do in primitive lands with great care; he had a bit of trouble with his gasoline which he overcame successfully after some set-downs. Our third *Arctic Tern* we sold to Sig Wien and it left the day after sale on a rescue mission to a submerged town on the Yukon, and that ship still does much good work in Alaska. The fourth *Arctic Tern* was again sold to Sig (who transferred our credit to the Cessna factory), and one of his pilots turned it upsidedown on floats in the John River, but it was ultimately recovered.

All our airplanes were painted alike with *Arctic Tern* on either side of the fuselage. They could hardly have been told apart except that the first two were Cessna 140's and the second two were Cessna 170's, the larger four-seat model. Because subjects in the arctic cannot always be completed in one year of work, we painted our airplanes alike in order that scenes in our films might be spliced together from various years. Also, we had a strong sentiment about the *Arctic Tern*. We always regarded "it" as one ship, although it actually grew into many.

The four-place Cessna 170 has a 120 pound baggage capacity which we were able to increase to a pay load of 750 pounds by taking out the back seats.

This ship cruises at 120 miles an hour, has a rate of climb of 690 feet a minute (at sea level), a service ceiling of 15,500 feet, holds 42 gallons of gas and weighs empty 1185 pounds.

It gave us satisfaction as we gazed upon the third *Arctic Tern* to realize that it would fill a good-size hotel lobby. Although its engine was a 145 horse, in general it looked exactly like the smaller airplanes, except that we had a special red paint job done on its wing tips and its big tail fin, like the army has on its B–29's which fly out over the polar ice.

We were bound yet further north. We were going out north of the continent to make a picture, and the red markings were for identification in the ice. With the larger ship we could do this — although it was still a very small airplane for such a project — and what's more, Bud and I need never be separated from each other again in the arctic, we thought.

While we were in the States Bud got his Commercial Pilot's License. He passed his exams with a grade of 100 per cent — an unheard of thing. He also became a member of the A.O.P.A. (Aircraft Owners and Pilots Association), in which fliers have banded together internationally to promote private aviation.

It was always fun visiting the Cessna Plant in Wichita where all the Cessnas are born. We were getting to be old-timers there and like one of that big family. Don Flower, Sales Manager, had taken us into his home many times for dinner. It had gotten to be a habit for us to spend Thanksgiving with his family sometimes when we were on the road. Duane Wallace, President of the corporation, with his lovely wife and two little girls, were special friends of ours — a relationship which grew in mutual respect over a number of years. Wallace got into the aircraft manufacturing business as a young Kansan who first won trophies and prizes in air races, and that gave him his first capital to start with. Every one of the men in the aviation business were young men. They had had various picturesque careers which gave them a sense of adventure in life and a willingness to take a "flyer" on various projects. We saw them in hard times making furniture to stay in business. We saw them increase their sales of airplanes steadily, invading one country after another until Cessnas were distributed practically all over the world, until Cessnas beat the fabulous Taylorcraft and Piper Cub in national sales, which was their greatest day. We saw them later go into ten and twenty million dollar orders for observation ships for the army. But Cessna remains the builder of airplanes for the public primarily.

An airplane in which you travel soon comes to seem like an animate thing. Our Cessna friends at their beautifully landscaped plant, from the executives to the test pilots, told us that it is not often, when they try to get an especially nice job off the assembly line, that they succeed in getting hold of an engine so perfectly tuned as this one.

Making engines is like making violins. They are all a little different. You can never tell for certain how an individual job will turn out. Some seem jinxed for no reason at all, while others make the angels sing. Ours was the latter kind. As we took off there in what is known as a "Wichita calm" — fifty-mile-an-hour wind — we knew then that she was going to prove a darling.

Our load was confused and miscellaneous. A manufacturer of cold weather clothing for the armed forces had given us some beautiful wool shirts in bright colors and a variety of fancy aviation suits to try out. With us we had the old sleeping bag and the primus stove; a .30–06 rifle; a caribou-hide portfolio carrying maps and papers; an airplane tool kit, somewhat larger than before; tie ropes; an army duffle sack with our furs which had been on lecture tour; a small kit of toilet articles and a few pounds of emergency food. We made it non-stop to Cheyenne and on to Dillon, Montana, the first day.

It was a thrilling experience to fly north each spring and see the flocks of ducks, snow geese, swans and cranes on their way. In Canada we made many friends as we passed. From lunch at the modern airport counter at Edmonton, we went on to sleep at that primitive but clean little hotel which is the landmark of Fort St. John, British Columbia. Because the roads were unpaved it was common during the spring for the taxicab to get stuck between the town and the airport, in which event the passengers were thoughtfully equipped with shovels. In the movie house that night, when the lights came on after the show, some people hailed us. It was our friends of the stomach ulcer.

There was a lunch to look forward to at Watson Lake, to whose personnel we had become familiar figures. We had spent a gala Saturday night with the air force officers and their wives on the trip outside last fall. Then came that part of the trip which means following the Alaska Highway winding into the mountains of the Yukon Territory. I have never seen it when it was not sleety and fog shrouded. There are several emergency fields in between with which we were well acquainted, formerly with the smaller airplanes, where we had been held over sometimes for days. But flying to Alaska with a Cessna 170 on wheels was merely a matter of about three days.

From Whitehorse we flew to Northway, Alaska, where I landed right into the middle of a women's club meeting. The women had driven seventy miles on the Alaska Highway from Tanacross and Tok for a home economics demonstration in rug making.

It was early in the season in April, one of those gorgeous days which come just before spring breakup when the sun in an azure sky bakes down on white snow and green spruce forest, giving promise of the awakening of spring yet to come. Although when spring does come, it brings disappointment. After the water opens in the north it seems colder again, and there are long days of fog and drizzle yet to endure.

Today was enough to make you weep at the sheer magic of being alive in this world, almost too precious to bear. In fact I did spill a few tears into my prime ribs *au jus* at the Whitehorse Hotel. We flew on. Bud dived at a yellow wolf standing on a frozen lake while I did my stuff with the movie camera — always ready on my lap.

We reached Fairbanks at 7:30 that evening just as a melancholy stratum of clouds moved in and obscured the sun. Weeks Field, unpaved, was a terrifying sight. Part of it was in mud, used by wheel ships working south; part of it was left in snow as a ski strip, for ships working north; and the rest was in water. We landed, and the same old customs inspector was there to meet us when our wheels touched the icy, pitted municipal airport; he charged us $9.75 for his services because we landed on a Sunday.

We had seen a lot of towns and a lot of airports since we left Alaska last November, but we were shocked at how primitive conditions were here. One soon forgets.

Piles of discarded cardboard boxes and trash, beer cans, bailing wire, old bicycle parts, lay in puddles of slush and filth as we ducked under parts of airplanes and crawled through Sig Wien's newest hangar into the inner offices. Sig's regular hangar had burned down during the winter. Over the door some wit had put up an elaborate sign which read: COCKTAIL LOUNGE, and in here were littered desks, a telephone, more bicycle parts, and a combined toilet and shower for the use of pilots which was sadly in need of an overhaul. We saw Sig at once about installing our skis for our new, larger-sized *Tern*, even before attending to our own lodging.

Taking our overnight bag we made our way five blocks along the mostly unpaved streets toward the downtown hotels. The lobbies were mudholes from the tramping boots of the clientele. It was impossible to keep any spot clean at breakup time.

We tried every hotel in town. My heart sank even as we crossed the lobbies filled with bearded men sleeping in chairs. Again I saw Alaska for a moment with the outsider's perspective as we were turned away homeless. The American Automobile Association had predicted that 185,000 cars would come up the Highway to Fairbanks this coming summer. What did they expect to find — the promised land?

At last we got a room on the third floor of the decent Fairbanks Hotel. The woman said that there had not been a vacancy for three years. We stepped in the moment someone checked out. Hotels in Fairbanks do not take reservations, for all out-of-towners come from the bush. There are no other towns; out-of-towners have no way of making reservations in advance.

All day Bud and I ran around town on those errands which always engrossed us during our brief sojourns in the terminal city. Skis for the airplane had been brought inside it from the factory, and we were able to get a tail ski due to the fact that an owner had cracked up his plane. A few days before great winds had turned all the airplanes on the field upside down, in which position many still remained, stuck in snowbanks. Wet snow fell, turning into rain, even as our skis were being attached in the hangar. Only a small section of the runway was left for ski craft.

We worried what we would do if that last ski strip melted before we could get off for the arctic. As the Fairbanks streets turned to water, we waded gingerly and detoured through alleys and over people's housesteps, while others now wore rubber hip boots. Of course, our waders were out at our cabin.

I was waiting for Bud in the lobby when a young man with a crew haircut came striding by. He was Dr. R. D. (Bob) Hamilton, biologist from the Museum of Zoology, University of Michigan, a fellow member of the Arctic Institute. Bob's great interest was in the distribution of frogs — and how far north they went — "A study of the ecology of Rana sylvatica in relation to permafrost, season, foods, and adaptations." Had he met Giddings yet? No, he had been out at the college all day and met a lot of the others, but had missed Giddings.

"I'll get Ruth on the phone right now," I said. "They will want you to come out with us tonight."

We took a cab out to the campus of the University of Alaska, where we clambered through snow in the woods to reach the Giddings's log cabin on the hill.

Ruth and Louie were snowed in and couldn't use their car. The sink was frozen and stopped up. But Ruth was always the perfect wilderness wife. She could make a dinner on a shoestring. The baby, who had grown immense, was playing on a polar bear rug before the fireplace, and they had a new Norwegian elkhound left by a Scandinavian scientist who was off to the other side of the world. Ruth made a Mexican dinner that night, in memory of our mutual heritage of the southwest. Louie told about a skeleton of a prehistoric man found by Dr. Rainey.

A caribou hoof protruded from the end of the skeleton's spine! As the scientist carefully uncovered it, he saw that a long slender piece of ivory had been thrust through the spinal column and the spinal cord of the human pushed out. The ivory was pushed thence into the skull of the man and finally protruded from the mouth in the shape of a small carved hand. Thus the entire skeleton was impaled in what would seem an ingenious and almost impossible way. We all shivered. The Eskimos of a thousand years ago knew how to literally remove the marrow from a man's bones.

Ruth said she was going out into the arctic this coming summer with Louie and expected to take the baby on her back.

"I think at last we're really on the track of something big," was all Louie would confide, but his face glowed. The discoveries they were to uncover were to make the front page of the *New York Times*. The little family that summer found "a new form of culture which appears to be the most ancient yet recorded for the Eskimo era."

Bud practiced take-offs on skis. Handling a ski ship was different still. The skis would freeze down on the soggy snow if the airplane stood parked for so much as a minute; it was necessary to shake it loose manually and then jump in to go. We had shaken many a dog sled loose the same way before now.

Bud found it difficult to make a turn on skis if a strong wind was blowing, much as it is difficult to turn out of the wind on floats, for the airplane wants to weathercock. How many times on skis it was to be my duty to jump out and grab one frigid, slippery wing end and hold the ship so that Bud could apply power and turn it onto the runway for the take-off! The chilly blast from the propeller as Bud gunned the motor to make the turn made this job none too pleasant, while I was usually dragged along the ground by the unmanageable airplane, only to lose my grip and be sent spinning headlong into a snowbank.

Once the airplane got straightened out on the runway, I would climb in, slam the door shut on my side, and away we would shoot. Over the snow the smooth skis would take us, and after a few preliminary jumps we would be in the air. Although many northern bush pilots like Johnny James prefer flying on skis to any other type of landing gear, I always felt a little squeamish about them as it seemed to me an airplane might easily start skidding and get thrown. This, however, never proved to be the case.

We were lucky to get off just as the Fairbanks field turned to water. Another day would have been too late. In a couple of hours we were winging over snowbound Hughes, where Johnny James's Stinson was parked on its skis below.

"We've got a new electric freezer for the ice cream that holds five gallons now," Mrs. James greeted us. It was as though we had never left the bosom of that family circle the months past.

"Pick yourself out twenty pounds of food from the store," Bud told me. "Anything your little heart desires."

"Oh, Bud, only twenty pounds? Isn't this new airplane big enough to hold a little more, for heaven's sake?"

"You can see for yourself we've got a full load of equipment now," said Bud. "Nanny's new sewing machine and material for new parka dresses and all. Would you want to leave that?"

In the end it always seemed that no matter how large the airplane, it never was large enough. The larger plane meant you carried more cameras and you had to carry more gas in order to be able to fly.

We flew to Takahula Lake in the morning before lunch. After a few preliminary circles we landed upon the snow-covered lake; the old snow shirt that Bud had tied to a pole on the ice for wind sock was still flapping as we last left it. The airplane plowed deep into the snow on the lake and settled with a heaviness that showed it was not going to be easy to get off again with a load.

"Do you suppose the bear has wakened?" I asked. All winter long we had kept asking ourselves that, wondering if our cabin was all right. Of course we might have killed him to have got rid of him. Many people would have done this.

We had endeavored to make our house safe from the bears. Realizing the futility of keeping them out by physical means alone, we employed psychological means. A welcome mat of spikes on the porch discouraged marauders from approaching the door. Several empty five gallon gasoline cans hung from the roof and from the adjacent trees, so that they would bang together in the wind, making a noise. Thus we hoped in this way to fool the animals into believing that we were always at home.

Fortunately the bear had not come out of hibernation. The cabin was safe. We floundered ashore, sinking in to the hips with each lunge. Crawling up the bank on our hands and knees, pulling ourselves up by spruce boughs, we reached the house, unlashed the log which was bound across its door, stepped inside, and put on our snowshoes. After unsealing the house there came trip after trip on snowshoes to unload the airplane and to beat down a "yard" for it where it would be safe from settling. Sticks of stove wood placed under the skis kept it from freezing down.

We had stayed at Takahula Lake over the spring breakup before now, and we knew by experience that we must not linger. It had been a warm winter and the condition of the snow was already such that a layer of water lay on the surface of the lake ice underneath the snow; all you had to do to get a bucket of water was make a shallow hole in the snow with the shovel and the water would come right up. This made it convenient for getting water but it also made it dangerous, for if the heavy airplane should break through the crust into this slush beneath we might lose the airplane. It would not be long, furthermore, before the ice itself would become unsafe. The way ice breaks up in a lake is an interesting thing. The rays of the sun apparently shatter the ice. The crystals separate from each other into vertical spikes about the size of a baseball bat. With the slightest pressure the ice, which may be three or four feet thick, may suddenly give way with no warning. Even thick ice, when it approaches this stage of rottenness, becomes unsafe to walk or land an airplane on.

We lingered at Takahula Lake only long enough to take a quick inventory of things in the house, repack the *Arctic Tern,* and get a few fresh fish from under the ice. The way to tell a good fish is by the width across its back and the curve of its belly line from nose to tail. We selected those whose bellies hung down.

In the twilight of the evening we saw a large wolverine come plowing through the deep snow. Following the shoreline he came almost up to the house while we watched from our window. He had a sturdy stride, swerving neither to the right nor left. Most creatures of the wilderness would give way before him. Never numerous at any time even in a state of nature, the wolverine has all but vanished from North America. It always irked us to read magazine articles embroidering on the superstitions already held by the public about the wolverine. It seemed a shame that there should be open season all the year around on wolverines in Alaska. For ourselves, we could see no reason to shoot the rare little wanderer of the wilderness.

Our take-off from snow-covered Takahula Lake with a big load was the worst I thought I had ever experienced. Bud said, "Oh you always say that."

After three trial runs we made it on the fourth. The snow, with water beneath it on the surface of the ice, was soft and squashy in the troughs, but at intervals of every thirty feet lay a hard-beaten drift. The airplane got its flying power by hitting just the tops of these hard drifts. Then it would fall upon the next drift with a crash, and bound into the air again. When we finally lumbered into the air to stay there, we had used all of the lake and we were pale and shaken.

"Did we break anything?" Bud kept asking me, as I craned my neck close to the Plexiglas window on my side.

"We've still got our skis with us."

We turned then into the snowbound Brooks Range, and headed straight north.

Many sheep tracks and "yards" covered the sides of the peaks on our way up the canyon for Iniakuk Lake. It was a good sight. Bud was grateful for a clear sky and bright sun which would cast shadows when we emerged upon the white featureless arctic coastal plain.

On a dull day it would be dreadful to fly there. Navigation must be perfect even on a good day; there must be no missing the mark to hit Oliktok Point.

"Always check your airplane carefully before each flight," was an axiom that every flyer knows. Bud faithfully followed these instructions but neither of us could have foreseen that from an unknown quarter would come an unexpected danger of which we never would have dreamed. . . .

The day was ideal. We had range enough with the bigger plane to go nonstop to the north coast — about 350 miles across the least known part of Alaska, with mountains about half the way. The temperature was slightly below zero. On our route, and for many miles in all directions, there wasn't even a trapper's cabin.

Bud of course had checked the gas and oil, given the skis and shock cords the once-over, and worked the controls to be sure that everything was free and unfrozen. The brand new airplane purred like a kitten. Bud and I relaxed in our furs. There was only quiet steady sailing across a dazzling world. With the spring sun pouring through the windshield, it was easy to go to sleep.

We were over the roughest part of the Brooks Range, nearly half way to our destination. Bud glanced at the instruments from time to time. "You fly awhile and I'll sleep," he told me, and as I took over, he dozed off.

Bud had been to sleep a few minutes when "Whop!" something let loose. Then, "Clank! Clatter! Clank!" A horrible sound, as though the airplane were ripping apart, shot through our nerves. Bud grabbed the throttle from me and eased back on it. I wondered what I had done now. What was it? The answer was soon apparent. The cowling was coming off.

The right side of the cowling ripped open before our startled eyes and started to flop like a bird's wing. With a shudder it then reared up and turned half around. We were cruising at 115 miles per hour; Bud reduced the speed to 70 as quickly as he could. It seemed as if at any moment the wildly-flapping cowling would either foul the propeller or break the windshield, to wrap around our necks.

We scanned the country. The fiercest crags in arctic Alaska lay below. One by one the screws that held the other side of the cowling in place began to work loose. Ping! the screws would strike the windshield as they ricocheted back. In a few minutes more the whole covering of the engine might be ripped free.

"Put her into normal glide and I'll get on the radio," Bud said.

He tried to get Bettles on the Koyukuk River but was unable to make a contact.

He had already picked his emergency landing. In the arctic we have what are called overflow glaciers. These are not real glaciers. They disappear entirely in the summertime, but during the nine-months-long winter they form in canyons by the continuous trickling of some little stream. The water keeps flowing and freezing down, and then the stream bursts out above through the ice and overflows on top again. This cycle of freezing and overflow continues all winter, until by spring many canyons have become paved smooth and blocked with great plugs of ice. The ice may form to a depth of several dozen to several hundred feet. The overflow glacier may be several miles long in some canyons. Such a glacier would make an ideal ski landing strip if it were not for the fact that it is always in the process of overflowing and freezing. You can usually suspect that some open water lurks in such a place even at 70 below zero. The ice may be in any stage, from just forming to several inches thick, and the water under it may be from an inch to three feet deep. About ten miles from us as we glided down, there lay such a glacier in a very steep canyon.

We had been flying at 10,000 feet in velvet air. When we lost altitude it became rough as we met air sweeping down through the canyon. The cowling held quietly braced by the wind. Bud kept the speed just above 50 miles an hour by using the landing flaps. The stall warning was just going wild and another screw had popped out as we limped over the overflow glacier. Clouds of steam blew from the open water at its head, but large frost crystals showed on the smooth green ice near the lower end.

"That ice will hold all right," Bud reassured me. We were thankful that years of snowshoeing around similar places gave us a basis of experience by which to judge the ice. As we dropped into the white canyon far north of treeline we both knew we wouldn't climb out of there again until that cowling was fixed.

In a thirty mile wind we came in and landed almost on one spot. We didn't slide seventy-five feet.

I pressed against my window watching the ski on my side. "Water coming slowly up in our tracks behind us," I announced. As the airplane slowed, I wondered, then decided it was all right. "The ice is just bending a little," I reported. "It's just soggy, that's all."

"We won't dare linger here long," said Bud.

The ice proved to be an inch or so thick over perhaps a few inches of water sandwiched in between the truly solid ice of the glacier beneath. Cautiously Bud climbed out and made his way along a ski up to the engine.

"Hand me the tool bucket behind you."

The cowling had only three screws left, holding it in place but to our immense relief it wasn't at all damaged. A few rivets were broken, but in a matter of minutes Bud straightened the cowling out and snapped the trunk fastener locks back into place. He replaced the lost screws with extras from the airplane emergency kit.

Exactly twelve minutes elapsed from the time our skis touched that glacier until we took off again. By the time Bud got back into the airplane the weight of the ship had caused all the ice around us to sag perceptibly and the skis were wet. Wet skis, however, would be no hazard as long as snow had no chance to freeze on them. We had seen how the Eskimos purposely coat their sled runners with water to freeze on a layer of ice for easy sledding. The main thing was that we dared not stay here long enough for the pressure of the airplane combined with the cold temperature to freeze us down.

When the engine started Bud allowed it to run very slowly so as not to put any undue strain upon the complaining ice. After the oil pressure gauge came up he opened the throttle and away we went. The stiff 30 mile headwind allowed us to take off within a few feet. As the canyon was too narrow to turn around in, we had to outclimb it. This of course is one of the most foolish practices in flying: to fly up a narrow canyon. But the headwind allowed us to soar, and we easily climbed above the pass.

Had we hesitated in that spot many minutes, the airplane would have settled into the slush, and within a matter of days the overflow would have poured clear over it, entombing it in ice until the fatal day of the breakup should carry it away. We ourselves, even with our Eskimo furs, our snowshoes and emergency equipment, would have had a long, hard walk out, to say the least.

What had happened to make the cowling come loose? Bud never permitted anyone except himself to touch the airplane, and he had carefully checked it the last thing. Then he thought more carefully. The oil gauge is on the left side of the C-145 engine. He himself never opened the right side of the cowling, yet that was the side which had caused the trouble!

Someone, unknown to Bud, had been tinkering with the airplane. People just can't seem to resist fooling around the controls or cowling of airplanes if they get a chance when nobody is looking. To some person at one of our previous stops miles past — possibly somewhere on the way to Alaska — the airplane had been an irresistible lure. Some person had surreptitiously opened those fasteners and then hadn't known how to close them properly again. The person had just pushed them back and partially locked them. Trunk fasteners go past center when they snap in place so that they can't come loose.

Yet the whole thing was the pilot's fault, reflected Bud. For he had been neglecting to check the fasteners on that side due to the fact that he never opened that side.

Ever since that day Bud learned to double-check his airplane for tinkerers and fiddlers who might have access to it even five minutes before flight: a good thing for any pilot to remember.

We emerged from the north side of the Brooks Range upon the sun-dappled arctic coastal plain. Fifty minutes' flight past Umiat, and the continent ended in sea ice. Now that it was covered with snow it was impossible to even guess at your altitude in this treeless void without the altimeter; and neither could you tell, unless you had a practiced eye, just when you reached the edge of the continent, for the shore.

line was not more than two feet high above the snow-covered ocean ice. A pilot could only hope to recognize the landscape he had known in summer by the contours of its indeterminate river patterns and its vague frozen ocean arms.

I couldn't recognize anything myself but the cliffs of the Colville River, which we picked up to the west of us distantly. Soon those cliffs dropped away.

"We'll come down and look closer," said Bud. Presently his eye spotted a fresh dog sled trail. That was the clue he needed. Flying just one hundred feet above it, we followed the trail until suddenly the dog sled itself was overtaken on the immense white plain. A little dark wiggling object, it was scarcely recognizable. Over the Eskimo driver we roared, while all his dogs crouched in the harness.

"It's Tagiluk," said Bud as we circled, "and he's got Old Black for lead dog."

Tagiluk, whose English name was Herbert, was an awkward nineteen-year-old orphan who had come to live with George and Nanny the past two years.

For a moment Tagi apparently didn't know what this monster was that had swooped down out of the sky. Then he waved, and standing stalwartly on the back of the sled runners, urged his team to greater speed. How slowly they traveled! How tiny they were on this immense stage: the little hunter in furs, the little sled, the little dogs.

Then suddenly out of the whiteness ahead there was a stovepipe and a radio aerial sticking up above the drifted snow, and dark figures erupted from everywhere beneath us beside a tiny sheet-iron warehouse. Only then did I know that this was Oliktok! It was the hub of a network of dog sled trails which converged upon it in the snow.

To make a landing we dragged the area several times and saw that the terrain was rough—cut across with rolling drifts beaten to the consistency of iron. There was no way to detect the present wind direction. As we circled I recognized, I thought, several of our friends, but I failed to find George or Nanny among the group. Suddenly I felt sick with apprehension. Had they died over the past year?

That was what we would always wonder. Bud made the landing by gliding down close beside the chained line of dogs. I couldn't recognize people for a minute. At this season they were burned black by the fierce glare of the polar sun on snow.

Martha fed us tea and ground meat cakes in the snug little igloo. She explained by shy signs that the parents were simply away on a trip to Beechey Point. Before the engine cooled, Bud and I hastened out again. Ten minutes later, with Apiak accompanying us, Beechey Point flashed under our silver wings.

A fresh young seal was just being butchered on the floor inside the abandoned old trading post, at Beechey Point, as we entered. Abraham Stine and Dora and their two chubby little dumplings, Ann and Evelyn, had taken up residence recently; the pilot, Red Crosslin, had brought them by charter flight from Barrow. I had forgotten we left a large picture of Bud's mother and father on the wall from the year we stayed there. The past years it must have looked down on many a strange scene. Its presence there never failed to surprise me.

Nanny and George looked just the same. Their love enveloped us. They had just got here, eight hours' travel by sled, and they would not let us take them home until they had completed their discussion with Abraham. The Eskimos made us a bed of blankets and caribou skins upon the floor.

Breakfast was caribou meat chopped out by Dora with an ax and boiled in large frozen chunks. It was delicious. We lived in our parkas inside the house as there was no fuel with which to fire the wood stove. The Eskimo costumes were splashes of exotic design. The Eskimo environment was frosty and pure.

Home at Oliktok for the spring months of April, May and June, we unloaded all kinds of surprises for our old Eskimo parents: a 12-quart pressure cooker for Nanny, new radio batteries; we brought colored hard candy and chewing gum, fresh lettuce, carrots, onions, celery, oranges, grapefruit, apples and bananas from Fairbanks — so that all might at least have a taste of these strange luxuries. Formerly with a small airplane, we had never been able to indulge such fancy. The fresh vegetables did not freeze in transit because of our excellent cabin heater and the insulation we wrapped them in.

The fact was, however, that this was to be no luxurious spring. It was to be the toughest photographic assignment we had ever tried — getting the day by day record of the people's lives in their winter phase while sharing with them existence in their igloo. Winter photography of the real arctic life is almost unknown. The severe temperatures are prohibitive to carrying your cameras out on the trail, and we find that almost all films in existence have been taken close beside heated dwellings. This is not only because cameras freeze up. Cameras may be winterized with some success, but even so, at temperatures of much lower than ten below zero, moving picture film becomes brittle and breaks. Our "winter" photography of life north of treeline was therefore actually done in the spring to get the benefit of milder temperatures as well as the return of the sun which is gone during the actual midwinter. Our studies were limited to merely the people's spring phase; there are many midwinter phases of the Eskimos which have never been photographed.

This spring was to be one of the hardest times Nanny and George and Bud and I ever shared together. For what we found, after we made our landing on that day, was that once there, our airplane was to be almost totally confined to the ground and we were reduced to the status of existence that the primitive dog sled could supply. The food we brought was gone in a week. We were their guests, and the Eskimos supported us. Bud added in his person an extra hunter to the family, but this was minimized to a pittance when the plague struck us all.

Disease was our greatest crime against the American Indians — and now against the Eskimos, who are the very last to be reached on this continent.

Why is it that native people around the world succumb as they do to disease? Why do they seem to have so little resistance?

The answer is probably something like this. We too have gone through in the past exactly what they are going through now. During the Dark Ages three quarters of humanity was at various times completely exterminated by the great plagues which ravished Europe. The people who survived the plagues passed down what scanty historical records we preserve of those times. We are the descendants of those survivors. We have a natural immunity to some extent to the standard European infections with which we have lived for many centuries.

Biologists say that there are probably no new viruses and that new or modern diseases of man may be but new phases of the very old ones. At any rate, we Europeans today, who are still busy colonizing what was until recently an isolated continent — America — have centuries of a certain natural immunization to our own germs behind us. But the virus which we carry with us all the time and which means little to us finds a splendid breeding ground in the more pure and unresisting system of the native who has not before come into contact with that virus in all the thousands of lives of his ancestral family tree. This is why, then, that even our most ordinary childhood infections such as measles, mumps, and whooping cough, to say nothing of our common cold may put into a new grave within three days the most stalwart Indian or Eskimo who has come into town from his trapping camp.

When we arrived the family had just emerged from one of those periods of hard times we knew so well. It was between seasons for good hunting of any kind of game. Last fall's supply of fish was gone. The warehouse was empty, the dogs starved. For just a week or so our arrival furnished a brief respite from insecurity.

Nanny fell in love with her new pressure cooker which she learned to operate with easy mechanical aptitude. I showed her how to make bread pudding to add to her repertoire: bread crumbs, sugar, powdered milk, a few raisins. But I did not allow for the extra sticks the stove must consume to get up heat and pressure. Oo-lak, age seventeen, went out with the sled after driftwood which he must go a half dozen miles for, and kick out from under the snow. The pressure came up slowly under the big cooker. We tried their primus burner to speed it up, but it was as weak as a candle. Even the use of a pressure cooker here was rendered most strange.

Many articles in the igloo told the story of our long friendship. Tagiluk wore a shirt that once belonged to Bud's father. I recognized familiar bath towels, one of which Nanny kept for wiping the sweat off her forehead when cooking, fish nets, a family alarm clock, our old meat grinder, a jeweled comb in Martha's hair. It made me not so much pity the poor Eskimos but wonder what will become of modern man with his many inventions. We don't know yet. It is too short a time to say. . . .

Nanny: scraping a sealskin on her knees in the igloo with the back of a butcher knife, the sharp blade clutched in her palms covered with a wrapping cloth. The strokes take power, as she bears down on her knees. The blade is grasped between her thumb and forefinger. Oh, if she should slip!

Martha: I can hear the gasp of her breath as she labors to pick up each dish. Her crippled back is yearly growing worse. A nerve is being pinched and shutting off control in her right arm.

The radio is going. Nanny's eyes close as she is carried away to lands unknown when hymns come to her over shortwave from a strong station in New Jersey. George's favorite program is the "Alaska Dance" every Saturday night. He remembers by this program the days of his boyhood over on the Koyukuk when pioneer figures whirled. We hadn't the heart to tell him that those dancers are no more but are today only a part of history, that the old-time music is only victrola records played there in Fairbanks. At the close of the evening's program the station signs off with the "Star Spangled Banner" and "Alaska's Flag," the territory's own anthem. I can see Nanny's workworn hand reach up and turn off the radio:

> Alaska's Flag, to Alaskans dear,
> The simple flag of a last frontier.

Bud hoped to go with Apiak and the dog sled to photograph the hunting of caribou on the white plain but the dogs were so weak it was improvident that any person other than the solitary hunter go. So Apiak went out alone and got us all meat.

I taught Nanny how to make chocolate cornstarch pudding, and egg noodles for the caribou soup.

Lydia, age eight, looking somewhat like bright little Margaret O'Brien in her braids, had no other children to play with, the rest of us in this family being adults. But she had a cringing half-grown pup. She dressed him up in human clothes and put sunglasses on his nose. She hitched him in a dog harness to a miniature sled, and then at times reversed the role by putting the harness on herself and pretending that she was a dog pulling him.

Nonetheless, Lydia was the only person who could approach the pup and they got on very well, apparently enjoying each other. The pup had no companionship with the work dogs of the team; they would kill him if he ventured near them. Every so often we would hear a shrieking and would know that the pup was being pinched between the jaws of the stern old lead dog. It is the lead dog's privilege to run loose about camp, while the others are chained. Like some ancient janitor or night watchman, the lead dog guards the human meat pile from thieves, and rarely turns thief himself. Old Black would pinch the pup now and then when he got bored with life; day after day we would see the pup relegated to a spot up on the roof of the igloo — he didn't dare leave it.

One morning we saw a dog team approaching. First it was a dot, then an elongated black line. It came fast.

"Something wrong," said George, standing up on the roof, using the ancient whaler's telescope. "Empty sled, driver sure in hurry."

Indeed something was wrong. A ten-year-old boy jumped from the sled before our house and reported breathlessly: "Carrie sick. No more speak. Empty igloo. Her man gone hunting. Babies cold."

The handsome young woman and her husband Jacob had come by with a big sail on their sled a few days ago, traveling with the wind. They unbundled two infants, Maugalok from the sled covers, and Wesley from inside Carrie's parka on her back. A third baby was not far from being born. They had come from Point Barrow where they had just been dismissed from the government hospital, after having recovered from the flu. They told the nurse there that they were going home. What they did not tell her was that home was 240 miles across the ice to a cold, fuelless and foodless driftwood igloo. They had visited every one of their friends along the way, and, stopping with us for the night, they brought the flu to all of us.

For three weeks we had all been coughing our heads off, spitting into an open can. Bud and I were pretty blue. Attacks like this can often be fatal among the Eskimos.

Bud glanced at the sky. A polar storm hovered in the offing as usual. He climbed inside the cockpit and looked at the airplane barometer; it was falling fast. But that airplane was Carrie's only hope. Often we had eaten and slept at her igloo; we had known her and Jacob ever since they were married.

It was foolhardy to fly on such a day. Bud looked at the trusting faces about him. No one could have blamed Bud if he didn't fly. I said nothing. Bud was thinking that Barrow has a radio range; he could find it even if he couldn't see it. Medicine for everybody was badly needed.

The minutes crawled by while the primus stove slowly warmed the engine. Six cylinders start harder than four in cold temperatures; the job took an hour. Elusive fog slowly rolled over the flat, white landscape. Bud had to pick up Carrie at her igloo and be gone before that fog really closed down, or he wouldn't be able to find her igloo at all.

The engine was warm and turning over slowly. The Eskimos stood by. Bud often took Apiak with him on his missions; I was hoping he would take me. Instead, today he said: "Oo-lak, why don't you fly with me today?"

George's seventeen-year-old boy weighed about 115 pounds. He would make a handy helper and survival companion in case the airplane was forced down.

We had taken everything out of the airplane so that the sick girl might lie upon the floor. As Bud began to taxi with the proud Oo-lak around the long line of chained dogs Nanny came running, waving a pair of extra fur mittens and a loaf of bread. She handed them up to Bud while shielding her face with the other hand from the propeller blast.

Bud found the igloo by the black stovepipe sticking out of the snow. No friendly puff of smoke rolled out, showing that the people had stuffed trash into the stove to give the pilot wind direction and velocity. Today all was still.

No figures bounded up from the white dwellings; as Bud with Oo-lak taxied to the door, there was no sign of life. Oo-lak led the way inside. There two terrified babies crouched. One was perhaps a year old, the other perhaps three. Carrie lay on a pile of skins in the cold, dark house. Making a bed of the skins in the back of the airplane, Bud carried the young woman out and laid her upon them, while the children screamed like wildcats. Between Oo-lak and himself, they managed to get the children into the back of the airplane and the doors closed, before they could get out. Meanwhile Carrie neither moved nor spoke.

A few minutes later we at Oliktok Point heard the airplane above the fog at one thousand feet heading on its way to Point Barrow. Bud turned on the cabin heater and threw back his parka hood. The fog beneath was as white as the trackless spaces. Bud swung onto the compass course, checking his position by the sun to make sure, allowing for the magnetic variation.

For an hour the party hummed along in a distanceless realm where they seemed to hang in space. The radio range beam rang loudly in the pilot's earphones. Carrie moved and Bud looked back and saw she was trying to open the window. He opened it for her. The blast of the thirty-degree-below-zero air caused her to motion him to shut it again.

An hour more and Barrow lay beneath them. But where? The radio signal changed from A to N to A to N as they circled the hidden settlement. Bud called to the radio operator and asked to have a stretcher ready as he landed. The man in the tower assured him that it would be waiting and that the fog lay just 100 feet off the ground, with visibility at 500 feet.

Down, down the *Arctic Tern* glided. The radio signals fairly blasted in, while the brilliant sky faded as gray fog enveloped it. The last the passengers saw was a fiery orange sun as they were swallowed in gray. Oo-lak sat like a statue. Carrie's children could be heard crying softly now that the engine was idling. The altimeter slowly unwound: Five hundred, four hundred — Bud cleared the engine to keep carburetor ice from forming — three, two.

"That radio tower is a hundred feet high," Bud said out loud, and Oo-lak who could not understand English, smiled confidently.

"If I don't make contact — see the ground — by the time the altimeter reads 100 feet, I'm going back up."

"Ceiling one hundred feet. Ceiling one hundred feet," came the calm voice over the radio. One hundred feet read the altimeter. Then below the pilot lay a beautiful sight: two rows of rusty 55 gallon oil drums lined up to mark the ski landing strip on the frozen lagoon back of Dave Brower's Trading Post. There is a good field at Barrow belonging to the navy, but civilian pilots are not allowed to use it.

Two minutes later Bud had taxied right up to the door of the hospital. Eskimos came forward with a stretcher and quickly loaded Carrie aboard it. Her father, old Cyrus, came forward and took the two children.

Calling the radio station, Bud reported in and then asked for the weather at Umiat. He was thinking that to find his way home he would ride the radio range to Umiat and then follow the Colville River down to the coast from inland. It occurred to him while he was at it, that he would like to see how Mathew's People were. The hospital supplied him with plenty of sulfa pills and cough syrup to distribute to the people he would contact.

Joe Crosson, an old time pilot, prepared some tea for Bud and Oo-lak and helped at the job of gassing up. Joe nodded with approval when he saw the full set of arctic camp gear, for all arctic pilots must be ready to camp and stay put if they are forced to land en route.

Bud and Oo-lak flew toward Umiat. As more fog closed in, Bud turned to intersect the willow-bordered Colville below Umiat and said that he would follow that little-known river toward the Arctic Ocean. If need be, he reported, he would camp until the fog lifted.

There is nothing harder for a pilot to see through than fog lying over snow. The fog rolled in, over and under the airplane. But up through it all came the dim line of willows, marking the frozen course of Alaska's third largest river.

Somehow, Bud felt, Mathew's People might be in trouble. Onward he persevered, just fifty feet above the river, following every bend, keeping to the east side where there were no high banks. Oo-lak was on his first long airplane ride and he was enjoying it. He studied the land below and watched the instruments with brown, almond eyes.

As darkness was settling around midnight they saw some spots that floated in space. Dogs. They were tied beside an invisible igloo. The river bed was wide here; two black cut banks defined the limits of the landing field. When no human being appeared beneath the circling airplane Bud knew for certain that all was not well.

Oo-lak helped tie the airplane by burying two toggles in the snow and roping down the wings to them. Taking the medicine, Bud walked slowly up to the silent dwelling. Bessie met him at the door; she waved him not to come in.

"We bad sick here," she gasped. Bud pushed on inside. It was as cold and still as a tomb. There was no food and no fuel. Mathew's family, a compound one, was made up of grandparents, many children and grandchildren. They all lay about on the floor, wrapped in caribou. Everyone was sick!

"Mother is bad sick," whispered Bessie. As Bud saw the old lady he realized that she was dying.

"Colliak is bad sick. But maybe better now," advised Bessie, pointing to her stalwart brother.

Speaking with several members of the stricken house, Bud directed how the medicine should be taken. Colliak, with whom he had often hunted, smiled and said he would soon be strong again and that he would go out and hunt and get meat.

Bud and Oo-lak pitched their tent beside the airplane for the rest of the night while the starving dogs of the Eskimo family whined and howled on their chains nearby. Daylight dawned gray with fog. The airplane was low on gas. Oo-lak walked a couple of miles to lug back ten gallons from a cache Bud knew of. The Eskimos had been securing our gas for us the past two years in this way: a raft of gas drums had escaped from the navy when they were unloading at Point Barrow, and our Eskimos picked up the drift barrels wherever they lodged along the polar beaches. They had gas for us every place, freighted by sled. Not a lot of gas, but enough for one small airplane. We paid our Eskimo friends for their labors and thus we had gas to use in this remote part of the world.

Bessie met Bud again at the door. "Old Mother is dead," she said simply. Then she added: "Colliak is dead, too."

Colliak dead! It didn't seem possible that the young hunter had passed away so quickly in three short days from contracting the white man's "cold."

Tears ran down Bud's cheeks as he helped wrap and carry two frozen forms from the igloo and place them out in the beached whale-boat. He pulled heavy sleds over the bodies to keep the dogs away. The dogs were being killed at the rate of one each day to feed the remaining dogs, and although the impoverished family never admitted it, he suspected that they were eating dog meat themselves. When a hunting people fall ill and cannot get their game and fuel each day they are abruptly reduced to a helpless plight from which the minis-trations of civilized charity — even were they available — cannot easily rescue them.

The fog lifted slightly. Promising to return with emergency dried foods as soon as he could, and with a last round of instructions con-cerning the medicine, Bud took off. "Why couldn't I have got there with the medicine just one day sooner?" The thought kept tormenting him.

When Bud and Oo-lak came over Oliktok Point we were fogged in solid. His ten gallons of gas were all but gone.

Around in a circle the airplane wheeled. The country was as level as a billiard table. If a pilot could only see, he could land anywhere.

*   *   *

I hadn't been feeling very gay while Bud was gone, for he had our one sleeping bag and I had plenty of worries about him. I had a big pile of caribou skins in Nanny's igloo, it is true, but they kept slipping off, leaving cracks and drafts. The coughing about me was something terrible. Ook-sook had arrived to take shelter with us. He told us Mathew's People were mighty hungry this spring and so he had gone a hundred miles to try to get polar bear on the sea ice. He had almost died out on the ice in his tent alone. He had come down with the flu there. A big polar bear came by and one of the dogs got loose and chased it away while Ook-sook lay "sleeping," as he described it, too delirious with the flu to get up and shoot it. Ook-sook came off the ice at our place, coughing in paroxysms.

Then Nanny got sick, and that was catastrophic. We had both meat and fuel for the moment, and Nanny had just made bread the day before while I had made an anæmic lemon pudding — the ingredients much stretched with water. The Eskimos were crazy over my pudding: sugar, canned lemon juice, powdered eggs, and cornstarch contained in small, precious packages.

Ook-sook hitched up his emaciated team and left for home inland. These people are strongly intuitive. There was no stopping him. He was coughing with every gasp.

Lydia had been a very sick little girl. A succession of violent nose-bleeds aggravated by her deep chest cough had caused her to lose what seemed to me like gallons of blood on several days. Nobody knows the exact cause of this kind of nosebleed. Severe and even dangerous nosebleeds are common among Eskimo children we have known.

We were all out of meat, but Nanny recovered sufficiently to find a hunk of sour meat she had forgotten someplace out in the snow alley under the washtub, and somehow we got by. An Eskimo always has some resource to fall back upon even after the last resource seems to be gone. George ground the small piece of meat up in the meat grinder, and Nanny made a kind of paste of it with flour, in the skillet, with a few spoonfuls of old meat fryings, which served us all. Lydia's pup came to the window every day on the snowbank and looked in, watching and waiting for Lydia. But the little pup came to a sad ending. He ate an old greasy dishrag and died.

When we heard the airplane come over the house at last, Nanny poured trash into the stove as Bud had taught her to do. But I saw in an instant that that course was useless.

"We must make a big fire quick," I told the family. They fully understood the danger and the emergency. Old rags and hides which could scarcely be spared were thrown to the sacrifice. We poured precious gasoline into the dog pans for containers and with these materials lit flares at each end of Bud's "runway" before the house, and kept them burning by running relays while the distressed aircraft above us could be heard futilely circling.

For a half hour the airplane circled while Bud with Oo-lak beside him debated upon coming down. You couldn't see twenty-five feet before your nose. No way for a pilot to tell the ground was there until he hit it.

From below an orange flame mushroomed up. It was gone as quickly as it came, but Bud saw it for one instant. As he let the airplane sink down into the gray fog there was utterly no sense of motion and no sense of danger. What a quick way it would be to die!

Then, with a slight bump the skis struck the white, invisible snow. The airplane came to a stop, and still Bud couldn't see the snow it rested upon. For a moment he wondered if he were sitting in eternity. Had he really seen a flare? Where was he? Had he missed the continent and gone out toward the North Pole?

Bud had come down about half a mile distant on the sea ice. We who waited could hear a succession of bumps and banging, which, muted by fog, might have been either a safe landing or a fatal crash at some distance.

It was with weak relief that presently we heard the sound of the airplane taxiing. It was so slow in approaching that I wondered if some part was broken. But Bud was back on the ground, and that was the main thing. The slowness was due to the fact that he must follow the steps of Oo-lak who got out and guided the airplane forward inch by inch.

Bud measures an ermine for making up a
specimen for Cornell University

A heavy snow falls and nearly sinks the *Arctic Tern*

We had to use care lest the float tails fill with water and the plane sink

We tie the *Arctic Tern* securely for the freeze-up

I set up the moving picture camera on its tripod. "Nanny, you take the pictures this time," I requested weakly, showing her how to press the release button and swing the camera on its turret.

"I do not know if I can do it," she said shyly. "But I try for you."

Frequently the Eskimos themselves turned photographer in a pinch to help us get the record of our lives. Unable to wait longer for Bud I ran out then before the camera lens and guided him in.

I appeared to Bud out of the fog dressed completely in Eskimo woman's costume, and he jumped out and hugged me.

"I've been worried," I said.

They were words long familiar, heard a hundred times in our explorations. Ours was a life of much danger but of much living, a strange life which probably wouldn't make sense to most people, involving a thousand skills to keep alive. I could see that all the airplane, including its windshield, was sheathed in ice.

George just had to go into the igloo and sit down when it was all over, while the boys tied up. "My boy," he said, over and over, referring to Oo-lak. "I lose lot of boys. I don't want to lose those boys."

I think we all agreed tacitly after that, that it was better to dispense with the airplane for the most part, and just stay on the ground with the sleds.

It was a consolation to learn later that Carrie, as well as her new baby, recovered in good health and that the remainder of Mathew's People made a hearty comeback. The year before, at this season, nineteen people had died of the flu along this coast — a quarter of the population. To get the record of their lives before it was too late was our self-appointed mission and project. Operating at the extreme end of our range, we were able to do this by means of our airplane, although we could do little to alter the people's essential condition.

15 THE LURE OF THE POLAR ICE

NANNY SAT CUTTING BOOT SOLES out of an ugrug hide that filled the whole house, while the big snow blocks she had cut and carried for drinking water settled and melted in the iron barrel behind the stove. Tagi, having had warm seal oil poured into his ear for an earache, sat strumming the guitar. Oo-lak came in with five ptarmigan he shot, and I commenced to pick them while Lydia chewed on and played with what I presently discovered to be a caribou teat, a kind of pacifier.

Bud worked with George at mending the fish net. George snapped the shuttle, pulling each knot tight. His ancient face was reflective.

"George," Bud said, "where were you born?" We realized his parents were Stone Age people. If it seemed primitive here now to us sometimes, when George was born there wasn't even an outside world to him.

Several more mesh snapped into place before George spoke.

"I am born Kobuk River, I think."

"But just where?" Bud prompted. "Were there any brothers or sisters?"

The wind rattled down the stovepipe vent. We never tired of asking George and Nanny to tell us stories of the old days.

"I have poor memory of my father," he began. "I was little boy, maybe four year old, maybe three. There are people all laid out in a row like seals. My father lie there. I run along and see my father. He is lay there very quiet and I crawl up and lay down and sleep by him. 'Maybe he be asleep,' I think. So I touch his face and lay down and sleep by him. People come and take me away. I never see my father any more.

"Yes, it was on Kobuk River, somewhere near ocean, I think. It was the time of big sickness. When I grow up I learn later. It come in fall time and many people die. I have brother, too, and mother left. We all leave that place quick."

"You buried your father first?" I put in.

"No, we no bury many people like now. There plenty loose starving dog and people too sick to feed them."

George explained: "We all leave, go up river long ways. Snow come fast and winter is very cold. There is maybe three sled and maybe ten people left, and no gun them days. There is nothing for people to eat, when come big storm, west wind."

George spoke as if he found his words somewhere in the fish net that covered his outstretched legs. The words came slowly as he tried to explain to us in comprehensible terms the Stone Age:

"Mother say to me, 'Kisik, there is no food. You nearly man now. You watch brother. I look food!'

"Mother wander off then. Storm coming. I never see her again. Maybe she little out of head, I think now.

"I have grandfather and few people living at Nariatok Lake. We all try to get to Nariatok Lake far inland. Storm is gone, we try to short cut for that lake. Little brother is left in snow. Too bad. Sometime I think about it. It is always that way when hard time strike. The baby is left in snow. Thrown away, I see many time.

"The people find my grandfather at that lake. Grandfather have plenty fish, plenty moose. He got gun from Koyukuk and we all have plenty eat."

"How many of you got there?" I asked.

"I don't know. Maybe five, maybe six. We all stay until spring, and those people leave, but I just keep stay with my grandfather. That old man, he sure a hustler. I remember him many time. He have old Eskimo fish trap in lake. He busy all the time fishing. Drying fishes, hunting and pick the berry. But my, I tell you that Nariatok Lake fish is fine one. Talk about fat! Many time I think, is any people living there now?"

"No," Bud reported, "nobody lives there. Connie and I fly over that lake every time we go to Hughes."

George's face retained its meditative smile as he thought of those delicious childhood meals with Grandfather.

"I'm maybe eleven when I hunt the sheep first time," he went on. "There is other boy call Tidalick — that mean little wading bird — and he have .22 rifle. Grandfather get me .22 single shot, and we go over mountain. There six, eight men, and we go over Noatak River and on across to John River. I kill my first sheep there."

We waited, and the hunt unfolded.

"Sheep is lamb," said George, "and I have shaking hand. I only break his back. I don't like waste bullet so I take rock and beat sheep on head. Sheep has hard head and take plenty beating," George chuckled ruefully. Then he added, "I shoot *sik-rik-puk*, that marmot, too.

"On John River we meet miners. I never see white man before. They say, 'Stop and work. We pay you plenty.' They have many things I never see before, and they got candy."

"Candy — did you like candy the first time you tried it?" we asked him, for many primitive people cannot abide the taste of sugar until they get the sugar habit.

George replied:

"No one else but me like it. But I am fierce for candy. So I stay. Everyone else go on, leave me with miners. Say, I have a time of it. For I no can understand. There are two miners and they say, 'hammer,' and I go get shovel or something. They laugh and show me hammer. They say 'ax' and soon I learn few things. . . .

"Well, fall is come quick and miners leave down river to Koyukuk. I go along and stop that place, and pretty soon I real surprise, missionary say, 'Come, school.'

"I come school. My, fine people, that missionary woman. She say, 'What is your name?'

"'Kisik,' I say.

"She say, 'That is bum name. Everybody must have real name,' and she put the name on me, George Woods. I am ever since George Woods."

"Did you like school?"

"School is fine, but I like the camps and so I go Bettles where big mine is work. I got no money, so I say to trader, 'Give me shoepack, give me rifle, little grub, and I hunt the sheep for you.' He good fellow, he give me everything, say, 'George Woods pay me when you get sheep.' I kill lots of sheep and bring them down river for sell. Those miners plenty good to me. They always hunt for gold. I look for gold, too, but gold is hard to find. I better look for the sheep and moose. Miners give fifty cents a day to me and I hunt and spend all fifty cents on candy.

"That candy cause me plenty trouble once. There is three of us find old miner's cache. Note there say: 'Eat or take. We tired dam' country, go United States.' There not much in cache but big glass jar candy. Other boy no care for candy, I eat whole jar.

"Talk about trouble. For nearly week I have awful time. That candy is strong. Call them laxative."

As we all laughed over the long-ago incident, we could see that George was winding up his story for today.

"I can read fine, but I don't know some words' meaning. I learn mostly from miners. They strong fellow. Fight and shoot people sometime.

"I am young man then and I decide to see arctic people so I get real fancy store clothes and leave in fall. It take me near one year go arctic coast. I nearly freeze. Talk about cold. People say, 'You need fur pants, fur boot, fur shirt too,' and I say, 'I will go back to other side.'

"But after first year I get good fur clothes and then I get married, and so — I am here."

It was the end of the day and about time to go to bed when Nanny, stepping outside, saw a polar bear on the ice a mile distant from our house. Pandemonium. Field glasses were grabbed. Lydia began to cry. I ran to the warehouse and got the movie camera. Bud started up the airplane: he and I would run the bear down, we thought, simply by taxiing.

The whole world was misted white in falling sleet. There was no horizon. Bud and I alone started off into the ice. George advised neither yes nor no. Would the bear lead us into some trap from which we could not extricate ourselves?

Snags in the ice even two feet ahead were imperceptible. As we taxied away from Oliktok Point with its faint brown line of exposed gravel and its small tin warehouse, it seemed to float in nothingness and the whole situation was a deceptive one. We might break a ski, harm our airplane. Anything could happen. Unable to see through the encrusted windshield, Bud stopped soon and jumped out with the glasses.

We had merely progressed in a large half circle. When Bud tried to start the plane again, it was stuck in soft snow! Abandoning the airplane temporarily, Bud ran on with the camera, hoping to walk down the ever-fading bear. I walked back to Oliktok. I was to send Tagi after Bud with the team. But George said Tagi was not strong enough to go yet. He was probably right. The dogs were too weak, too, said George. Finally Bud gave up trying to catch the ghostly dweller of the ice, returned home with the airplane — which he managed to extricate — and we all went to bed.

The arctic is a strange place, I reflected. The more I see of it the more respect I have for it. It is not like the old West, a place that can be "conquered," although this is an analogy you frequently hear. You may conquer it one year, but the next year you will have to do it all over again.

I used to think that if a person lived one year north of the Arctic Circle he had seen it all. Not so. For a place whose type of scenery is limited and whose animal species are few and whose weather is generally souped in, the arctic holds many paradoxes.

Playing with an airplane, for instance, is a suicidal ambition of man. The polar ice lying offshore here is hostile, with its sudden strange ground fogs that travel on invisible wings at fifty miles an hour.

Everything is unreal in the high latitudes. The quality of the light is different. There is day after day of leaden, even overcast, having no shadows. I walk from the igloo to the warehouse a few yards and stumble over a snow hummock six inches high because I can't see it. Even after I fall, I can't make it out. I can only feel it with my mittens.

The arctic is as uncompromising to mechanized modern man as it is to primitive man, maybe more so. You'll do all right with a dog sled stumbling over this half world, groping your way inch by inch. You are not apt to come to much harm, as long as you don't starve to death. But when you get into an airplane and travel over the polar regions far from your base, far from the environment which modern man can sustain himself in, you're asking for trouble.

It was clear enough today to try a flight out over the ice. The thing we had been yearning for from Nanny's igloo, that alluring vista which had beckoned for so long, was at hand. It was time to move camp out onto the ice to hunt for the seal and the polar bear.

Usually it is only the men who venture out there. Bud and I intended to establish a camp using the airplane, and Bud would hunt with the sleds even as he photographed the hunt that we all might augment the desperately needed supply of food. There was nothing to eat from the land at this season. The human beings at land's end were forced to turn to the ice for survival, but this time we would see how an airplane could help out in the pinch.

Apiak went out first with the sled and selected the camp on safe, landfast shelf ice forty miles from shore. But although we covered hundreds of square miles of the tumbled ice fields by a succession of flights, Bud and I were unable to find Apiak in the ice. His little sled tracks were totally erased in the last blizzard. When he came home days later he unloaded from his sled a fresh polar bear hide and meat and two seals. It seemed a miracle. Where did the hunter find them in such a waste?

Strengthened by the fresh fat meat the family quickly constructed a new sled out of a single good drift log Oo-lak found. Many sleds get broken in the ice. The new sled, strong and flexible because it was not nailed together but was bound together with elastic seal rawhide, was ready for ice work.

Not until Bud had flown Apiak out over the ice and Apiak had pointed out the camp, was Bud able to locate it; thereafter he and I flew out to stay.

We slipped through the weather at 1:20 one afternoon in early April. During the forty-minute cruise much open water was sighted to seaward.

"That's splendid," I said. "Can't we camp pretty near that and shoot the seals swimming in the open water?"

Bud shook his head. "Not the way it is this season. Look at that stuff down there. Your life wouldn't be worth a plugged nickel."

The aerial survey indicated all kinds of little lakes and cracks which had opened up throughout the entire mass for many miles, showing that the whole thing might crush up at any time. The ice hunter must beware that he does not get out upon ice that, with an offshore wind, may carry him away from the continent or crush in storms beneath him. An old iceman although young in years, Bud was probably but one of a half dozen men in North America today who could read polar ice reliably. I often thought that if radar stations should be erected out on the ice near the Pole, as appears the likely thing in the war of tomorrow, competent men, who understand ice action, should select the sites.

I was glad that Bud and Apiak knew what they were doing when they chose our camp. It was ten miles by air or about twenty-five miles by sled, from the danger area.

Carefully we scrutinized the strip Apiak had marked out on a great ice plain surrounded by rough pressure ridges. A safe landing can be made practically anywhere upon the polar ice by even our largest aircraft, if the pilot can read ice and is lucky enough not to plunge a ski into some drifted-over crack, thus wrecking the airplane. The pilot must also know the tricks of taking care of the airplane or a polar gale will soon waft it away.

Bouncing lightly on its skis, the *Arctic Tern* came quietly to a stop, and there we were. The country about us resembled the southwest desert in monochrome. It was flat, with tumbled fifty-foot ridges outcropping here and there, where the normal five-foot level ice had been pushed up in former storms and then resolidified. These are known to the polar traveler as "pressure ridges."

"Let's put the tent over there by that tall hummock," Bud indicated. "That will be a handy lookout for hunting."

For equipment we carried with us ordinary camp gear: our common seven foot by eight foot canvas wall tent, our Woods Arctic Three-Star Sleeping Bag, a couple of caribou bed skins, a rubber air mattress (convenient when the ice begins to run water in spring), a common Coleman two-burner gasoline stove, a couple of boiling pots, a snow knife, matches in a jar. Our food was a few days' supply of biscuits from Nanny, tea, sugar, salt, pancake mix and a skillet, some dried fruit, and two days' supply of meat from shore.

Bud and I have spent six months altogether living on the ice: three months once before, supporting ourselves with a dog team; and three months now, again supporting ourselves with a dog team.

I had my .30–06 and Bud had a new .300 Magnum this year. My rifle was equipped with a 2¼ power 'scope and Bud's had an 8 power 'scope. We had formerly used .30–30 carbines — only since acquiring a generous-sized airplane had we got so fancy. Because of its long range and flat trajectory, Bud hoped with his new Magnum to do wonders in augmenting the blubber supply for our friends this spring.

Then, of course, we had our old 8 × 30 Bausch and Lomb binoculars, an indispensable item in the life of the explorer or professional hunter. We had ropes to tie the airplane with, an ice chisel brought from Takahula Lake, a shovel, and the airplane tool kit and engine cover.

We expected to live entirely in furs while we were on the ice except when we slipped out of them to get into the down sleeping bag. Our feet were clad with waterproof sealskin boots with fur stockings under them; we had a number of changes of boots and many changes of insoles. For this the tent was equipped with a line along its ridgepole, both inside and outside, for hanging out spare clothing, especially the footwear; spring hunting on the ice is a damp occupation and skin clothing will quickly rot unless properly aired and cared for. We wore amber-colored sunglasses all the time except when in bed. Without them a person would quickly become snowblind.

The camping procedure we followed was simple. Bud tied the airplane by chipping two holes down about ten inches into the ice, one foot apart. When the holes were cut he chipped out underneath them, and running a rope beneath the ice bridge, made a secure toggle to tie to. Such a tie-down will hold any airplane in a gale. The Eskimos have held whales by such tie-downs, which are made with a pocket knife. It is easier to tie an airplane to either ice or snow than to tie it on ordinary land, if you know how. One such tie-down on each wing and one on the tail; with the airplane set facing into the wind, and that was that.

I, meanwhile, unloaded the airplane of the camp gear. For pitching the tent Bud selected a hard drift that was flat and which bore his weight when he walked upon it. One must not camp directly upon bare ice itself. I spread out the little tent on the drift and stretched out the tent ropes. Again, it is easier to tie a tent to snow than it is to stake it to land. We scratched holes in the drift ten inches deep, tied the ropes to little wood toggles we had brought out from shore, and tamped snow over the toggles. This tie solidifies shortly and becomes amazingly strong.

With the four corner ropes tied we raised the tent. I crawled under the spread-eagled tent and fitted the rear tent pole into the ridgepole socket, and then lifted it into place. The front tent pole came next, and I simply lifted the ridgepole and set it on top of the front tent pole. The tent was up.

In nearly any gale one man can pitch a tent in this way. In a few moments we had tied the remaining tent ropes to the snow, tightening them so as to make the tent perfectly taut.

Bud handed in the canvas floor to me and I tucked the bottom of the tent under and patted the floor cover in place. This patting caused the bottom of the tent to freeze to the snow so that wind could not whip it loose. Then came the blown-up air mattress, the caribou robes over that, and finally the sleeping bag. The grub box and primus stove set up on the floor on a number of small sticks completed the interior of our ice camp. Bud cut a few snow blocks and stacked them around the back and sides of the tent up, about five feet in height, to make a dead air space. Such a makeshift shelter would be sufficient for this time of year; by winter a real snowhouse would have had to be made for safety. With proper clothing and a mere tent, plus the knowledge of how to use them, the polar traveler is perfectly comfortable. Properly dressed Eskimos never suffer from the cold.

During these operations it was easy to work barehanded much of the time because our long loose parka sleeves were so designed by Nanny that the cuffs came down almost to the ends of the fingers; by shifting your shoulders you could withdraw your hands completely inside your parka, next to your body, to warm them at any time. This is such a valuable innovation in saving hands from freezing — for even the best of mittens may fail in a land of no heated shelters and no camp-fires — that we have never been able to understand why factory cloth-ing has not imitated it.

Another factor which factory clothing for the arctic seems to miss altogether is the principle of the parka hood. The Eskimos know that it must be a proper distance from the face, so that the breath in gather-ing upon the ruff condenses in the form of frost crystals which can easily be brushed away. But if the parka hood is worn tightly up against the face the condensation of the breath turns to ice and after some thirty-six hours out-of-doors without shelter the man dressed in such an arrangement as those now on the market becomes the man in the iron mask: his face will be burned and scarred and he is on the way to die soon of exposure.

The most arresting principle, however, is that polar life is not a life in which human beings can be regimented to a set tempo. The natural tempo of each person's body and metabolism is an individual matter which shows up in the low temperatures as in no other environ-ment. Great care must be taken by the individual, if he is living con-tinuously out-of-doors with no established shelter or heat, other than a primus stove, that he does not perspire and get his furs drenched with sweat. Perspiration, which goes on as long as the body lives and breathes, along with the problem of proper ventilation for the body, are the greatest problems in the design of arctic clothing. The exhalations of the body turn to frost and ice in the clothing unless this moisture can escape through cracks and drafts, and unless the individual is equipped with sufficient complete changes. The Eskimos have solved this by learning how to control the layers of clothing they wear to fit their occupation and the day. But most important of all, they are fortunate in wearing animal skins that are not commercially tanned, but skins which are themselves alive and which breathe. These natural untanned skins are something which the white man so far has not been able to duplicate in his factories.

Although we brought out on the ice the best and very newest factory clothing to test for the manufacturers who were making it on consignment for the army and navy, there was not a piece of the clothing which proved to be trustworthy as judged by Eskimo standards.

Apiak arrived with the dog team, seven hours travel from Oliktok. As we greeted that handsome figure, the young face noble in its sculpture, his dogs slant-eyed and furry, I thought how right it is that the Eskimo should grace this environment. It will be a sad polar world the day that the airplane replaces the Eskimo and his dog sled altogether, a sad day when this fine and gentle race of people are seen no more with their sleds.

Actually, it will be a less safe world, too. The airplane is good, but when it comes to survival you need the dog sled along. You need a dog's nose to scout out seal breathing holes; you need the sled for hauling meat and for the hunting. You must never be separated one minute from your camp outfit which is hauled on your sled with you when you hunt. For us, the airplane was only an accessory to the dog sled.

I felt a lot safer as soon as Apiak and the sled arrived.

I awoke in the tent to the stirrings of Apiak starting breakfast on the primus stove by my head. It was lazy to lie there before leisurely dressing in the warm sleeping bag. The air being forced into the little pressure stove always made me think early in the morning of the compressed air of organ music. As I dozed, the grand strains and thundering chords of an organ rang out, then faded, just before I could find the pattern of the melody and just as I began to smell the mixed aromas of coffee and boiling meat.

"The music of the spheres is what I hear," I thought. "If you could hear it any place on this earth, the place would be here." It was all harmony and you could construct of it what you would, according to the whims of imagination.

Each morning abed, as Apiak stirred and struck a match, and outside our tent the dogs basked and the omnipresent glare pressed down, I would listen for the music. Somehow it got mixed up with those pleasant breakfasts in the tent, the hot sunshine, white ice, and deep ocean lying somewhere beneath, until one could hear it in the silence of the fixed pressure ridges themselves, as one wandered hunting the seals and polar bears.

The seals we were after — *phoca hispidae* — hair seals which have no commercial value, freely inhabit all the oceans, but they are probably the most difficult game to hunt, when you hunt them here.

All winter long the seals live under the ice by keeping numbers of breathing holes open to the surface. Each seal has several holes scattered over many acres of ice. But their breathing holes are so minute on the surface and so cleverly hidden under snowdrifts that they are usually not discernible to the human eye, and thus for years polar explorers assumed that this frozen ocean was completely lifeless.

However, Eskimos along the shore learned to use a dog with a good nose for smelling out the seal breathing holes, and learned to station themselves there, waiting with a spear. For untold centuries Eskimos knew how to get the seals. Today, modern Eskimos may set a trap gun. This, too, is a good survival trick for anyone to know who goes out on the ice.

But in mid-April, May and June the seals gnaw their way clear through the small breathing holes, and come out on top of the ice to bask in the sun. It is at this season that the Eskimos work hardest to get them. The seals are their best, of all the year, in the amount of blubber they carry, yet a few weeks later they will have nothing of their present golden yield. The harvest of the seals must be taken, furthermore, when they are ripe for their skins. For after a short period of basking in the sun, rolling about from side to side like bathers at a beach, the seals contract such a powerful sunburn that their skins are worthless for boot soles.

Sneaking up on seals that are sleeping on the ice, beside their holes, for the brain shot that is necessary to bag them, is a great art about which much can be said. It is not easy, but the expert hunter may manage it, and will find seals visible in most areas on the polar ice — even to the North Pole — during the spring and summer season.

We who went out on the ice to hunt were confident that we could make our living there. Bud cut steps in the sixty foot ice hummock which overshadowed our small camp; he and Apiak climbed up on top of it each day, where they sat for hours at a time, immobile with the binoculars. It was two days before they found anything. Then suddenly, there were five small black dots which were basking seals discovered in the neighboring miles of ice. While the two hunters with their seven-dog team started out after them, I remained in camp. Two hunters at one time are about all that one sled can accommodate to advantage; I would guard the airplane and the camp from marauding polar bears.

With one camera and my rifle, and a book I read with sunglasses on, I took my stance inside the upholstered airplane parked beside the tent on its skis, where I could easily see about on all sides. The airplane was warmer than the tent. It was up off the damp ice, and the sun came through the Plexiglas windshield. It soon became very humid inside the tent in which people lived and breathed, and in which, of course, the innumerable boilings of snow tea and meat took place. I kept the two-burner primus in the tent. Bud and Apiak used a tiny single burner with a small trail tent and a separate grub box for their treks abroad.

Bud was pleased that he was able to quickly brush up on his seal psychology. Seals are wary. The polar bears ate the sleepyheads centuries ago and those living today are descendants of light sleepers.

The seal lies with his head right beside the open hole, watching for danger. He trusts his nose to tell him about an upwind approach. It is downwind from the seal or crosswind that the hunter must stalk. This means that during the stalk the seal is usually facing the hunter.

As the seal drops his head to nap every few seconds, the hunter moves forward during the nap interval. Wearing a white canvas "snow-shirt" over his furs which hangs to his knees, and carrying his rifle in a white canvas case until the moment he is ready to use it, the hunter simulates the environment of ice and snow. The seal cannot recognize him if the approach is made on a *straight line* directly to the seal, and *not* wavering from side to side for obstacles. If the hunter wavers in his course and weaves about, the seal is quick to detect that something has moved in his landscape, and he will dive down his hole into the ocean beneath.

On long flat approaches where there is nothing for the hunter to hide behind, a stalk may take as long as three hours, while a decent shot is considered to be all the way from 175 yards to 300 yards. The seal must be killed instantly with an expert shot which severs the brain or spinal column.

As I lounged in the solar-heated airplane and visualized Bud and Apiak out hunting, I keenly recalled my former days on the ice. One time, having crouched waiting for hours for swimming seals at the edge of a lead, I began to retrace my way to the tent. I had just topped the first rise when I saw a long white object in the blue water of the open lead before me. It was exactly the size of our dog sled. The white object moved; it cut through the water like a shark. Squinching up my eyes against the glare, I saw that seals gave way to it in the peaceful polar pond. It was a polar bear I had come upon, swimming about leisurely among the cooling ice cakes before our little tent in solitary reverie.

I took just one step towards him. Then the swimming white monster swerved accidentally in my direction. In an instant he was just twenty-five feet away. What a rare sight for a naturalist to stumble upon in an untrammeled part of the world! Yet the rapidity of that swerve told me more than any words. It was like a power launch putting on steam.

The litheness of the water animal that can hunt out anything it goes after, the animal that can dive and swim under ice caves, and may weigh three quarters of a ton: the biggest and at the same time the strangest bear that lives, had not a whit of difficulty in intimidating me.

Never have I been able to convey to other people my race with my rifle down the ice for Bud and Ook-sook. It little mattered to me that Abraham Stine told us he once killed a polar bear whose hide measured 11 feet, 9 inches, by putting just one shot behind the ear with his little .25–35 at close range. Although the polar bear never knew he had an audience, I was certain that he was panting on my heels as I fled down the edge of the ragged lead, leaping over yawning chasms beneath which the sea came in. When at last I saw Ook-sook and Bud on an ice point across the bay, I couldn't even whistle.

The screech, "Polar bear going to get our dogs," brought the enthused hunters on the run, and again I was left to tag behind on the way home, as I couldn't keep up with them over that ice. Of course, by the time we all reached the tent the meandering bather was gone. He had returned to the far side of the lead to the moving ice pack from whence he had so mysteriously appeared, and nobody ever saw him but me. I always have queer things happen like that.

"What if a polar bear comes to camp now while I'm sitting in the airplane?" I asked Bud the second day. "How will I ever muster up the courage to shoot it this time?"

"Oh, you've shot lots of big game. You won't have any trouble," Bud replied confidently. We both knew that as soon as we had seals in camp the odor of the meat and blubber would draw any polar bears from a great distance across the ice. In hunting polar bears which range over vast areas, the camp — and the hunter himself, aromatic with seals as he is — is the bait.

"When a bear comes it will only be a small one in all likelihood," Bud pacified me. "One you can handle."

"Why do you say that?"

"The winds we've been having all spring. He'll come from downwind, following his nose. That means he'll come from landward. If the winds hold as they are we're going to have a hard time to get any

A wolf track and our .30-30 carbine

Ready to leave for the States — Connie loads up

Changing from floats to wheels at Hughes

The floats come off and wheels go on

good bears. If only the wind will change and blow off the land to sea, we'll have a chance to draw one of the really big bears that stay out in the pack."

It was 63 degrees out on the ice at 2 P.M. Bluebottle flies and bugs flew about, landing on our warm canvas tent, forty miles from shore. The shore seemed to breathe outward of heat and bursting fertility. To-day's wet clothes were hung over the tent, while the wings and tail of the airplane looked like a clothesline on wash day. Flock after flock of multicolored king eiders — largest of the ducks — bore low over me, with a swish of rapid wings. The host emitted a melodious thrilling cackle as they flew, their long wavering lines numbering from 2000 to 5000 in a flock, as they headed unerringly for some remote breeding grounds. Whoever said the polar ice is lifeless? Not only do these flocks skirt the shores of the continent. By the time we would be eating supper that very night they might be swimming around in some open lead in the ice devouring shrimps not far from the North Pole. Wild swans and loons and squaw ducks were their erstwhile companions.

"I want to get the first load of seals to Oliktok without delay," said Bud, the next morning. "I think I might get through the weather today." The rest of the people were waiting anxiously on shore in a state of semistarvation.

So I stayed behind on the ice that the airplane might take a pay load of five seals or approximately 800 pounds to our waiting family. As Bud took off I saw a large army transport ship flying along the edge of our arctic horizon to shoreward.

"I suppose that's filled with five-star generals and things," I thought. "They're getting thicker every day."

If so, they never saw our camp. Had they sighted it in the ice they probably would have circled for an observation.

Bud got back by the time I got the seal meat boiling for breakfast. Apiak had boiled stomach and mammary glands (which he enjoyed with the spring milk in them), Bud had heart, I had the liver, and Bud brought back some newly-made cinnamon rolls from Nanny. By 1:20 the hunters started off with the sled into the ice, and I took my seat in the tethered *Arctic Tern*.

The strange ice forms about our camp looked like pure marble Greek statuary in the white sunshine. The statues were in attitudes of action, some as though they were about to spring to life. Some were crouched, some huddled. Gigantic faces — beneath which the dog sled wound, loaded with seals — assumed expressions of nobility, their beards dripping with icicles. As wisps of horse-tail clouds trailed across the sky the shadows lengthened and one looked out upon the distant buttes of Montana and Wyoming as they used to be. Again, as one ventured among the thickly-strewn, jumbled blocks of the crushed ice, he might imagine himself surrounded by the exotic flowering shrubs of a king's gardens.

But the noble statuary with the benign faces composed in hoary meditation, and the busts with angel's wings poised for flight would change meaning to a person who was lost in the desert of ice. Every ice hummock would be transformed into a horrible grinning gargoyle. I was glad that both Apiak and Bud were seasoned ice men who knew what they were doing.

The pilot who flies above this ice knows how hopeless it is, how endless. He sees the danger in its signs, its patterns from the air. The airplane to persons camped out on the ice means unsuspected ease in the middle of hostility; it means a challenge, an effrontery to this eternal polar icecap. It means possible rescue.

Seeing a dog sled slowly approaching across the vast plain, skirting ice ridges and detouring the violet buttes, is one of the strangest sights in the world. In the evening I usually saw the hunters come home. At first I could make them out only by the telescope on my rifle — a dot out there. Slowly the dot changed its relationship to the scattered ice domes. As the dot lengthened out into a thin line I knew that the dog sled had swung sideways; it contracted and lengthened alternately as it wound its tedious way. As it became visible to the naked eye it reminded one of a ship on the ocean. The driver standing up behind the sled on the back runners with his arms on the tall bars was the ship's mast. The ship glided over a trackless sea. At times it seemed to float suspended in space, for there was no distinct horizon. The last half mile of its progress disclosed the two human figures, the one standing and driving the dogs, the other seated on the sled. Dressed in long white gowns, their white hoods outlined faces of mahogany black side-lighted by a low orange sun. The immobile figures with their featureless dark faces rose out of the foreground as if they, too, were some of the ice figurines which had come to life before me.

The appearance of man on the ice was like the first revelation of his existence on earth. As the sled rose over the last undulating snow-drift into our camp one could surmise that the dark faces staring out of the white hoods were possessed of some intelligence which was alien among the ice. One could feel the intensity of their glance.

A moment later here was Bud driving and Apiak sitting, their sun-burned faces creased into the familiar pattern of welcoming smiles for me, and I hastened to set the tea to boiling and saw that they had four big seals, like drooping blimps, on their sled. The dogs pulled and panted the last yards to the tent. The hunters were home. It was ten o'clock at night.

Photography of the polar ice is not easy. We have seen a lot of beauty in Alaska and elsewhere in nature, but one can say that any mortal has to go out to the drifting ice floes of the polar ocean on a spring night to see the most beautiful colors that exist on our planet. He has seen nothing at all until he has seen this spectacle, dangerous though it is to see it. I saw it once.

It was an experience in being a trespasser in an age gone by. It was the Ice Age again, or some dim dawn of unrecorded time when mists come and monsters rise from the deep. And great dawn, a mon-ster did rise and I saw it!

Ook-sook was just reeling in the line of his manok from the twilight seas. Then, whoosh! The ocean erupted right in front of the three of us. A creature raised its neck four feet out of the water where we stood on the ice ledge and looked us right in the eye. The glassy eyes stared so close that we could almost reach out and touch them. Then the creature arched its body and slid beneath the cold black surface. We just stood gazing at the spot where small waves sucked hollowly beneath the ice.

Ugrug! The giant bearded seal that weighs nearly as much as a moose.

Bud and Ook-sook threw themselves prone on the edge of the ice, rifles cocked. I shoved the gun, which I was carrying, into Bud's hand, removing at the same time the leather cap from its telescope. No word was spoken. We just crouched.

The giant reared far out in the lead and dove again. He was traveling on. When he rolled the next time along our ice shelf he was 100 yards away. Bud got the crosshairs of the telescope into line at the exact moment and shot him in the brain in mid-roll. That was one of the nicest shots Bud ever made.

The ugrug stopped in mid-roll and turned sluggishly on its back. It floated! We on the ice reef howled for joy. Get a line on it! We ran forward to cast the manok. Then — bubbles came up. Clouds of wine-red blood stained the black water and trailed off. Tipping slowly backwards, keel up, the wonderful monster sank before our eyes into the inexorable enclosing waters of the Arctic Ocean. Oh, cruel loss! Sometimes an ugrug will float in winter or in spring — never in summer. It depends upon the amount of an animal's blubber and the buoyancy of salt water. The polar sea had reclaimed its own.

I looked now at my boot soles curled up beneath me on the luxurious airplane upholstery. They were made, of course, of durable ugrug.

Life here is the most primitive now existent on our planet and it can be cruel. We lost about 800 pounds of meat and blubber that time, not to mention the many needed pairs of boot soles. The Eskimos lose three out of every four seals, walrus or whales they shoot in the water. It amounts to tens of thousands of animals each year in Alaskan waters.

Shaking with cold in the lowered temperatures of midnight after our vigil at the lead, our little party worked barehanded at retrieving seals shot hours past, and at the difficult job of photographing them. We had to stand on the ice and wait for our seals to float in on the breeze. Other seals popped up in their swimming farther out, sticking their heads up through the glassy cold water; again, that time, I had seemed to hear all the while that strange music of the spheres.

The sun was gone an hour when we lost the ugrug and then it got lighter. A mist began to form. Cautiously the sun sneaked back into our vision, hanging just over the North Pole, as dim as some boarding-house electric light bulb. Squaw ducks and king eiders in the golden lanes between the silent ice cakes greeted it with a chorus of cries. Revealed gradually before us were standing ice cliffs of pearl, etched on their edges with turquoise green, reflected in the motionless water of copper brown, and a quarter of a slim lemon moon hung over all.

The scene changed by the moment as it lightened. Fragile and delicate were the stalagmites of the ice boulders caused by the thawing of spring. Little ponds lay at their base, having frozen during the night. The drinking water in the ponds which form on the ice in spring is fresh. For some unknown reason old ice which has existed more than one year, loses its saltiness into the ocean beneath and becomes fresh for camp use. At midday the ponds would melt again, pouring down scalloped, jade-green ravines of ice like mountain brooks, with a tinkling everywhere of millions of chimes.

I sat in the luxurious airplane, a modern explorer now, and continued my reverie. Black smoke came swiftly over the sea as we looked. I had time to complete a picture or two, and hustled my camera back into its parka of caribou fur.

What was it? A foreboding clutched us. Ook-sook rolled his eyes and looked foolish. He was an inland Eskimo and didn't know any more about the ice than Bud and I did. We were forty miles from shore and it was June.

Of course it was fog, just another variety of it. It meant that the sea was getting more open everywhere around us. Inky black, as black as midnight is supposed to be, the wicked tentacles of the fog sped towards us in a great engulfing mass, shutting out the sun. I hurried to take a last picture of Ook-sook. He had a dead seal caught in the young ice some yards from "shore," and was at work tossing ice blocks into the water to break a pathway through the solidifying slush so that he could drag the seal in with the manok. The camera was ready to freeze up. It had been out of its case half the night, waiting for ugrugs that never waited to be photographed, and its shutter sounded very slow. Fearing that overexposure was resulting from a sticky shutter,

I closed the lens down to a wild guess, and hoped for the best. This opportunity would never come again in a whole lifetime. Nothing would ever get me out here again, I thought.

Then, far away down the ice corridors from our camp, an uproar reverberated. It came to us much as it might have come through limestone caverns. The sound was dim and faint. We had wandered two miles from our tent and dogs. Polar bear in camp? We were sure of it. The chained dogs wouldn't have a chance!

Bud dashed for home. The disturbance turned out to be just another dog fight, but I was left with Ook-sook as the strange black fog closed in. Would Ook-sook never get that last seal? He started to walk out to it impatiently. Grabbing him by his clothing, I pulled him back. I couldn't stand the sight of that new ice bending with him over unknown thousands of feet of ocean.

"No, no, Ook-sook. Dangerous," I exhorted him in Eskimo. That time he seemed to agree with me. He did get the seal, however, just as the fog hit us.

With Ook-sook dragging the seal on a line behind, I started leading the way to camp. Turquoise and pearl ice hummocks stood out stark before the lapping wavelets of the cold ocean in which they drifted, while the sun came through the black shroud only as a flattened orange ball, very much as if it were in eclipse. "Stand right there, Ook-sook," and I got another picture along our way. Even though death and the world's end seemed imminent, I had my camera in hand. "For heaven's sake, can't you smile?"

Long hoar frost covered our furs from the fog as we three met at the soiled brown little tent among the ice boulders. Yes, *that* had certainly been one summer night out on the ice I wouldn't forget. *Life* Magazine ran 14 pages in color, the longest color assignment that they had ever done. I shivered and snapped back to the present.

Soon this white ice statuary will turn to yellow and green, I thought, for the sun daily shrinks the snow upon it. When the ice begins to look dirty, George said that's a sign that it will rot out fast and you had better get to shore.

As we slept in our tent it was difficult to imagine that some five feet beneath lay the ocean with strange fish swimming by. We wondered occasionally about the fish. Are there flounders and halibut in this ocean? Are there octopus and crabs? It seemed conceivable because we know these creatures inhabit adjacent northern waters just as cold. Yet we were under the impression that fisheries of the Arctic Ocean would prove rather limited. There might be a shortage of vegetation over large areas on the bottom because this ocean, enclosed by continents, is not much disturbed; locked in the Ice Age as it is, there are not the currents which might easily bring in living organisms from the other oceans. We know that whitefish, sea trout, and arctic char run along the edge of North America and utilize many of our arctic rivers for their spawning. But we have little idea of what life inhabits the Arctic Ocean far from land.

Out on the frozen ocean we were obliged to renounce all land game and live on seals. Bud found his powerful .300 Magnum with 'scope could get them at distances hitherto undreamed of. Each animal was encased in a layer of blubber up to four inches thick running around the entire body, which weighed again as much as the animal itself: the pure profit for which we hunted. Total weight of each seal ran from around 120 pounds to 150 pounds. Dogs and humans together consumed almost one seal a day with a small amount of blubber to balance the lean. We ate females more often than bull seals because their flesh seemed milder. I have often been asked how I liked the diet.

The person who has lived on land animals all his life is not going to like the taste of sea animals at either the first or the second attempt to eat them. The strange odor of the cooking meat and its tarry black appearance are far from prepossessing. My silver forks turned black on the tines from it, much as silverware becomes discolored from the yolk of a soft-boiled egg. My pressure cooker accumulated a kind of glue from the meat, which no scouring agent I thereafter discovered was able to remove. In order to keep from ruining my pressure cooker, I was shortly obliged to turn back to an ordinary cooking pot which could later be thrown away following sufficient encrustation.

After living upon seal two or three weeks we got so we could eat it pleasurably provided no other thing was around. I have no doubt that it was a treasury of minerals, including quantities of sulphur and iodine, with the vitamins doubtless presented in a highly condensed form. Never in our lives has either of us been more bursting with vitality than when we were forcibly on the straight seal meat and blubber diet. Physicians say that a quality which is doubtless contained in the sea animals as in few of the foods that are eaten by modern people today is the steroids, of which not a great deal yet is known except that they are a tonic for the glandular system of the body, having to do with resistance to old age and the aging processes.

George Woods could hardly bring himself to eat seal meat, although the children loved it. He still clung, like Bud and me, to the food preferences of the inland Eskimo. He said: "Them old Eskimos that lived on the whale and the seal, they were strong fellow. They make us people look weak today. Those old fellow would laugh at us. Only, I don't think maybe people today have the strong stomick to take that strong meat."

Mixed in with George's observation there was some possible truth. The old Eskimos *were* stronger. They had a better diet than present-day Eskimos have who supplement seal meat generously with flour and beans. But even present-day Eskimos like George and Nanny have a better diet than average Americans. As for our stomachs being weak, is it possible that people today lack the vital enzymes that are produced by plentiful steroids in primitive animal food?

George had advised taking the seal meat diet slowly or we might get sick. A half pound of this meat eaten straight down, unless you are used to it, will make you as dizzy as breathing pure oxygen or swilling down a straight pint of cod liver oil. You get used to it by practice and develop a tolerance to the condensed vitamins and minerals.

First I learned to like boiled seal heart, then boiled liver which are not unlike these organs in other animals. Bud liked the boiled ribs from the beginning, while Apiak liked best the head, complete with eyes, teeth and whiskers. As we only had one meat pot and had to economize on fuel, I soon got used to cooking these sections together in the same pot, and each person would grab for the part he preferred. Apiak liked to crack the thin skull of the head with the back of his hunting knife and eat out the cooked brains with a teaspoon. I coaxed myself into eating seal meat regularly, as I had no intention of courting some disease of malnutrition by living only on biscuits and tea.

One day a crack in the ice was discovered, having opened up four inches on the far side of the airplane by the tent. Bud simply moved the airplane by taxiing it across the crack. The crack never opened any wider.

Had we not been vigilant the diverging ice to which it was roped would have pulled our airplane in two. Cracks in the ice, caused by winds and currents, may come at any time but they occur slowly.

Intense light was with us on the ice both night and day, its rays even penetrating the canvas tent to burn our faces while we slept. Bud's lips became so caked and cracked that he could hardly open his mouth to eat. Apiak's tougher brunette skin was black. Even I who kept out of the direct sun to a great extent became deeply freckled and my skin felt dry and leathery. Eagerly the hunters shared my cold cream jar with me.

We had just crawled into the sack at midnight when Apiak from his separate trail tent spotted a dog team coming. It was Oo-lak and Tagiluk. We expected them to get a sled load of seals — our transport crew. Some of the seals were too bloody and soft to go in the airplane.

We welcomed the arrivals with tea in the white light of an early morning sun which was 10 degrees above the horizon at 1 A.M. The boys had sledded by night because the snow was firmer during the cool hours. Alas, they brought no bread, and our provisions other than our pile of seals amounted to just ten pounds.

The next morning almost all our last remaining flour and corn meal went into huge pancakes which I fried in the skillet to fill the crowd up and provide them a trail ration. Then Apiak announced that he would return to Oliktok with Oo-lak, leaving with us only the awkward Tagiluk and the poorest team. It had not occurred to us that we would lose our chief hunter as well as the star of our film. But he would come back as soon as he could. His father and mother and sisters on shore were hungry for caribou. The thought that he would bring back for us a small piece of the delicious caribou — if it went that far — cheered us.

Tagi, the big nineteen-year-old orphan, a lovable and blundering boy, anxious to please, had his own little trail tent to sleep in. This was the first time in his life he had been alone on his own with white people; he spoke no English. He had been kicked around all his life. We hoped to show him a good time. Bud, seated in his usual royal place upon the sled, disappeared into the overcast ice-scape with Tagi as driver.

The day dawned mild and partially clear, seeming almost tropical, without a wind. I was alerted for a holiday because Bud had promised that on Sunday, weather permitting, he and I would fly to Oliktok and to Beechey Point to visit.

All there was to eat in camp other than seal meat was some soy bean soup mix which Mrs. James had been unable to sell to her Indians at Hughes and had donated. Leaving Tagi in camp, Bud and I took off with the airplane and within 20 minutes landed at Oliktok.

At Oliktok we found all of Mathew's People encamped, having arrived emaciated and belatedly on the coast for the sealing. Noble old Mathew dressed entirely in caribou skins without a stitch of cloth clothing on him, was saddened by the loss of his wife. But his seamed face could still muster a smile and it held no bitterness toward life. To study his face was to see written the testimony of a man who considered that he had had full measure of all good things. What could I say? As I shook hands with him I found myself squeezing his hand a little harder than usual, but words couldn't come, either English or Eskimo. Then with admirable composure he straightened himself like an old soldier as the tears started to his eyes and he said to me, "T'ank you. T'ank you." I bolted, gulping.

After shaking hands all around with Mathew's grown sons and daughters and grandchildren, a group in which stalwart Colliak's absence was conspicuous, I noticed that George and Nanny had moved into the old summer tent. They had just moved out of the igloo yesterday. George explained that now the warm weather had come the igloo had a "strong smell."

As I took my place for my cup of tea and slice of bread in Nanny's summer home, and the tent flap rustled in the spring breeze and the snow birds twittered, it was very good. Lydia had fattened up a little, I noticed. She was absorbed with several little balloons. They were made from the inner membranes of the crops of ptarmigan. Her mother, upon preparing an occasional bird for dinner, removed the crops without breaking them, and blew them up for the child, tying up the openings with sinew thread. Inside Lydia's translucent balloon, you could see dried willow buds shake about and rattle — the unfortunate bird's last meal.

Lingering a couple of hours, with an eye on the weather every moment, Bud and I then flew over to the Jones Islands where we learned Abraham Stine was now encamped; he had with him there the key to the Beechey Point warehouse. While Bud and the storekeeper flew to Beechey Point I stayed on the Jones Islands with Dora who treated me to the best: a kettle of Pacific eider boiled with rice soup, hot sourdough biscuits and real canned butter. I ate and ate. Probably one of the extreme delights of the vagabond's life is that you are always hungry, and when visiting you know you will be fed.

The smell of wood smoke was good again after weeks on the sterile ice. It was good to be on firm, solid ground, to sit on a warm, dry floor. Dora was a cluttered housekeeper with unemptied kettles of entrails setting about waiting for the dogs. I noted that the two webbed feet from the Pacific eider were thrown among the bedding for the two little girls to teethe on, and I never saw more perfect dental arches than those two cherubs possessed. Showing their white blood prominently, with great rosy cheeks, they were children who would have taken a baby prize in any magazine except that to some people they might have evidenced a strangely attractive wildness about them, somewhat like lion cubs.

16 DOG TEAM AND AIRPLANE

AT OUR CAMP on the ice the spring blubber hunting was showing profit. We had a new supply of grub from the Beechey Point warehouse. A typical meal might be boiled seal, bread and peanut butter, stewed dried pears and tea. I had sat around so much this spring that Bud urged that I try my hand at hunting. Tagi, with his battered .25–35 and open sights, only got one seal last spring out of twenty shots, Bud reminded me; certainly I couldn't do any worse than that. We needed to augment the supply for the ice cellar on shore by every possible seal we could get as the harvest season passed. I had to agree myself that it was a shame for my fine .30–06 with 'scope to just be lying around unused, for nothing much seemed to be happening at camp.

"Pretty soon Mathew's boys will be out here," Bud said, "and I'll hunt with one of them, probably with Ook-sook, and help them out, and you can have Tagi and his sled. So you had better begin to practice up. There're seals everywhere now, even right around camp."

Consequently, as soon as the fellows were gone into the gloaming one morning, seeing the dark form of a basking seal within easy walking distance of the camp where I kept vigil, I donned a white snowshirt over my parka and set forth to try my luck.

I had not gone far with my eyes focused on the seal when everything blurred. I stopped, sat down on the level white plain, and tried to locate the seal again through my telescope sight by resting the rifle over my knees. It was a dead overcast day, with indeterminate visibility of perhaps one mile.

In a few minutes I found the seal again, although it persisted in fading out intermittently, a blob that seemed to float suspended in the shimmering whiteness. I progressed some distance when I discovered that I had dropped my mittens where I last sat. Oh well, it was a warm day, and it was better to pursue the seal and pick the mittens up on my return.

Again the blob toward which I walked dimmed out, as my eyes behind their sunglasses smarted in tears; once more I patiently searched with the strong rifle telescope.

This continued for what may have been a number of hours. Time dimmed out too, and there was only me, the black glob, and my determination. My confusion may be imagined when at length, upon taking my last and final observation through my rifle telescope, I discovered that I had wandered in a circle right back to where I was in the beginning, and the black glob in the whiteness that I had been carefully stalking for the last hour turned out to be my own mittens!

Meanwhile, the seal which lived in the vicinity had either dived in boredom or for reasons of his own retired under the ocean. The hunt was ended. It was with a peculiar feeling of unreality about the whole business that I slogged back to the camp. One can be made to feel awfully foolish on the ice.

At first out on the ice I had been afraid to walk about for fear of plunging through some crack into the sea. Bud urged me to be more bold. Pools of water now lay around the base of the hummocks while snow covered many ice boulders and their sockets. It was spooky. One year in late spring Bud had plunged through an enlarged seal hole and saved himself only by throwing out his arms. In the rough ice, where I had no intention of wandering alone, an adventurer could sometimes see down fifteen feet into a crack as he stepped across; a misstep there could mean literal entombment.

Abraham Stine arrived. "White man live on seal meat all spring," he greeted me grinning. "I never see that before." We were all up next morning by 9 A.M. and Bud went off with Abraham's sled and I rode on Tagi's. I had a glorious day of it, winding in and out through the jumbled ice. The dog team gave you something real to look at and deal with.

"Oh, please, don't you think we can photograph today?" was the eternal question I put to Bud. "Even if there's no sun, let's shoot film while we're here."

"No, it won't work," he replied. "We'll just have to keep on waiting for sun. You can't photograph *nothing*."

"That's the trouble with this whole subject," I said. "This polar ice is just a study of *nothing*. There are no shadows, no vegetation. No familiar objects anywhere. Yet it certainly produces some strange effects upon the person visiting it. Our problem is: can emotional effects be photographed? If they can be," I ended, "you know I think we're on the track of getting one of the world's most original films."

There was absolutely no perspective on an overcast day and very little at any time. You couldn't tell distance or the size of things because there were no known objects for comparison.

I saw an obelisk-like figure sticking up on an ice cake. I watched it as Tagi drove our sled slowly forward.

"It might be Bud," I thought. "He's dressed all in white. His sled may be waiting just behind that ridge, and he has climbed up there to take an observation."

However, as the figure did not move and it had no face, I determined that it was just more ice. "It must be about fifteen feet high," I concluded.

It was only during the last yards of approach that a complete transformation took place in my psychology. The ice figure began to shrink. When our sled passed close by, it dwindled abruptly to a figure just two feet tall.

One of the difficulties of mapping the boundaries of lands of the Arctic Ocean, far out near the North Pole, is this deception of the human senses which repeatedly occurs. Only by walking over a given area inch by inch can its real dimensions and conformations be determined. The army's project of aerial photography of polar lands is not too satisfactory, for even the camera lies; the days that photography is possible are numbered to only a few out of the year.

Yet awkward Tagi was a master at maneuvering a sled through rough ice, as Bud had already discovered. The dogs had legs like coiled springs. I couldn't understand why their legs didn't get broken. Although Tagi and I conservatively followed only old established hunting trails, and stuck to "smooth country" it seemed to me at every bend that we had surely entered an impasse. Yet, like the cowboy with his horse who finds a way through the wonderland of rocks, Tagi always found a way. In a few places I had to get off the sled and walk or run, and then each step was a surprise. Covered with a rounded, deceptive layer of snow, the jumbled blocks offered many a crevice into which to plunge a leg. Many spills were inevitable. Usually they weren't painful because the snow cushioned us, and we were, like the dogs, encased in soft skins.

Bud was anxious that I shoot some seals. The first one Tagi and I found was right in our trail. It should have been a cinch. You could creep up upon it, behind a boulder. But I was cautious. No wind today; I thought the seal would hear me. I had just about decided to make the best of a fairly long shot when Tagi reached my side and led me forward. But when he peeked around the ice boulder the seal saw him and dove. Tagi's indifferent approach alarmed it.

The second seal I had Tagi stalk, using my rifle, but he scared it. The third seal the dogs rushed and scared.

"Pore eye," laughed Tagi, referring to himself and me. We should have seen the third seal but it had its burrow in a depression with foot-high ice all around, so we didn't know it was there until we were upon it.

As we had to return to camp with some game by any means, I told Tagi to stalk the next one, and he got it. I studied his approach from where I parked with the dogs, just out of sight behind the ice. Tagi made a fine shot at 85 yards, nailing it. At the shot the dogs broke into a wild chorus of howls and before I could catch the sled, galloped away. I enjoyed a nice walk.

Tagi then sewed up the hole in the seal to prevent mess and loss of blood and we made a "seal snow house" at the site of the kill, covering up the carcass with snow to pick up upon our return; then we traveled on. Tagi climbed an ice pinnacle at intervals with his old, handed-down whaler's telescope to announce a seal in the offing.

"Bud, track," Tagi advised suddenly. And there were Bud's tracks in the snow where he had killed a seal from that very seal hole previously. All I had to do to take a lesson in stalking was to follow the tracks right to it and do what the tracks did.

The tracks led around and through a conglomeration of snow-encased ice shapes, many of which I had to hoist myself up on by bracing both mittens and knees. A shower of snow crystals tinkled audibly at every move. While Bud's long legs had moved over this terrain with ease, I sank hip deep into cracks from which I was minutes extricating a leg. To step in the exact tracks he had made proved noisy, the snow having stiffened. At this time the fickle sun burst through the haze for its only appearance of the entire day and I was drenched with sweat and my sunglasses fogged.

Emerging into an idyllic little valley, I now ran into the most common difficulty of seal stalking. I knew the seal was near some place, but exactly where? The exact position of the seal should be memorized before you start. Ultimately, just when I was about to give up in the belief that the seal was gone, I saw it. It was a little farther yet over the next valley, still peacefully rolling and basking.

The closest approach I could make was 120 yards. I shot. The seal dove. The world was empty. The dogs yelped and around the end of the ice valley Tagi and the sled careened.

We found blood spattered about and the water in the seal hole was thick with blood. Tagi got down on his hands and knees and poked with the long stick he carried. No luck. Sometimes a dead seal will float in the hole just beneath the surface.

Time for tea. We stopped at the same picnic grounds where Bud and Tagi had tea before. The dogs lay in their traces panting, while Tagi expertly unloaded the tea things from the sled.

Our sun had dimmed out for the day. My sweaty body grew cold. When I told Tagi I was cold he improvised a little tent by simply draping his sled cover over the edge of the sled and over our shoulders where we sat down, using the primus stove for a heater, sheltered in the upturned side of the grub box. By sticking my face and hands into this heat crouched with Tagi while drinking hot tea, I was immediately warmed, even though our own backsides furnished the side of the tent. Tagi was proud, attentive and respectful. I felt like a girl with a new beau.

The last part of our hunting day was damp and foggy, with wet mittens, soggy feet, and faces flaming with a severe polar burn. Tagi shot one more seal, a very lean one, while I assumed control of the team. We got home at ten o'clock that night, Tagi in great joy that "we" had got as many seals as those top hunters Bud and Abraham, together.

"It sure is nice of these people to let us ride around on their sleds with them," I remarked to Bud. Far from expecting guide's fees or salaries from us, the hunters were proud to come from miles around to the camp we had established so that we could make our film and, principally, all have a good time together.

I was alone in camp when I saw a long black apparition move slowly into my horizon: two dog teams. "Well, it's about time," I thought. "Mathew's boys are coming out at last."

Each driver, lounging or half sleeping in his sled, came on with a tremendous number of dogs: Ook-sook and his young brother, Uke, sixteen. Like ours at the commencement of the season, their dogs were in such a starved condition they could hardly pull one man with an empty sled. Mathew's People always were noted for the number rather than the quality of their dogs. A lot of them had been eaten during the winter. The others were being brought out here to fatten.

Ook-sook had on regular Eskimo dress for the ice. He looked wild enough. He had with him the old rifle which he had hunted with the year he lived with us.

The rifle barrel was an old Winchester model 1894 with an octagon barrel. It was around fifty years old and loose in every joint. Many sled accidents had broken the tang while the stock was held in place by wire so that it drooped about four inches. By now completely smoothbored, the old .30–30's chamber was so badly worn, with head space so great, that every time the rifle fired it blew the cartridge cases in half! Ook-sook countered with a hook. He first pulled out the back half of the shell case, and then he reached in and hooked out the front half. As much fire flew out the breech as out the muzzle every time the rifle went off. The original sights were gone, but a set of homemade brass sights had replaced them. With this now single-shot rifle, Ook-sook supported himself, his family and his dog team. The rifle had strong days and it had days (due to low temperatures which affect the accuracy of bullets) when it was "no strong." This rifle had killed, we would estimate, some fifteen thousand head of big game altogether.

The two brothers were ragged skeletons. First I hastened to revive them with tea and graham crackers in my neat dwelling — the quickest thing at hand. Then, realizing their hunger for meat and blubber, I told them to boil all they wanted for themselves and their dogs from our big meat pile. After they had set up their shabby little tent and prepared their feast, I surprised myself by succumbing to a strange urge to join them. Bringing my own tin plate and knife and a stained fork, I sat with them in their tent and we ate quantities. Uke, with his hunger for fat, after lean caribou inland, cut so much blubber we couldn't eat a quarter of it, but we did succeed in getting away with eight or ten pounds in all.

When Bud and Tagiluk got home from sealing, I had them all to my tent for more seal meat and an apple strudel, which I made in a vessel borrowed from Ook-sook, that exactly fitted inside the pressure cooker.

As Bud and I slept, the happy bachelors frolicked half the night; the sounds of a harmonica and coffee drinking could be heard.

We had only been asleep about two hours when at 4 A.M. we were roused by the dogs. A seal had come walking right up to our tent!

Once in a while a seal coming out on top of the ice to bask will lose its burrow and not be able to find it again. When that happens the seal is stranded in a hostile world and will drag itself countless miles over the ice by its front flippers. The end is freezing, starvation, or certain death at the fangs of bears or the white foxes that live on the ice.

So far will these destitute seals travel on their flippers that Richard's

People reported one found 75 miles inland, still looking for water. Richard's People were trapping on the prairie when Richard remarked one morning, "We are getting hungry for seal blubber. I think I will sled to the ocean and hunt the seal." Richard opened the door. And there, right at the door of his igloo, was a lost seal which had walked all the way from the ocean directly to him!

I had seen the track of a lost seal leading over the surface of the ice when I was out with Tagi. That such a seal would come flopping into our camp was fantastic, but it actually happened!

"Hurry! Get up!" cried Bud jubilantly, as he withdrew his head from peeping out the tent flap. "We've got our chance in a million for the cameras. It's a sunny day!"

The miracle of our only sunshine coming just at the moment the seal arrived was beyond words. But I am so inadequate at four o'clock in the morning. My eyes wouldn't stay open. Even the bachelors, peeking out their tents and seeing only a seal, wouldn't get up, aside from loyal Tagi, and he retired again shortly.

In the glaring sun which lighted the shadowless polar world, Bud dragged the seal by the hind flippers, and it squirmed and snapped at him with fierce teeth; he dropped it in a hurry. Next he decided to lasso it, whirling a noose and running after the flopping animal like a cowboy. The noose caught. But roping a seal is just like trying to tie up and hold a glob of jelly. The jelly slipped out of the noose where the rope squeezed it. I ran to the airplane and got a gunny sack. We bound and sacked the seal. It was my half-articulate intention to just go back to bed, and we could photograph our captive later. Bud suggested that we get Tagi to stab it with a hunting knife the way he killed crippled seals occasionally. At four in the morning I couldn't think what kind of pictures we wanted of the seal, but certainly *not* that. The yearling seal was so cute that already I loved it.

We unsacked the seal and went to work at photographing its movements and facial expressions. It reminded one of a little fat man in a pettish mood, for even though the seal realized it should flee for its life, it had to stop to sleep every two minutes for naps of several seconds' duration. The need for naps seemed constitutional. When we poked and roused it, its lips curled back in an exasperated snarl, and the round opaque eyes registered alarm. Yet the sleep compulsion was so strong that it dozed off again, and so did I while standing up.

Thus two hours passed and the total of 38 dogs on their chains screamed and lunged, while the bachelors tried to sleep, and up and down the icy glades beside the brilliantly painted airplane and the little tents we pursued our annoyed fat prey.

At six o'clock we sacked the seal and went back to bed. But neither of us could sleep. I kept wondering if the seal was slowly suffocating in the sack and the thought permitted no rest. Bud was excited over the hunting and photography which such a day would offer, and he wanted to get an early start.

We all had a miserable breakfast at 9 A.M. when Bud hailed the sleepy bachelors into our tent at a time when my pancakes were burning and my hair was hanging down into them. I went off to hunt with Tagi, while Bud trekked with Ook-sook. Bud and Ook-sook freighted the sacked seal across the ice on the sled to the nearest seal hole and as a reward for its having been such a good actor, allowed it to escape under the sea where it belonged.

Our assembled camp was now composed of five Eskimo bachelors and Bud and me, and dogs which numbered up to almost fifty. When you have fifty dogs in camp you have bedlam.

There was water-sky on the horizon shoreward, showing that the big Colville and Kuparuk Rivers had flooded the ocean ice along the continent for many miles. This water separated us all, including Mathew's and Abraham's families on the Jones Islands, from the continent, except for one strip of ice a mile wide which still permitted sled passage. The rising water and rotting ice did not worry the Eskimos who would not leave their sealing until the last moment. Uke went to shore with a load of five seals for Mathew, and Tagi went with a load for our family. Apiak and Abraham Stine were back and Ook-sook remained, while Bud helped him hunt.

It was about one in the morning and we had all just gone to bed. The dogs commenced a frightful uproar and we thought, "Ho-hum! Just another dog fight." As the barking continued, I urged Bud to peep out the tent door.

"*Nanuk!*" was all he said. In his tone was all the magic we had been waiting for.

I looked out and saw the visitor approaching at a slow ambling gait like a great yellow phantom out of the night fog. Polar bear!

All the weeks on the ice I had kept my clothes within instant reach, waiting for just this moment which was most likely to come during the cool shadows of night. All I had to do was slip into my long woman's parka which was under my head and thrust a fur stocking onto each foot. As I reached for my rifle and crouched, loading a shell into the barrel, I felt suddenly light and buoyant, filled with purposeful energy. For after six months on the ice I was at last getting used to polar bears, and Bud and I had planned exactly how I was to shoot the bear when he came.

Scrambling over to Abraham's tent in a half crouch, I found Abraham already stationed there with his own rifle, while Tagi with the glasses was kneeling behind an upturned sled. It was all up to me. The Eskimos had promised Bud they wouldn't shoot.

The bear was approaching upwind, following his nose. I believe the Eskimos would have waited until he got right into camp, but a person had a hard time to hold steady with all those dogs trying to break loose at once. Only one thought was in my mind: get him before he gets into camp.

"Can you lie down to shoot?" Abraham whispered.

"I will shoot sitting down," I replied, and opened fire without further delay. Bud wasn't there to counsel me. What I had never stopped to hear Bud say was that he wanted above all to photograph the live bear.

At the shot, the bear jumped and poised broadside, offering a perfect target. I reloaded and carefully aimed through the crosshair 'scope. There was no doubt in my mind as I fired. A split instant before I fired, Abraham opened fire with his first shot. He had a 'scope we had got him, mounted on his .30–30. Then, just after I fired, we saw the white bear slump on his haunches.

"You got him," Abraham said.

We waited then. I held the sight steady on the bear, and in a few moments the great supporting shoulder gave way, the head dropped, and we all knew he was dead.

Bud, who had been rummaging in the airplane in a state of undress to get the camera going, came up to offer lame congratulations. He had given me one pep talk too many about how easy polar bears are to kill. The deed was done. Everyone there had killed polar bears before but Ook-sook and me.

Returning to our tents, we dressed leisurely and pushed the light sled over to the carcass. It was three hundred yards! I had shot at an inadvisable distance, but somehow luck was with me, for the shot had broken the bear's neck, killing him instantly. Bud dug out my bullet.

It was a two-year-old male weighing only about 300 pounds. He had a very nice coat although not much blubber was on him. At one in the morning we took moving pictures in the dim reflected light, the Eskimos assisting even though the job kept them up all night. Pushing the bear on the sled over in front of our tent the boys skinned it, Bud doing half the work, and cut the meat into piles. Had they delayed doing this for even a few hours the strong muscles would have set and made the job extremely difficult. I served hot tea and a "party" in my tent for all at 4 A.M.

Late the next noon we had our breakfast outdoors without our parkas, in front of the tent, setting up the primus stove and using the two dog sleds for seats and picnic table. Boiled polar bear ribs, because of changes in our taste perceptions caused by living on seal, tasted as sweet as beef to us. Bud told the Eskimos about the danger of trichinosis in eating polar bear meat that is not well cooked. A recent issue of the journal *Arctic* had reported infestation in some of the polar bears off Norway, and we bore in mind that polar bears are international animals.

Abraham sledded off for the Jones Islands carrying my polar bear hide for Dora to scrape; he would pick up a number of seals for their household on the way.

My lips began to swell from sun blisters and when I awoke the morning following, after a feverish night, my mouth was almost unrecognizable. For several days I sat in the tent applying salve, and dipping a washcloth into a pan of hot water, steaming my lips in an effort to "draw out" the poisonous rays. The men hunted in shirtsleeves, wearing only their white snowshirts over their woolens, their parkas carried unused on the sleds. Everything was soft and slushy. My lips festered and finally began to heal and scab over.

All over Alaska the snow had long since melted and another summer was here. The steel-shod runners of the dog sleds, crossing the ice toward shore with their final loads, ground over barren sand reefs through patches of shy pink tuliplike blooms without stems. Little rivulets flowed over the ice surface, joining bigger ones until they formed brooks rushing like water mains toward holes in the ice, the old seal breathing holes.

As the hunters sledded they had to be careful not to step into a hole. The dogs didn't care about that; they would swim over bottomless puddles with the sled floating behind them as well as through the safe ones. The hunters looked sharp when their dogs began to swim; as long as the dogs kept walking they knew it was all right ahead.

Bud and I broke camp quickly one fine day and flew back to Oliktok over open ocean.

"We didn't do so bad this season," Bud summed it up. "We must have got over five thousand pounds of blubber altogether. It will help those folks out more than anything you could do for them."

The salmon fisheries on the southern coasts of Alaska, jealous of the fish which hair seals were eating and not willing to place the blame on their own greed for the steady decrease of the salmon pack, had recently got the territorial legislature to place a six dollar bounty on these seals. Some people were making a summer's living just bounty hunting, a wasteful slaughter. It seemed a great shame when the poor Eskimos demonstrated in their lives how useful common seals can be!

Out from the little tin warehouse came the wheels for the *Arctic Tern* which we had stored during this time. While I photographed the process Bud took off the skis of winter exploration and put on wheels for flying south. The C.A.A. inspector, according to regulation, is supposed to see such work before you are authorized to fly your airplane, but the closest inspector to us was 520 miles away at Fairbanks, and Bud reckoned that he could inspect the job later. I was used to seeing Bud take the airplane apart and put it together again in many out-of-the-way places.

Our farewell with Nanny and George was sad, not knowing when or if we would ever see them again. It was also a strained farewell because they expected to see us killed before their eyes on the take-off.

The wind was all wrong for a take-off on the short sandy exposed beach. So all day long George and the boys, at Bud's direction, worked at shoveling a runway through the snow on the level sea ice in front of the igloo. We had never before tried to take off on ice with wheels, but we would try it. Yet the faster they shoveled, the faster the sun melted holes and pock marks into the salty ice. We were pale beneath our tan and even the *Arctic Tern* trembled like a frightened bird as Bud held the brakes and opened up the throttle. As the wheels began to slide along the ice he released the brakes.

The airplane didn't gain speed. It just lunged forward down the runway. Water flew as we hit the first foot-deep hole, obscuring the windshield with slush. We had nearly gained flying speed but this slowed us down.

Again we charged down the strip in a second attempt. We just barely gained flying speed as the runway ended in a three-foot wall of snow. Bud brought the wheel back and we climbed above the drift, missing it by inches, but the tail didn't. It caught the snowbank a sharp clip and we came down with a shattering crash into the deep wet snow, the propeller throwing up a cloud of ice crystals and snow as we hit.

Emerging with some difficulty from under the pile of duffel, we climbed out of the airplane to survey the damage. Bud expected a broken propeller but only the shock cord on the tail ski, which we had left attached, was broken.

The Eskimos arrived with shovels and dug the airplane out from the snow where it had stopped suddenly, from a speed of 45 miles an hour, in a distance of five feet. All of us there were emotional wrecks. Practical Nanny fixed supper.

"No use to try that again," said Bud. For the only time in his life, he was definitely and finally foiled in a take-off. I knew he would think of something.

He turned to study the beach which at first he had regarded as hopeless.

The sand beach had been thrown up by violent storms; there were a few snowdrifts left from winter stretched across it. There was just a narrow strip about wide enough to accommodate the wheels, with the frozen Arctic Ocean on one hand and the snowbound prairie on the other. Removing the worst of the drifts, some miscellaneous whale bones, a caribou antler and a wooden grave marker, Bud marked out a path there.

It was near midnight when a slight breeze of the kind we wanted came down the beach. Since this strip was crosswise to the wind practically all the time, except during wind shifts, we knew that a change of wind was brief and we should act fast.

Once again we said good-by. The airplane moved sluggishly over the cloying shifty sand to take-off position. It would hardly pull itself in the soft sand, but as Bud pushed in the throttle to full power and it gained speed, the airplane grew lighter and the wheels climbed up until they at last scarcely marked the sand. Down the curve of the narrow beach we passed adroitly through the holes in the snowdrifts. Bud lowered the flaps. We sprinted off into the sky.

All our friends stood beside their tent waving a frantic farewell as we circled in a wide arc. That was good-by to the small speck that had been home, to our beloved Eskimo family, and to the low arctic sun that hung over thousands of miles of mysterious polar ice.

We reached Hughes at three o'clock one early spring morning. Johnny James, asleep in his bed, always had his ear tuned for the various airplanes that came to Hughes. At the sound of ours he jumped up. "That's Bud and Connie," he said. Already his family were pulling on their clothes.

"Good God," Les James said, as we sat around their early dawn table and Bud and I ate canned fruit and cookies and all of the bountiful provision set before us, "we thought we had seen the last of you that time

The army reports you have been missing from the north coast of Alaska for two months. I wish you wouldn't worry a person that way. I'm getting to be an old man. I can't stand this kind of worry any more."

We learned that flyers out of Point Barrow, having become accustomed to seeing the *Arctic Tern* parked beside Nanny's igloo at Oliktok Point, had reported our complete disappearance as a consequence of our going out on the ice for the sealing, and this disappearance had mystified Alaska. We were sorry to have caused our friends this worry due to a misunderstanding. Mrs. James reported us located on her 6 A.M. broadcast.

At Fairbanks we sold our airplane. We flew down to the United States on the airlines in a few hours. I got a dress along the way, and Bud a new pair of pants and the trimmings.

We were in wonderful health. The reason we had gone to the States in summer was to get a new Cessna 170 equipped with floats. There were no float fittings in existence for this ship, so it was necessary to go to the United States to get them in order to return to Takahula Lake.

17 THE FUTURE GENERATIONS

The problem of having the right landing gear on your airplane at the right season keeps an Alaska pilot busy. Will there be enough snow for a ski landing? Will the lake be open for floats? When will the freeze-up occur? Sometimes, as in this case, it is necessary to detour to the United States to buy the right landing gear, and while you're at it, buy a new airplane. We got the first Cessna 170 on floats that was produced, and flew floats back to Alaska in July.

By now we had friends, like the folks at Cooking Lake, to visit all along the way. When we came down on Bear Lake, western Alberta, friends took us into their farm home as week-end guests and held a neighborhood party, to which were invited the Mac Prentisses, of Saskatoon Lake, who had befriended us before. Flying on to Alaska, we carried gifts of strawberry plants for the garden at Takahula Lake inside the floats.

This time, instead of continuing inland via Whitehorse, we turned off to Juneau on the coast. At the capital of Alaska, we added many substantial statistics to our years of field experience, and wrote a report on conservation needs for the Conservation Foundation of the New York Zoological Society — a private organization backed by the Rockefellers. To the Foundation, which has begun the gigantic task of drawing up reports on all the continents of the world, we made several recommendations regarding Alaska.

Perhaps the foremost of these was Bud's pet project for a caribou reservation called the Colville-Mackenzie Caribou Reserve; to be successful, this would probably have to be operated jointly with Canada. Much could be learned from such a project, used as a wildlife laboratory, patterned after the tracts which have been set aside to preserve the game in Africa.

The whole question of Alaska's colonization, in our opinion, rests on how many people a given area can accommodate on a sustained yield basis, by other than the extractive industries. We must recognize that Alaska has a different kind of geography from the United States and that it was not designed by nature for a great deal of agricultural expansion.

A number of weeks passed and I didn't feel quite myself. A trip to Fairbanks and home to Takahula Lake entails almost six hundred miles of flying, so it was some time before I got to a doctor to confirm my suspicion. (Bud didn't like to go to Fairbanks in summer because it was so hard to get a ship off the Chena Slough there, and we had a great deal of photography to complete yet that season.)

When we were told by the doctor that we were going to be parents, it seemed absolutely incredible! He saw no reason why I shouldn't finish up that season in the arctic, since I was used to life there. The fish and meat diet was exceptionally good; in fact, the most recent views on maternity recommend a high protein diet for normal individuals. Since flying is the best means of transportation, much to be preferred over the automobile, generally speaking, I could fly as much as I wanted. The way it turned out, Bud and I flew, I suppose, between five and ten thousand miles camping about the arctic during this time. We even did some of our most head-spinning photographic stunts which had to be done to complete our studies of the mountain peaks.

Garbing ourselves as Eskimos, we flew north of the trees and to Oliktok Point on the Arctic Ocean where we visited George and Nanny. Crippled Martha had died. Often Bud and I had discussed flying her out to the Mayo Clinic where we had friends who might be able to do something for her strange back affliction. But the lovely, primitive girl would not have survived the trip nor the loneliness among strangers in a strange land.

There was good eating at Oliktok Point in the summer; we ate boiled caribou joints and raw bone marrow. I consumed too much marrow in my exuberance in visiting and got sick, but only temporarily.

When I told Nanny about my expected baby I thought she would be thrilled and delighted, but her face became sad. I couldn't understand the way the Eskimos took my big news until I realized that they figured that if I had a baby, Bud and I would not come back. I asked Nanny if she would start sewing some tiny caribou clothes for her new "grandchild," and the thought brought a smile to her loving face. I wondered: Would my baby's Eskimo layette ever be used? We were going back to the United States to have the baby, we explained.

I laid in a specially big supply of blueberry and cranberry preserves that fall at the cabin, and even picked many horrible ground berries that we never customarily used, and put up the product. Perhaps it was just because there was such a big crop of these horrible berries that I thought they ought to be used. Or perhaps it was my subconscious wish to return for sure. I also dried a big supply of moose meat. When we thought of the future generations to come, it wasn't hard to talk ourselves into that piece of arctic real estate at Takahula Lake — and it was all free!